*John F. Kennedy's
13 Great Mistakes
In the White House*

John F. Kennedy's
13 Great Mistakes
In the White House

by

Malcolm E. Smith

Suffolk House
155 East Main Street
Smithtown, N.Y.

Contents

John F. Kennedy's
13 Great Mistakes
In the White House

Foreword

JOHN F. KENNEDY was a political phenomenon. In all American history no President ever rode the crest of a popular wave such as his. Everywhere he went, smiling, gracious, confident, he was hailed with enthusiasm, often with cheers, frequently with adulation. When an assassin's bullets felled him, the world was stunned. Men and women wept openly without shame.

The inspiration for much of this hero worship was in Kennedy's personality. He was the embodiment of young America: fresh, vigorous, good-looking, charming and witty. He had plenty of money and style to match. He had served in World War II and survived the war experience only to carry a souvenir of it in an injured back. He chose to endure dangerous surgery and long painful convalescence in order to recapture full health. He used the convalescence to write a book which was good enough to win a Pulitzer prize.

Kennedy had more than his share of special gifts and graces, and he possessed as well a magnetic and magic quality. In great measure, he had the enthusiasm of youth and a desire to right the world's wrongs. He was imbued with the desire to win, a quality which had been drilled into him from his earliest years by his father, Joseph P. Kennedy.

9

Joseph P. Kennedy, whose own father and father-in-law were run-of-the-mill Boston politicians, was determined to break loose from the Boston Irish pattern. He, himself, was graduated from Harvard, and it was to Harvard that his four sons went.

There is ample evidence to show that Kennedy Sr. argued and bullied and trained his sons to fight their way to the top. He made competition a way of life for them. And because he was obsessively set on the Presidency as the goal worthy of a Kennedy, he directed Jack's intellect into the hard vulgarity of American politics.

Financed by his father, coached and directed by him and by cronies schooled in the brass knuckles ward politics of South Boston, Jack Kennedy entered politics in his native state.

When he made it to the White House some fourteen years later, he was well-educated, but untrained, and young. However, his youth appealed to the young voters. It appealed to many older ones, too, who remembered that Theodore Roosevelt had been even younger. "TR" became the nation's youngest chief executive at 42 years, 10 months and 18 days when William McKinley died in office on a September day in 1901, the victim of an assassin's bullet fired eight days earlier.

The first Roosevelt was younger than Kennedy when he assumed the Presidency but the parallel ends there. Roosevelt came to the White House after a dozen demanding years as a Federal Civil Service Commissioner, New York City Police Commissioner, Assistant Secretary of the Navy, and Governor of New York State.

In contrast with Roosevelt, John F. Kennedy took over the nation's biggest job without any experience in business or in public administration. All his civil service had been in the Congress and there he served mostly as a fair weather sailor. Even his biographer, Arthur M. Schlesinger, Jr., a sympathetic observer, admits Kennedy never became one of the "cloakroom boys." He was never chairman of an important committee. No outstanding piece of legislation bore his name.

Proper and efficient administration of public office is no sinecure. Our Founding Fathers realized that and for almost two hundred years the road to the Presidency of the United States almost invariably followed one of two roads. Presidents were either career soldiers who received their administrative hardening in the Department of the Army, or they won their advancement step by step up the civilian political ladder.

No one can dispute George Washington's exceptional qualities of leadership. At sixteen, he showed a flair for business. At twenty-one, through the long ordeal of the French and Indian War, he was a lieutenant colonel with the fate of England's American colonies in his hands. Then, at 43—the same age as Kennedy when he ran for President—Washington became the Commander-in-Chief of the Continental Army. Through seven years of adversity, from Lexington and Concord to Yorktown, he led a young nation to victory and independence. The Constitutional Convention and the Presidency claimed his middle and declining years. And throughout his life he was responsible for the management of many farms which, at his death, comprised 110,000 acres. He was a man who never knew freedom from responsibility.

In 1765, when he was 30, John Adams argued taxation before the Colonial Governor of Massachusetts. Thirty-one years later, after serving in the Provincial Congress of Massachusetts, the Continental Congress, and as Commissioner to France, Delegate to the Netherland, Minister to England, and eight years as Vice President, he felt himself qualified to fill the highest office in the land.

Thomas Jefferson was a most accomplished man. He read the Greek and Latin classics in the original and was an inspired and inspiring writer. One has only to visit Monticello, his home and masterpiece, to see his architectural and inventive skill, his genius for creating.

Despite Jefferson's gifts and attainments, he studied and trained and served for thirty-one years before he became President. He was a legislator in the Virginia House of Burgesses, the House of Delegates, and the Continental Congress. He was Minister to France, Governor of Virginia, Secretary of State and Vice President.

As for Presidents of the more recent past, almost all of them have held to the same strict pattern. Grover Cleveland rose from Assistant District Attorney, Sheriff and Mayor of Buffalo to Governor of New York State. William McKinley set up the practice of law in his native Ohio, served several terms as Representative and was twice elected Governor of that State.

Another Ohioan, William Howard Taft, prepared for the Presidency as a County Prosecutor and Solicitor, State and Federal Judge, Governor of the Philippines and of Cuba, and Secretary of War.

Woodrow Wilson was a theoretician in government, a professor of jurisprudence and political economy who became president of Princeton University and put his theoretical knowledge to practical test as Governor of New Jersey before seeking election as President.

One of the most thoroughly trained administrators was Calvin Coolidge. His record as Councilman, City Solicitor, Clerk of the Courts, Member of the Lower Massachusetts House, Mayor of Northampton, State Senator, Lieutenant Governor and Governor of Massachusetts for two terms, covered more than thirty years before he succeeded to the Presidency on the death of Harding.

Herbert Hoover's career in administration was unique. Renowned in the world as a mining engineer, he was only twenty-six when he turned temporarily from his mining duties in China to use his great organizing ability in helping feed the victims of the Boxer uprising there. He became a world figure in relief work, distributing $5,000,000,000 worth of relief in war-devastated Europe between 1914 and 1923. And for seven years he served in the Coolidge Cabinet as Secretary of Commerce.

Franklin D. Roosevelt's preparation for the Presidency included a term in the New York State Senate and service as Assistant Secretary of the Navy. He was another of the many Presidents who learned political and executive administration as Governor of a large State.

Even Harry S. Truman, perhaps the least qualified President from the standpoint of executive experience, learned command as a soldier, had some business experience as a merchandiser, and practiced the elements of administration as lay Judge of the Jackson County Court. When he went to Washington to represent Missouri, he was an active Senator, a vigorous, astute politician, who was chairman of several important committees.

Dwight D. Eisenhower was well prepared to undertake the complicated administration of government when he succeeded Truman. His military career over two decades prepared him for the demanding responsibilities as Supreme Commander of the Allied Expeditionary Forces in Europe. Eisenhower interrupted his professional military career with a sojourn in the academic realm as President of Columbia University. Subsequently, he returned to the uniform and life of the professional soldier as Supreme Allied

Commander in Europe of the North Atlantic Treaty Organization. In organizing and running this peacetime complex of twelve nations— three more joined later—for mutual defense, Eisenhower once again demonstrated his rare skill, akin to genius, for the orderly management and diplomatic handling of diverse personalities and temperament at high level.

In contast to all of these past Presidents, John Fitzgerald Kennedy, 43 years of age when he entered the White House, was without prior experience in business or in the executive branch of state or local government. Moreover, he took little cognizance of the fact that all over the nation there were mature men of high character and brilliant mentality, successful, patriotic, eager for his Administration to succeed, who would have given him the best they had for the asking. He drew away from his father's counsel now that he had won the gift Joe Kennedy had so avidly desired. He did not seek the advice of many older men. Instead, as his mother said frankly, "John Kennedy brought into politics, and relied heavily upon, youthful men of his own generation. Like himself, they were originally political amateurs outside the regular party apparatus."

Her words revealed her son's greatest weakness. It was this defect that Henry Brooks Adams undoubtedly had in mind when he wrote in *The Education of Henry Adams* that, "Power is poison. Its effect on Presidents has always been tragic, chiefly as an almost insane excitement at first, and a worse reaction afterwards; but also because no mind is so well balanced as to bear the strain of seizing unlimited force without habit or knowledge of it, and finding it disputed with him by hungry packs of wolves and hounds whose lives depend on snatching the carrion."

The young advisors John Kennedy brought to Washington were, like him, men in a hurry. Their youthful idealism appealed to the new President. But their advice to him often did not work and caused him to blunder. *Newsweek* magazine in 1973 wrote of the criticism which by then was being expressed: "The main argument against him is that he was what he said he was—a young man in a hurry, a free-floating pragmatist, an activist, a short cutter. In his haste to 'get this country moving again' after the snooziness of the Eisenhower years, he surrounded himself with gung-ho types who were as impatient as he with the clog of bureaucracy. ('They may be every bit as intelligent as you say,' Sam Rayburn told Lyndon

Johnson, 'but I wish just one of them had run for sheriff once.')"

Lacking experience himself, Kennedy soon adopted the idea of relying on "the opinion of the people." He seldom made major decisions without testing the political climate. Perhaps he was simply, and understandably, anxious to please and be popular but in so doing he was foredoomed to error. For the people were not privy to sufficient inside knowledge to make wise decisions. Nor is it ever up to them to do so. When they elect a President they give him the power and authority to speak and act for them. The responsibility of leadership is his; decision-making is the President's job.

Edmund Burke, the brilliant Dublin-born statesman and writer who influenced 19th century political thought in Europe and America, described the obligation of political leadership succinctly:

"Your representative owes you, not his industry only, but his judgement; and he betrays instead of serving you, if he sacrifices it to your opinion."

The Founding Fathers distrusted popular opinion for its heavy emotional content which always obscures reason and often defeats justice. Thomas Jefferson, our third President, believed the minority must be protected against the tyranny of the majority. He had a wholesome fear of what he called "elective despotism."

Our values are different today, although the principles of leadership in a Republic are constant. President Kennedy was a practical politician who seldom thought of acting without checking the opinion polls which he followed avidly and believed in. The majority view was all important. Yet he sometimes had to acknowledge how false a barometer of public understanding of his administrative effectiveness the polls could be.

Soon after the Bay of Pigs fiasco when the young President was close to the nadir of his political fortunes and emotions, and while he was still smarting from the disaster, he saw an advance copy of the latest Gallup poll. It showed an unprecedented majority behind the President.

He tossed it aside with the bitter comment, "It's just like Eisenhower. The worse I do, the more popular I get."

The President's failure at the Bay of Pigs, one of the 13 Great Mistakes described in this book, brought forth another side of his personality which has seldom been discussed. One of the few who mentioned it was columnist Patrick J. Buchanan, who wrote, ". . . The Kennedy legacy . . . has been permanently tarnished by the investigations of Frank Church. Rummaging through the secrets of the CIA, it was Church's committee which called national attention to the unknown fact that while John F. Kennedy was calling for a free Cuba, his brother, the Attorney General, was privately discussing the murder of Fidel Castro.

"Beyond that, a clumsy committee cover-up resulted in enormous publicity for the fact that "our first Catholic President" carried on a clandestine affair with the paramour of the Mafia mobster who was given the contract on the Cuban premier."

The shocking truth that a President of the United States, while in office, would have an affair with a Mafia mobster's girl, and plot the assassination of anyone, is a hard bullet to bite for most Americans. Yet both are true.

On June 1, 1975, the *New York Times* ran a story which reported that in testimony before the Rockefeller Commission, officers said there could have been "several" plans to assassinate the Cuban leader following Kennedy's blunders which resulted in the failure to overthrow Castro by means of the Bay of Pigs invasion.

The story continued, "Yesterday, General Lansdale (Maj. Gen. Edward G. Lansdale, retired) said that in November, 1961, Attorney General Robert F. Kennedy ordered him to prepare a secret contingency plan to depose Mr. Castro. General Lansdale confirmed that Robert Kennedy was acting on behalf of President Kennedy. . . . In preparing this plan, General Lansdale acknowledged, the matter of assassination as one means of removing Mr. Castro may have been contemplated."

Whether or not the Mafia contract to kill Castro, which the Church committee uncovered, is the same assassination plot General Lansdale referred to is not known. But it is certainly illuminating to realize that the same man to whom the contract was given, Mafia chief Sam Giancanna, had spoken with Jack Ruby in Dallas prior to the assassination of President Kennedy, and it may well be that the Kennedy plot to have Castro killed resulted in Kennedy's own death.

In November, 1977, the *New York Post* wrote of a document which indicated Fidel Castro was linked to the assassination of President John F. Kennedy:

"The document, a report written by an investigator for the Senate Internal Security subcommittee, places Jack Ruby in Havana two months before Kennedy's assassination.

"Part of the report, written Jan. 27, 1964, by agent Al Tarabochia . . . tells of Jack Ruby, the killer of Lee Harvey Oswald, meeting with a Castro agent."

The article then quotes Watergate burglar Frank Sturgis, "Ruby almost certainly organized the killing, may have actually been a second gun and then he covered his tracks by taking care of Oswald."

A *New York Times* story in 1977 lends credence to this. It quotes G. Gordon Liddy as saying that he would not be surprised "to discover that Lee Harvey Oswald was acting for the Castro government when he shot John Fitzgerald Kennedy. . . . In short, it is as logical and appropriate that the Government of Fidel Castro should kill John Kennedy as it was for the Kennedy government to seek to kill Castro."

The above may or may not be the story behind the Kennedy assassination but polls show that most Americans do not believe the story of the assassination has ever been fully told.

Also never fully told is the "other side" of the John F. Kennedy record as President. An almost unending outpouring of praise for the fallen President has led millions, especially young voters, to have a completely distorted view of that record. Within 36 months after President Kennedy was killed a flood of books appeared praising the fallen leader. Nothing like this outpouring of praise had occurred in America since the death of Abraham Lincoln under equally tragic circumstances.

In his book, *The Lincoln Legend,* Roy P. Basler wrote, "Lincoln was suddenly lifted into the sky as the folk-hero, the deliverer, and the martyr who had come to save his people and to die for them . . ." This was a spontaneous and natural result of the passing of a great President.

100 years later there is reason to believe that some of the continuing praise of President Kennedy has been motivated by those seeking to return to positions of power in Washington by building a 'legend' around the man under whom they served.

It is time that the "other side" of the John F. Kennedy record be fully told. For, as *Newsweek* once wrote in describing the views of the few writers who have reported on the "other side". . . .

"Kennedy, far from offering the nation any new torch to follow, was a traditional, trigger-happy cold warrior in his foreign policy and an ineffective and unconcerned leader domestically. In this view, the missile showdown over Cuba was not Kennedy's finest hour but his most needlessly reckless, and everything about his Administration— from the inflated rhetoric of the Inaugural Address to the cocksure academic warhawks around him to the 15,000 so-called advisers he sent to Vietnam—pointed the country down the road toward the Indochinese swamp and all that came with it."

Perhaps Richard Whalen summarized this view best when he wrote of Kennedy's "splendid fakery, the vain arrogance of the courtiers and the transparent improvisations of bold initiatives . . . quickly forgotten."

As America approaches its Presidential elections, voters must learn about John F. Kennedy's Great Mistakes, and must learn that the qualities he had in such abundance—charm, wit, good looks and charisma—are not enough in an American President, and that we must choose future leaders not on charisma or glibness or promises made, but on the basic qualities of experience, sound judgement and the ability to be right in decisions of momentous import, any of which, if wrong, can have the most ominous consequences for all of the American people.

The Election That May
Have Never Been Won

AS THE KENNEDY family gathered together with Presidential
candidate John F. Kennedy on election eve 1960 to see the results of
the long uphill battle against Richard Nixon, the result was far from
certain.

As the campaign ended it was almost impossible to predict
whether Nixon or Kennedy would emerge the victor. More Americans cast ballots in the 1960 presidential election—over 69 million—
than in any previous election in U.S. history. It was a cliff-hanger
and, as the evening went on, it became clear that the key could be
Illinois.

As tension was growing, Jack Kennedy placed a call to Chicago.
He wanted to talk to Mayor Richard Daley, to learn what was going
on in that most crucial state. It was from Richard Daley's lips that
Kennedy was first addressed as, "Mr. President."

"Mr. President," Daley told Kennedy, "with a little bit of luck and
help from a few close friends, you're going to carry Illinois."

Close Kennedy friend and *Newsweek* correspondent Ben Bradlee
was with the candidate at the time of the phone call. Later he
recalled that he "often wondered about Daley's statement," about
whether it meant that, somehow, something dishonest was at work.

Not until the last minute were Chicago's results made known. Finally, Mayor Daley reported, an avalanche of votes from Cook County offset losses downstate to give Kennedy a slim 8,585 plurality in Illinois.

The official tabulation shows that Kennedy defeated Nixon nationally by 119,450 votes. Counting write-in votes and other votes for minority tickets, Kennedy did not receive a majority of the 68,836,385 votes cast. The official tally gave Kennedy 34,227,096 votes and Nixon 34,106,646. In electoral votes, Kennedy had 303 and Nixon 219. Senator Harry F. Byrd of Virginia received 15.

In the final official tabulation, Illinois cast 2,377,638 votes for Kennedy, and 2,367,937 for Nixon, a difference of only 9,801 votes.

Almost immediately charges of fraud in the Illinois election were made. Mrs. Marie H. Suthers, a Republican member of the board of elections commissioners, made the charge that at least 10,000 Chicagoans were barred from voting. She said that their names had been wrongfully removed from voting lists in the official canvass of voters made October 12 and 13. U.S. Attorney Robert Tieken said on November 10 that his office would investigate these charges.

Hundreds of irate Chicagoans violently protested to the election board offices that their names had indeed been mysteriously removed from the voting lists. Many of them had been voting from the same addresses for years, but when they went to the polling places they found that they were no longer listed as eligible voters.

Frank Ferlic, first assistant state's attorney, angrily charged that the election was loaded with cases of fraud. He pointed out that his office had received calls concerning more than 1,200 cases of irregularities at the polling places.

Two persons had the misfortune of encountering Robert N. Caffarelli, an assistant U.S. attorney, near the polling place at 930 W. 17th Street. "Are you the man who is supposed to give the money?" a woman asked Caffarelli. "Oh, I'm sorry, I see him over there." Caffarelli handed the woman and a man subpoenas.

On November 11, State's Attorney Benjamin S. Adamowski said that he would request a preliminary recount of votes in certain areas. He was attempting to upset the apparent 25,000 vote victory of his Democratic opponent, Daniel P. Ward. Adamowski said that there is "not the slightest question that there was enough vote fraud to justify" his challenge of the totals. He said that he had heard stories about "skullduggery that were shocking and disgusting."

It is "tough enough" to run against the Democratic machine, Adamowski stated, without having vote frauds practiced as well.

Albert F. Manion, first assistant U.S. attorney, called the First Ward a "morass" of vote frauds and said he wanted clearance to subpoena every voter of one precinct in the First Ward and possibly the voters in precincts in other wards as well. He said that hundreds would be asked by the jury to tell whether they were offered money and whether they were paid money to vote a certain way.

Frank J. Durham, instruction chairman of the Committee on Honest Elections, on November 12 charged that the Democratic machine had "stolen" the election from Nixon and State's Attorney Adamowski. Durham said he had never seen fraudulent practices more "vicious" in his 25 years of poll watching.

The pluralities rolled up, Durham charged, were unbelievable for both Kennedy and Daniel P. Ward, Adamowski's opponent. He further charged that his staff had found as many as 45 fraudulent registrations in just two apartment buildings in the Fourth Ward. In that ward, Kennedy received 25,770 votes to 7,120 for Nixon. Durham said: "The vote frauds carried out by Mayor Daley's henchmen on election day were the most flagrant I have seen."

At the same time, William H. Fetridge, chairman of Midwest Volunteers for Nixon and an investment banker, declared: "I look at those figures and see the fantastic totals the machine rolled up and I cannot help but become alarmed. Certainly, there has been a history of thievery and corruption on election days in these wards. Perhaps what happened was traditional."

In Washington, Republican officials were concerned, believing that the evidence that the 1960 election had, in fact, been "stolen" was growing and was persuasive. Acting independently of Richard Nixon, the Republican National Committee asked party officials in 11 states—including Illinois—to probe complaints of vote frauds.

Nixon himself was reluctant to challenge the vote. His special campaign director, Robert Finch, said that, "As far as the Nixon national camp is concerned we are standing on the vote as reported, leaving to the individual states any questions of investigating irregularities or demanding recounts."

"We have no grand design at all to question the result," said Herbert Klein, Nixon's press secretary. "We ran a good race, the votes have been counted and we accept the decision."

Republican leaders in Washington, however, asked party chairmen in ten states to review the election results. In addition to Illinois, they included Delaware, Michigan, Minnesota, Missouri, Nevada, New Mexico, New Jersey, Pennsylvania, South Carolina and Texas.

Senator Thruston B. Morton of Kentucky, the Republican national chairman, put the stress on Illinois and Texas. Morton also announced that ballot boxes had been impounded in 13 counties in New Mexico.

Democrats made light of the charges. Visiting Chicago on November 13, former President Harry Truman termed the idea of recounts in 11 states as "a lot of hooey." He branded the Republicans as "a bunch of poor losers."

Mayor Daley attempted to turn the stories of vote fraud in Chicago around—charging that such frauds were even more likely in downstate Illinois, where Nixon had received large pluralities. "In certain downstate counties," said Daley, "the results are so fantastically, overwhelmingly Republican that there might have been error in their eagerness. It is a great disservice to the thousands of fine men and women who worked as judges and clerks in the election to make these general and unsubstantiated allegations for political purposes."

"You look at some of those downstate counties," said Daley, "and it's just as fantastic as some of those precincts they're pointing at in Chicago. The people of Chicago are just as honorable and honest as in any section of the state."

Daley's demand for a state-wide recount was met by Republican leaders with enthusiasm. "If that's the way he feels, we'll be happy to invite him to participate," said William Fetridge, head of the Nixon Recount Committee. "We're not planning to recount in all areas downstate. There has never been any history of fraud down there. But we just want the facts to be sure that each candidate receives the votes to which he is entitled. If he feels the same way, he should ask for a recount of whatever downstate precincts he wants."

Cook County Republican Chairman Francis X. Connell, on November 13, charged that the Democratic machine swung the presidential vote to Kennedy by a slim margin through "the systematic looting of votes in 12 city wards and parts of two others . . . There is no question that they stole the election. The work was mainly done by the professional vote thieves. Those we'll never catch. But we think that through a recount it will be possible to catch the careless and the over-ambitious ballot thieves who stuffed the ballot boxes and reported 'loaded' vote tallies."

Republican officials met secretly on November 18 and made a spot check comparison of the votes actually recorded by voting machines in some traditional Democratic wards with the tallies that were reported November 8. They said that they found large numbers of discrepancies favoring the Democratic candidates.

Francis X. Connell, Cook County Republican chairman, said the checks were made of figures reported by precincts in some Democratic river wards and south side party strongholds. "What we found leads me to believe that there were extensive vote thefts. It is apparent that votes were stolen from Vice President Nixon. . . . It appears they manipulated the count reported to the board of election commissioners to favor the Democrats."

In one West side precinct, a ward long a part of the Democratic county machine, Connell charged that as many as 46 votes more than actually were recorded by the voting machine for the Ward were reported to the election commission by precinct polling judges. In the case of Nixon versus Kennedy, a dozen or more votes were reported to the election board for Kennedy than were recorded on the machines.

"These large gaps between what the machines registered and what the election judges said was the count shows that there was large scale stealing," Connell said. "I have no doubt that as our comparison continues we will find many more such instances. Some of the differences in the tallies can be accounted for by absentee ballots, which would not be recorded on the machines, but there were not that many absentee ballots in those types of wards."

The county chairman said that his staff had also assembled information indicating the Democrats had "loaded the election polls with fraudulent registrants."

"In some cases, we know that they (Democratic precinct captains) marched the phony voters right into the voting machine booths, pulled the two levers for a straight Democratic ticket, and then marched them out again. Then they gave them $2 or $5 or whatever the going rate was for buying votes."

Chicago's newspapers had already expressed concern about the mounting evidence of vote frauds. *The Tribune* declared that, "The election of November 8, 1960 was characterized by such gross and palpable fraud as to justify the conclusion that Nixon was deprived of victory."

At the same time, author Victor Lasky reported that, "It develops that Mafia chief Sam 'Momo' Giancana may also have played a decisive role. Giancana often boasted to Judith Campbell that he used his power to elect Kennedy. 'Listen, honey,' he told Judith, 'if it wasn't for me, your boyfriend wouldn't even be in the White House.'"

Republicans in Illinois continued to do everything possible to arrive at the truth about the Cook County vote. A grand jury investigation began on Tuesday, November 29. Four hundred and sixty precinct election judges were subpoenaed to appear. David H. Brill, chairman of the non-partisan Committee on Honest Elections, reported that his group had compiled evidence indicating that the number of ineligible voters left off polling lists exceeded 10 per cent of the total Chicago registration. In one precinct alone, Brill said, his investigators found 103 registered voters not listed. In another precinct, the 6th of the 4th ward, 45 "floater" votes were found in two apartment buildings. In other words, persons registered as being eligible to vote from two addresses did not exist. Yet, it was charged, ballots were unquestionably cast in their names.

A demand that a special prosecutor be named to conduct the grand jury investigation of voting frauds was made by two leading members of the Chicago Bar. Albert E. Jenner, Jr., former Illinois State Bar Association president, and Charles A. Bane, first chief counsel of the city council's crime investigating committee, recommended that the special prosecutor be named from a list of top lawyers compiled by the Chicago Bar Association.

Just as the November 29 grand jury investigation was to begin, records vital to it "disappeared." Sidney Holzman, chairman of the board of election commissioners, said ballot applications from the 2nd ward's 50th precinct were missing from a third story vault in City Hall. They had been stored there under federal court order along with applications from all other city precincts. This is the precinct Republicans were using to bolster their charges of widespread voting frauds. Seventy-seven votes were cast for President in a precinct with only 22 eligible voters. Asked if he considered the "disappearance" a "theft," Holzman replied that he did not know. He said that he did not plan to call in police but would handle the matter himself.

Asked about the continuing investigation and the mounting evidence of fraud, Mayor Daley on November 29 said simply that, "Ward won the election and so did Kennedy. In the words of a former President (Harry S. Truman) they are damned poor losers."

Although Mayor Daley discounted the charges of fraud, U.S. Attorney Robert Tieken on May 30 disclosed that he had turned over a large amount of evidence to the F.B.I. He said: "We have collected evidence from citizens who were deprived of their votes because they cast absentee ballots that were not counted because they were not delivered to polling places before they closed on election day. Responsibility for counting these ballots rests on the county clerk and the board of election commissioners." Mr. Tieken recited, in addition, the familiar litany of citizen complaint of fraud.

State's Attorney Benjamin S. Adamowski, on December 1 charged that Chicago's Democratic organization stole at least 100,000 votes on November 8 and asserted that Mayor Daley has become "the most powerful political boss in America through a rigged election contest." He charged that the Democratic machine headed by Daley virtually "stole" the White House for John F. Kennedy.

He charged that, as one phase of the operation, enough legitimate Republican voters were deprived of their voting rights by the mysterious disappearance of their names from precinct polling place binders to shift Illinois from Nixon to Kennedy.

As for the hesitancy of the Democrats to look into charges of fraud, Adamowski said the delaying process was "all part and parcel of the technique of taking the election any way they can. If Nixon actually won in Illinois, Kennedy goes into the White House with a cloud over his head which will never dissipate."

At this point Illinois Governor Stratton assailed the "disgraceful, planned, stalling and confusion" in the Democratic recount and attacked "flagrant vote frauds" in Chicago. He said that the state electoral board may not certify Kennedy's unofficial narrow victory if there is sufficient evidence of fraud. Mayor Daley, for his part, charged the Republicans with "conspiracy" to upset the Kennedy election.

Republican officials in Washington were following events in Illinois very carefully. They were convinced that Richard Nixon could still be named the winner and they believed that everything depended upon the recount in Chicago. Republican National Chairman Thruston Morton said on December 3 that he would pursue every legal means "to preserve the sanctity of the ballot." He traveled to Chicago to observe the progress of the recount and said he had "a duty to give the widest exposure" to disclosures of fraud and other irregularities in the Presidential election.

"I have a specific and definite duty and responsibility to pursue this investigation," he said, "so that the people of this country can see and know what went on. The issue is not just the electoral votes or who won Illinois, it is the sanctity of the ballot. I'm here because I believe in that sanctity. . . . I didn't come into this half cocked on a fishing expedition. I could have done that the Thursday after the election. We sent attorneys into 11 states including Illinois to learn what the facts were before the national committee made any moves. Now that we have the facts, we intend to pursue every legal means to assure honest elections and an honest count."

The same day as Senator Morton's visit, broken and missing seals on a large proportion of boxes containing ballots of the November election provoked protests from Chicago Republican leaders. *Chicago Tribune* reporters saw that seals were broken or missing on 13 of 47 corrugated cardboard boxes containing ballots. One day earlier, they spotted similar defects on 14 of 21 boxes. In addition, reporters noted that in the case of four boxes the precinct judges had not written their names across the paper seal of the box as required.

"This represents either fraud or gross irregularities, we don't know which," said Republican attorney Ralph Berkowitz. "The law provides for a seal to keep the boxes safe from tampering. The situation raises reasonable presumptions that some of the ballots may have been tampered with. They (the Democrats) have had plenty of time to do things."

As the ballots were re-checked, evidence of fraud mounted. Republican watchers declared on December 4 that in seven of the 34 precincts which had been checked, "apparent" erasures of Republican votes were found.

Attorney Berkowitz reported that Republican votes had been erased in the circle designated for Vice President Nixon and a mark inserted in behalf of Senator John F. Kennedy, the Democratic candidate. He said: "This is one of the most flagrant situations we have found in the recheck of the 863 paper ballot precincts in Chicago. This again points to the utter disregard for the election laws that the Democratic machine practiced on election day."

Mayor Daley responded to all of this by saying that there was, in fact, no evidence of fraud and that the Republicans were employing "Hitler-type" propaganda.

While Mayor Daley denied any evidence of wrong-doing, the facts became too difficult to so easily dismiss. Thus, election officials in precincts in which glaring vote discrepancies were uncovered found themselves unable to explain how tallies marked on ballot boxes could vary so widely from the ballots inside.

In a typical case, Annete Mazius, a Democratic judge in the 8th precinct of the 31st ward, where discrepancies were found, said: "We spent 18 hours working in the polling place at 1312 N. Honore Street, and there were two Republican watchers breathing down our necks all the time. What could have gone wrong, I don't know. It doesn't seem possible that we could have made an error like that. It's amazing."

A re-check of the votes in this precinct showed that the vote for Kennedy was overcounted by 33 and the Nixon vote undercounted by 32.

While most of the nation's attention was riveted upon the Illinois election results, evidence of fraud elsewhere in the country was also growing.

Texas was often discussed. Among the examples:

**Fannin County, which went for Kennedy by 3 to 1 had 4,895 voters on the official "poll tax list" but 6,138 votes were counted.

**In the 27th precinct of Angelia County, 86 individuals were officially recorded as having voted—but the final result was Kennedy, 147 and Nixon, 24.

**In Fort Bend County, in two adjoining precincts: in one, which voted Nixon over Kennedy 458 to 350, 182 ballots were declared void "at the discretion of the judges." In the other, which went 68 to 1 for Kennedy, not a single ballot was declared void.

In Texas, every phase of the state's election machinery from the local to the state level was in the hands of the Democratic organization, which was dominated by Lyndon Johnson. A series in *The New York Herald Tribune* disclosed that the stuffing of ballot boxes reached a new high and that dozens of election machines in Republican precincts jammed mysteriously. Tens of thousands of ballots disappeared overnight. *The Herald Tribune* declared that a minimum of 100,000 votes tallied for the Kennedy-Johnson ticket never existed in the first place. The importance of such charges was clear because the Democrats carried Texas by the slim margin of 46,000.

Offers of money and lawyers to mount a challenge against the 1960 results continued to flood into Republican offices in Washington.

Leonard Hall, who had co-managed the Nixon campaign, recalled how Admiral Lewis L. Strauss, former head of the Atomic Energy Commission and Secretary of Commerce, said: "Len, you get the lawyers. Don't worry about money for legal fees. We'll get that."

Richard Nixon was faced with the choice. Should he challenge the results of the 1960 election in the courts—for which the legal case seemed promising—or should he accept the results of what more and more Americans were coming to view as a fraudulent election?

In his book, *Six Crises*, Nixon recalled the dilemma:

"From the evidence I examined, there was no question but that there was real substance to many of these charges. But substance or not, when I looked into the legal aspects of the situation, I found that it would take at least a year and a half to get a recount in Cook County, and that there was no procedure whatever for a losing candidate to get a recount in Texas. Many of my close friends and associates urged, nevertheless, that I demand a recount. They felt it was important for me to continue fighting so long as there was any hope whatever of winning. They also thought that, even should the effort fail, the publicity that would result from my taking the lead in demanding a recount would carry over and be most helpful to Republican candidates in the 1962 and 1964 elections. This was a compelling appeal in view of my responsibilities as a party leader."

After much soul-searching, and against the advice of his wife and daughters, Richard Nixon came to his decision. He would not contest the election.

The New York Herald Tribune began publishing a series of articles by Earl Mazo charging that the election had been "stolen." Twelve pieces were scheduled for publication but after four of them appeared, Nixon asked Mazo to come and see him. Much to Mazo's surprise, Nixon asked if it were possible for the paper to stop publishing the series.

In his own memo of the conversation, Mazo wrote: "Right off as we shook hands, Nixon said, 'Earl, those are interesting articles you are writing—but no one steals the presidency of the United States.' I thought he might be kidding. But never was a man more deadly serious."

Mazo reported that, "We chatted for an hour or two about the campaign, the odd vote patterns in various places, and this and that. Then, continent by continent, he enumerated potential international crises that could be dealt with only by the President of a united country, and not a nation torn by the kind of partisan bitterness and chaos that inevitably would result from an official challenge of the election result."

At some point in the conversation, Nixon said: "Our country can't afford the agony of a constitutional crisis—and I damn well will not be a party to creating one just to become President or anything else."

Because of Nixon's request, the *Herald Tribune* cancelled the remainder of the Mazo series.

When Leonard Hall went to Nixon with Admiral Strauss' offer of financial assistance to pay for a recount, Nixon said no, explaining the damage that would be done to the American image abroad should he challenge the elections.

Nixon also telephoned the editors of the *Chicago Tribune* and *Chicago Daily News*—Basil L. Walters and Don Maxwell—and asked them to end their editorial campaigns demanding a recount of the Cook County vote. Thus, Nixon put an end to the growing movement in Illinois and elsewhere that might well have led to what he feared, a "constitutional crisis," and which may have led, in addition, to a paralysis of the presidency.

Recalling the difficulty of making the final decision, Nixon recalled: "But I finally made the decision against demanding a recount for what appeared to me, on balance, to be several overriding considerations. If I were to demand a recount, the organization of the new Administration and the orderly transfer of responsibility from the old to the new might be delayed for months. The situation within the entire Federal Government would be chaotic. Those in the old Administration would not know how to act—or with what clear powers and responsibilities—and those being appointed by Kennedy to positions in the new Administration would have the same difficulty making any plans."

"Then, too," Nixon argued, "the bitterness that would be engendered by such a maneuver on my part would, in my opinion have done incalculable and lasting damage throughout the country. And finally, I could think of no worse example for the nations abroad, who for the first time were trying to put free electoral procedures into effect, than that of the United States wrangling over the results of our presidential election, and even suggesting that the presidency itself could be stolen by thievery at the ballot box. It is difficult enough to get defeated candidates in some of the newly independent countries to abide by the verdict of the electorate. If we could not continue to set a good example in this respect in the United States, I could see that there would be open-season for shooting at the validity of free elections throughout the world."

"Consequently," Nixon concluded, "I made the decision not to support the contest and recount charges. I know that this greatly disappointed many of my best friends and most ardent supporters—but I could see for myself no other responsible course of action."

After the decision was made, Richard and Pat Nixon traveled to Key Biscayne, Florida, to rest and recover their strength after the arduous campaign.

Two days after their arrival the Nixons were having dinner at the Jamaica Inn with a party including Bob Finch, Herb Klein, Don Hughes, each of them accompanied by his wife, Bebe Rebozo and Rose Mary Woods. Suddenly, a call came from John F. Kennedy.

Nixon remembers that, "When I picked up the phone, Kennedy was already on the line. . . . He began the conversation pleasantly and informally by asking me how the weather was and if we were finally getting some rest from the campaign. I replied in the same vein and then quite casually he said, 'I would like to fly down from Palm Beach to have a chat with you—if it won't interfere with your vacation.' I replied that I would welcome the opportunity to talk with him, but added: 'I would be glad to come up to Palm Beach to call on you. After all, that's the proper thing to do in view of last Tuesday's results.' He laughed and said, 'No, I have a helicopter at my disposal and it would be easier for me to come to you.' I asked him what day would be most convenient and we agreed to meet at the Key Biscayne Hotel on Monday, November 14."

Later, Nixon found little appreciation of the historic significance of the occasion when he reported it to daughters Tricia and Julie the next day. They berated him: "How can you possibly talk to him after what he said about you in the campaign?" Nixon replied: "After all, he won the election and this is the only proper thing for me to do under the circumstances." Julie still protested: "He didn't win. Haven't you heard about all the cheating in Illinois and Texas?" Nixon recalls that, "I could see that I was not going to win this argument and, quickly as possible, I changed the subject."

Florida's weather was at its best when Kennedy arrived to meet with Nixon at the Key Biscayne Hotel. Nixon stood at the hotel entrance with Bob Neale, the manager, surrounded by scores of reporters and photographers, waiting for Kennedy's arrival. After a short wait, the Dade County police escort came up the drive followed by the Secret Service escort car. Kennedy was in the next car, riding in the back of a convertible and, as Nixon remembers, "despite the officials surrounding him looking almost lonely."

As the car pulled up, Nixon opened the door for Kennedy and they shook hands for the photographers. Then they walked together through the hotel grounds to a private detached villa where Nixon had stayed before on his visits to Key Biscayne and which the hotel had made available for the conference. Nixon insisted that Kennedy walk on his right, as his new rank now entitled him to do. Both men joked about the protocol.

When they reached the villa, they sat on the porch and Nixon fixed soft drinks. Kennedy started the conversation by saying, "Well, it's hard to tell who won the election at this point." Nixon agreed that the verdict had been close, but said that the result was pretty well determined.

When Nixon returned to Washington he was still being pressed by his staff to contest the election. At this point, the popular vote margin had been whittled down to 113,000, out of 68,800,000 votes cast. A change of half-a-vote per precinct nationwide would have shifted the margin to Nixon. A swing of between 11,000 and 13,000 votes—properly distributed in just a few states—would have reversed the election results. But Nixon's decision had been made. The election would not be contested.

In the years following the conclusion of the 1960 election much has been written about the question of who was the real winner, Nixon or Kennedy.

Look Magazine ran an article entitled "How To Steal An Election." It said: "For the first time, many thousands of Americans suddenly realized that elections can be stolen. They only half believed it before 1960, as part of our historic lore. . . . Many, many thousands of voters and civic minded people in several leading states no longer take the easygoing attitude toward election frauds."

In a foreward to Neil R. Pierce's book, *The People's President,* published in 1968, *New York Times* columnist Tom Wicker observed: "A shift of only 4,480 popular votes from Kennedy to Nixon in Illinois, where there were highly plausible charges of fraud and 4,491 in Missouri would have given neither man the electoral majority and thrown the decision into the House of Representatives. If an additional 1,148 votes had been counted for Nixon in New Mexico, 58 from Hawaii and 1,247 from Nevada, he would have won an outright majority in the electoral college."

Wicker added: "Any experienced reporter or politician knows that this few votes can easily be 'swung' in any state by fraud or honest error."

Thirteen years after the election, the pro-Kennedy syndicated columnist, Marquis Childs, conceded: "That the Daley-controlled wards in Chicago supplied the 10,000 votes to put over the Kennedy-Johnson ticket can hardly be questioned. . . . In hindsight it might have been better for Nixon to have faced up to the frauds of 1960."

Theodore White admitted that perhaps enough votes were stolen in Texas and Illinois to win the presidency for Kennedy. In his book, *Breach of Faith,* which deals with the downfall of Richard Nixon, White states: "Democratic vote-stealing had definitely taken place on a massive scale in Illinois and Texas (where 100,000 big city votes were simply disqualified); and on a lesser scale elsewhere."

In Washington there was a widespread feeling that the 1960 election was marred by fraud. When J. Edgar Hoover was congratulated by his good friend Philip Hochstein, then editor of *The Newark Star-Ledger,* upon being reappointed by President Kennedy, Hoover launched into an attack of "election frauds" and said that as far as he was concerned, "Kennedy is not President-elect."

Hoover complained that he had not been "permitted" to investigate the election frauds which had led to the final Kennedy victory. Hochstein asked who prevented him from launching such a full-scale investigation. Hoover replied: "Ike and Nixon."

Eisenhower and Nixon had jointly decided that, despite the closeness of the election and the widespread evidence of irregularities, the welfare of the nation at a time of trouble abroad demanded that a new President be inaugurated without a controversy that would prove divisive to the country.

In his book, *Kennedy,* Theodore Sorenson, a close ally of President Kennedy, declared that, "Eisenhower and Nixon merely by meeting with Kennedy, were patriotically recognizing the certainty of his election, and thus helping to put an end to the bitter charges of fraud, the demands for recounts and the threats of Southern independent electors."

Victor Lasky recalls that, "Probably the most interesting thing about 1960 was the general unwillingness of the media to pursue allegations that the election had been 'stolen' by the Democrats. Only a handful of newspapers (and they were generally Republican) were excited enough to look into a story that could easily have developed into one of the biggest political crimes of the century."

On January 6, 1961, Richard Nixon, as Vice President and President of the Senate, presided with House Speaker Sam Rayburn over a Joint Session of Congress for the ceremony of counting the electoral votes.

An hour before the session was to begin, Earl Mazo called Nixon's office to suggest that in view of some comments in the press gallery that this would be an embarrassing moment for Nixon, he might make some statement at the time he announced the official outcome.

"This was," Nixon remembered, "a most unusual occasion. Only once before had the defeated candidate had the responsibility of presiding over his own 'funeral' by announcing his defeat in a Joint Session, and this had occurred exactly one hundred years before when John C. Breckinridge announced the election of Abraham Lincoln."

Nixon took Earl Mazo's advice and when the counting had been concluded and announced—to no one's surprise it was 303 for Kennedy, 209 for Nixon, with the balance of 15 for Harry F. Byrd of Virginia—Nixon made this brief statement:

"Mr. Speaker, since this is an unprecedented situation I would like to ask permission to impose upon the time of the members of this Congress to make a statement. . . . This is the first time in 100 years that a candidate for the presidency announced the result of an election in which he was defeated and announced the victory of his opponent. I do not think we could have a more striking and eloquent example of the stability of our constitutional system and of the proud tradition of the American people of developing, respecting, and honoring institutions of self government."

Nixon continued:

"In our campaigns, no matter how hard fought they may be, no matter how close the election may turn out to be, those who lose accept the verdict and support those who win. And I would like to add that having served in Government for 14 years . . . as I complete that period that it is indeed a very great honor to me to extend to my colleagues in the House and Senate on both sides of the aisle who have been elected—to extend to John F. Kennedy and Lyndon Johnson, who have been elected President and Vice President of the United States, my heartfelt best wishes, as all of you work in a cause that is bigger than any man's ambition, greater than any party. It is the cause of freedom, of justice, and peace for all mankind. It is in that spirit that I now declare that John F. Kennedy has been elected President of the United States, and Lyndon B. Johnson, Vice President of the United States."

The audience rose to its feet. The ovations from both Democrats and Republicans went on for such a long period that Nixon had to stand several times to acknowledge it. Sam Rayburn broke precedent and joined in the applause himself. He grasped Nixon's hand warmly as the Vice President left the Speaker's rostrum and said, "That was a fine speech, Dick. I will miss you here. Good luck."

Two weeks later, at a few minutes past noon, John F. Kennedy took the oath of office as the 35th President of the United States.

1

The First Domino Falls

THE NEW STATE Department auditorium in Washington was packed. Word had gone out that President John F. Kennedy, just sixty-two days in office, was going to drop a bomb at his news conference. A record number of 426 correspondents picked their way through the confusion of cameras and wires and sat blinking in the unnatural glare of bright lights for the President's first televised meeting with the press. The new satellite Tel-star would bounce the waves across the Atlantic Ocean into millions of British, French and German living rooms.

Just before the scheduled hour a press aide rolled out a six by eight foot map of Southeast Asia on a metal stand.

One country, drawn in blue, was shaped like an extended finger out of which three red bites had been taken at the big knuckle.

A few moments after the unveiling of the map, the President himself appeared. He moved to the podium with that stiff-backed carriage to which newsmen were becoming accustomed. In a matter-of-fact way he addressed himself to what Madison Avenue advertising men call "the presentation."

The blue finger on the map, he said, was the distant land of elephants and parasols, the Kingdom of Laos; and the three red bites were the inroads made by the communist guerrillas across the borders, from the neighboring countries of Red China and North Vietnam.

The bites were mere nibbles on August 7, 1960, the President said, but . . . State Department Press Aide Lincoln White removed the first map revealing a second.

By December 20, 1960, six weeks from the day Kennedy won the Presidential election, the communists had really sunk their teeth into Laos.

White whisked away the second map. The third showed how things were on that very day, March 23, 1961. The hungry red mouth was ready to devour Luang Prabang itself, the seat of Royal power.

The President's talk was tough and realistic. He demanded strong measures in Laos. He had been briefed well on this and he believed what he had heard.

Admiral Arleigh Burke, who had just resigned as Chief of Naval Operations, had described the strategic importance of Laos in a speech which was censored by the State Department. He said, "Laos is the key to control of the whole of southeast Asia. It adjoins Free Thailand, Free Cambodia, Free Vietnam. Free Malaya is just to the South. Indonesia is only a short sea distance farther south. In the hands of the communists, Laos would be a pistol pointed at the heart of every free country."

Under French rule there had been no separate Laos, no Cambodia, no Vietnam. The area was known as Indochina and it remained a political entity until World War II when France had to withdraw large contingents of her hard-bitten Legionnaires to oppose Adolf Hitler in Europe. This withdrawal left dissident elements free to flex their ideological muscles, and during the war years these rebels became strong and bold. One of them, Ho Chi Minh, had set up a communist organization called the Viet Minh in the southern provinces of China bordering on Indochina, as early as 1941.

During the war years when France was occupied, she was excluded from the Yalta Conference, and from Potsdam, where she was deprived of her overseas possessions. At the close of hostilities, the surrender of Japanese troops in Indochina north of the sixteenth parallel was entrusted to the Chinese, and south of that line to the British.

Meanwhile, Ho Chi Minh had been able to set up military units under a very able leader, the man we know as General Vo Ngygen Giap. The contingents were composed mainly of veteran fighters seasoned in jungle warfare with the Japanese.

Giap won an ally in a remote member of the royal family, Prince Souphanouvong, who had returned home dazzled by French Socialism. He hurried off into the northern jungles to visit Giap who taught him how to employ guerrilla tactics to the best advantage.

"Use the peasants as your eyes and ears and your main source of supply," Giap advised. "Descend on the villages at nightfall. Kill or kidnap village leaders and thus destroy the will of the peasants to oppose you. Exact a handful of rice from each woman. Implicate a peasant in the killing of a soldier, and so implicate him in the war."

Prince Souphanouvong learned the lessons well. In three years he formed the hard core of the Pathet Lao. By that time, General de Gaulle had assembled an expeditionary force, put it under the command of the famous General Jac Philippe Leclerc, and sent it to the Far East to save Indochina from the new and insidious enemy waiting in the northern hills and jungle.

At first Leclerc was successful. He drove the Viet Minh north to the Chinese border where Chiang Kai-shek, involved in a life and death struggle with the Reds, forced them to disperse. For a while, the Indochinese communists were reduced to guerrilla activities, mainly in the lush jungles along the Mekong River.

In 1949, when the Chinese Reds, under Mao, reached the Indochina frontier, Ho Chi Minh, Giap and Souphanouvong found a sanctuary and a base. The Viet Minh revived rapidly. By October, 1950, they were strong enough to strike a blow at French rule. Through brilliant tactics, General de Lattre de Tassigny, successor to General Leclerc, was able to contain them. But unfortunately he fell ill and died soon after.

After de Tassigny's death the tide turned, and the flood rolled south. General Eisenhower, in the White House, at last saw Ho Chi Minh clearly for what he was and threw our support behind the French. As their position deteriorated, especially at Dienbienphu in 1954, Eisenhower ordered Admiral Arthur Radford, chairman of the

Joint Chiefs of Staff, to give top priority to French requests for arms and materiel.

It was too late. General John "Iron Mike" O'Daniel, chief American adviser, said of the French surrender in Indochina, after the fall of Dienbienphu:

"The French gave up—not because of Dienbienphu—but because French public opinion was fed up, French domestic politics was in turmoil and the French economy a mess. The Viet Cong never defeated the French in any decisive way. They broke France's will to continue the struggle." The battle was lost inside France.

The United States had made some desperate, last-minute attempts during the siege of Dienbienphu to bolster France's morale.

These came to nothing because the British would have no part of them. Besides, Washington and Paris were working at cross purposes. The French were determined to negotiate their way out of Vietnam.

Between the opening of the Geneva Conference in April and June 20, 1954, the French Government was swept away by the formation of a new government headed by Pierre Mendes-France. He made it plain publicly that he was determined to have peace at any price.

The Geneva agreement partitioned the former French colony into separate states. The communists got North Vietnam. Laos, Cambodia and South Vietnam were declared independent neutral states.

Neither the United States nor South Vietnam signed the final declaration at Geneva and President Eisenhower's Secretary of State, John Foster Dulles, inspired the formation of SEATO, the Southeast Asia Treat Organization, with several Western and Southeast Asian countries.

The Dulles philosophy was to build and strengthen the Royal Laotian Army. To that end we poured about $50,000,000 a year into the kingdom, and the policy seemed to work.

Although the communist Pathet Lao, armed with Soviet and Red Chinese weapons, kept trying to overthrow the government, the Royal Laotian Army held its own. As a matter of fact, early in December, 1960, these troops, under General Phoumi Nosavan, went on the offensive and managed by adroit maneuvering, despite the presence of Russian artillery, to recapture the administrative capital of Vientiane.

It was a great victory for the pro-American forces. A few days later, on December 14, 1960, pro-western Prince Boun Oum took over as Premier.

At this point the Russians openly intervened in support of the Pathet Lao. In the period between the United States November elections and the January 1961 inauguration of a new president, Eisenhower refrained from moves which would commit his successor. And now Russia joined in a large-scale push by Soviet-trained North Vietnamese troops. Russia also introduced a substantial airlift into northern Laos which put heavy pressure on the Royal Laotian Army.

That was the situation when President Eisenhower turned over the administration of government to President Kennedy, warning the new President it might take the intervention of American troops to redeem our pledges to the Laotians and keep Laos from falling under communist control.

The young President listened courteously to the elder man. But he had some positive ideas for change and naturally wanted to do things in his own way. He felt the Eisenhower Administration had been too slow and hesitant, and that the staff system had been largely responsible. He decided to take personal charge of all major policy and action, asking for advice only when he felt he needed it to reach a decision.

So far as the Defense Department was concerned, the advice he got was direct and unequivocal. The Joint Chiefs of Staff believed, as they had under Eisenhower, that the challenge in Laos demanded firm handling. SEATO should send a mixed allied force, they said, including United States troops, to hold the important cities, while the Laotian army, protected from subversion in the rear, dealt with the enemy in the field.

While the President held meetings and talks in Washington, the situation in Southeast Asia deteriorated. Kennedy was doing his best to cope with the problem, but he was new to the task and on unfamiliar ground. While he cautiously weighed his options, the Red forces in Laos advanced foot by foot and mile by mile.

At a briefing on March 9, the military advisers favored strong measures. The majority suggested the landing of units in Thailand, South-Vietnam and the government-held positions in the Laos panhandle. If this failed to produce a cease-fire, then the military men suggested air attacks on the Pathet Lao positions, and use of tactical nuclear weapons on the ground.

The phrase "nuclear weapons" was a red flag to the new President. Alarmed, he asked, "Are you telling me I can't do anything without starting a nuclear war?"

The military program of direct intervention in Laos became known as "Track One" in White House parlance.

But there was another school of thought. Some of the new advisers on the White House staff were professors who had visited Russia late in 1960 and been persuaded that Nikita Khrushchev was in a mood to do business with the United States. In spite of the Soviet-supported Pathet Lao attacks, they thought that the Russian Premier was merely indulging in what they termed "salami tactics" and that he could be stalled for an indefinite time with a small slice of Laos.

Their policy was to maneuver the Russians into a compromise—a neutral government in which the Pathet Lao would have a minor representation. This policy became known as "Track Two."

Early In March, while the President was still debating which line to follow, a sudden attack by the communists dislodged General Phoumi from his position commanding the Astrid Highway.

A hurried summons was sent to U.S. Pacific Commander, Admiral Henry Felt, to come to Washington. He flew in from Pearl Harbor and reported to the President that "the Russian-backed rebels are spreading in Laos like the measles."

At one of these sessions Kennedy is reported to have said belligerently, "The Russians have been pushing us around. Let's push them around a bit."

It was against this background that he conducted his historic televised news conference of March 23, 1961, with much of Europe watching the proceedings bounced across the Atlantic by the satellite Tel-star.

"If in the past," President Kennedy told his vast audience, "there has been any ground for misunderstanding our desire for a truly neutral Laos, there should be none now."

His words were firm, his attitude stern and seemingly unyielding as he went on, "My fellow Americans, Laos is far away from America, but the world is small. Its two million people live in a country three times the size of Austria. The security of all Southeast Asia will be endangered if Laos loses its neutral independence. Its own safety runs with the safety of us all, in real neutrality observed by all."

He warned the communist world, "No one should doubt our resolution to preserve an independent, neutral Laos," and added, "If there is to be a peaceful solution there must be a cessation of the present armed attacks by externally supported communists. If these attacks do not stop, those who support a truly neutral Laos will have to consider their response."

They were strong words, and to put teeth in them the new Commander in Chief mobilized his forces in the Far East. The sleek, 62,000 ton carrier *Midway* quietly slipped her mooring buoy in the green harbor of Hong Kong and sailed to join the attack cruisers *Lexington* and *Coral Sea* off the Indochina coast.

Two thousand marines were pulled out of Japan where they had been making a Hollywood potboiler aptly entitled: "Marines Let's Go!" and moved to an undisclosed position near Laos.

The Army's strategic strike units and special jungle fighting outfits at home were put on the alert. Technicians were airlifted into northern Thailand to help service helicopters flown by Royal Laotian Army troops.

Editorial writers hailed the decision and supported the President. "Mr. Kennedy emphasized the resolution of the United States to counter communist aggression and preserve an independent, neutral Laos, but it was clear the primary aim of his declaration was to bring about a peaceful solution of the Laotian crisis," one said.

Everyone recognized that the test of wills was on. It was a test not only of wills but of nerves. And it was taking place on the brink of the abyss that all men dreaded.

The intent of the President was plain and unmistakable. The Pathet Lao must stop their attacks on the Laotian government. The President warned further "that the United States would otherwise, however unwillingly, be required to intervene militarily on the ground to prevent the takeover of Laos by force."

That message was conveyed through Warsaw to the Red Chinese; through the British to the Geneva Conference; and by India's Nehru and Ambassador Llewellyn Thompson directly to Khrushchev.

The air was still crackling with expectant tension when, two days later, the President flew to the Key West Naval Station for a conference with Britain's Prime Minister, Harold Macmillan, whose government had conveyed new proposals for a cease fire in Laos to Moscow.

Although the Key West parley produced a public statement by the Prime Minister and the President that the situation in Laos "cannot be allowed to deteriorate," the fact of the matter was that the young President failed to win over the wary old Prime Minister. Macmillan declared flatly that Britain wanted no part of a SEATO action in Laos. General de Gaulle, disdaining protocol and courtesy, had already told the President the same thing in even blunter language.

The President drew two blanks, and from that point on it became apparent that the idea of a military showdown in Laos looked less and less attractive to him.

However, President Kennedy did issue one more warning to the Russians that might have been construed as a threat of military action. It became known in Washington that when Soviet Foreign Minister Andrei Gromyko called at the White House, the President took him into the rose garden, out of earshot, and told him, "The United States does not intend to stand idly by while you take over in Laos."

But that was the last vestige of a firm stand by the President. After having stated unequivocally before the listening and watching world that he would pursue a strong policy of military intervention against the Pathet Lao, he suddenly abandoned the idea for one of compromise.

As events moved forward it became increasingly clear that the President was now relying entirely upon the chances of getting a negotiated peace in Laos. The means to that end had already been communicated by Britain to Moscow, but had been overshadowed by what seemed to be the President's fighting words. Americans awoke to the truth of the matter. The President favored the British proposal of a committee of Canada, India and Poland—one Western, one neutral and one Communist country—as a Control Commission to supervise a truce. He was willing even to let communist China take part in the conference if that would work out a settlement.

Here, tragically, President Kennedy was walking into a trap. The young President was handicapped by his lack of experience in dealing with the devious devices of diplomacy. In his anxiety to do the right thing he leaned on advisers who were "specialists" and "experts." Unfortunately, many of them were academic theoreticians, not hard-nosed bargainers like Soviet Foreign Minister Gromyko whose own careers, their lives even, depend on undeviating adherence to the Kremlin line.

He also apparently believed, as his father had before him, that differences with dictators can be resolved by negotiation. Kennedy's father, when he was Ambassador to the Court of St. James in 1938, had spoken strongly in support of Chamberlain's appeasement of Hitler, urging an accommodation of British and German interests.

This is the businessman's illusion which Kennedy senior brought to diplomacy. There is no reason to believe he ever changed his views. He never apologized for them or explained them. It is reasonable to suppose he conveyed this philosophy to his son who now had to deal with another dictator, one Nikita Khrushchev.

The young President, then, undoubtedly suffered from the dual handicap of exposure to parental and academic concurrence in a fatal decision that he could get along with the communists. He did not seem to mind that communist countries had for months been calling for just such a conference set up in just such a way as he was now ready to accept. Nor did he appear to mind that Khrushchev, once he had received the Kennedy proposal, took his own time about replying, and that meanwhile, the fighting in Laos continued.

About that time, the Bay of Pigs invasion rudely jolted President Kennedy's attention from the Far East to the Near West.

But the communists did not relax their concentration on Laos. Khrushchev stalled off the British proposals for a cease-fire for a full five weeks while the Pathet Lao tightened their grip on the little kingdom. The guerrillas moved through the jungles toward Vientiane and Luang Prabang; and down the western border of South Vietnam. Russia stepped up her airlift, flying weapons and supplies into the country.

Even after the British-Russian agreement for a ceasefire, which came when Khrushchev was good and ready, the Pathet Lao rebels continued on the offensive. By the middle of April it appeared that the communists would go to the Laos peace table, scheduled for May 15 in Geneva, not as defendants charged with criminal acts, nor even as plaintiffs pleading their case, but as military victors able to dictate their terms and demand their spoils.

It was six weeks since the President had broadcast to the world that "no one could doubt our resolution." Peace of a sort settled upon the Asian Kingdom of Laos. But it was relief without joy, for the cease-fire in Laos came as a cold war defeat for the United States.

A political cartoon by Bill Mauldin in the *St. Louis Post Dispatch* showed Khrushchev, a napkin tucked under his fat jowls, sitting down to a plump pigeon labeled Laos and remarking to an onlooking Kennedy, "Mind if I eat while we talk?"

So, drop by drop, while the President did nothing, Laotian independence dripped slowly away. His military advisers urged intervention with at least 140,000 men. One day they suggested landing troops on two air-strips in territory held by 5,000 Pathet Lao guerrillas. But Kennedy rejected that proposition with the remark that the Pathet Lao might counter-attack before all our troops were landed. Haunted by the prospect of a nuclear war, he did not know what to do. Finally, he sent Averell Harriman to meet Prince Souvanna Phouma of Laos and report on the situation.

The Prince was one of three men of royal lineage who had been contending for power in that lush land of princes and peasants. The most powerful was Prince Souphanouvong who had long ago let it be known he was an ardent communist and the boss of the Russian-backed Pathet Lao which had kept the small Kingdom in turmoil for years.

Then there was pro-western Prince Boun Oum. Hostile diplomats called him "a sort of Buddhist Falstaff." The rifles of General Phoumi Nosavan had put him in power and the dollars of American aid had kept him there.

Somewhere between these two stood Prince Souvanna Phouma, as difficult to categorize as to understand. Until the army ousted him, he had been recognized as Premier by the Russians. Afterwards, while Laotians warred on each other, he spent his time cultivating gladioli in voluntary exile at a royal villa he had borrowed from Prince Norodom Sihanouk of Cambodia. Whenever the press waited on him, he spoke vaguely of a doctrine he called "neutrality in neutralism," which he consistently refused to define because Laotians dislike precision.

In their New Delhi meeting, Souvanna impressed Ambassador Harriman. The Prince told him the people of Laos did not wish to be communists. It was not too late, he said. Laos could be saved.

Then he made a proposition, which was a variation of an old refrain: form a coalition government, take in the Pathet Lao, and let the coming fourteen-nation conference at Geneva guarantee neutrality. This was the troika line communist nations had been advocating for months—team a Western ally with a neutralist and a communist and let them pull one against the others. It was an old trick that had done irreparable damage in China, Czechoslovakia and elsewhere.

Harriman hastened back to Washington with the message. The President, after listening to Harriman, was infected with his enthusiasm and decided to take a look at the Laotian Prince who had impressed the roving Ambassador so favorably. He decided to invite him to Washington for an official visit on April 19.

Secretary of State Dean Rusk, however, took a dim view of the proposal. The State Department believed Souvanna Phouma was hand in glove with the communists. Rusk passed the word to Kennedy. The Secretary said, with diplomatic caution, he had a speaking engagement in Georgia and would be unable to receive Souvanna on that day. Apologies were made. Instead of coming to Washington, Souvanna gravitated to Moscow.

For a time this ended Washington's dealings with Souvanna Phouma, but only for a time, for the President did not forget the advocate of "neutrality in neutralism."

For some time the Kennedy Administration had been seeking a summit conference with Khrushchev, and the President now went off to Vienna for the historic confrontation. From the first it appeared obvious that the President wanted to talk about problems, while the whily old Russian, less impetuous, delighted in needling the young President about capitalism. If Kennedy wished to accomplish anything, he had to get in a few words between ideological exchanges. It must have amused Khrushchev, because the President's words and manner showed plainly that nothing in his previous experience had prepared him for jousting with a negotiator as cunning and skillful as Khrushchev.

When finally Kennedy got the conversation around to Laos, he admitted to Khrushchev that the Pathet Lao enjoyed certain advantages. The next time they met, he conceded that Laos was a land without strategic importance. And, if Kennedy had forgotten or ignored the fact that this was almost a complete reversal from his earlier Tel-star statement that the safety of Laos ran with the safety of us all, Khrushchev remembered it.

Finally, the President weakened his bargaining position even further. The United States, he confessed to the Russian dictator, wanted to reduce its involvement in Laos which, he said, was not important enough to bring the U.S. and the U.S.S.R. to grips.

The well-meaning Kennedy thus answered the mocking question Khrushchev had put to Ambassador Thompson earlier: "Why take risks over Laos. It will fall into our hands like a ripe apple."

Kennedy had sold himself on the three-nation 'troika' solution Harriman had grabbed so eagerly from Prince Souvanna Phouma. He decided to send Harriman to Geneva to carry out his wishes. But the State Department voiced some objections.

Nevertheless, Kennedy went right ahead and let it be known Harriman was his man and after some jockeying to preserve departmental "face," Kennedy had his way. He named Averell Harriman Assistant Secretary of State for the Far East. And in that role Harriman flew to Geneva to take charge of negotiations for the United States.

His first act was to cut the 126-man delegation to approximately one-third of that number. At the top of the delegation he had put William H. Sullivan, a Class 3 Foreign Service Officer who, he knew, sympathized with a soft line toward Russia. When the State Department objected, pointing out that Sullivan could not be put above men of higher classification, Harriman simply sent home those delegates who were in Class 1 and Class 2.

Harriman's goal was to achieve the Kennedy-Khrushchev objective. He saw certain obstacles, of course; and the biggest was General Phoumi, who could not bring himself to believe that Kennedy would let in the communists after the long American-Laotian fight to keep them out.

Even as the talks opened, the fighting in Laos continued and the Pathet Lao, shrewdly avoiding an all-out assault, continued to flow in and around the towns and villages and consolidate their positions. So swift was their advance that President Kennedy admitted ruefully, "With a few more weeks of fighting, the communists have every military prospect of picking up the entire country."

Yet he was unable to come up with any plan to prevent it.

In June, when Kennedy, reporting on his meeting with Khrushchev, said he was hopeful Soviet assurances could "be translated into new attitudes at Geneva," Russian-supplied guns derisively opened up on the Laotian village of Padong.

In Geneva, Harriman said the United States would boycott the conference until the fighting stopped, and the British and French backed him up.

The fighting did not stop. Undeterred, the Communists went on with their military takeover, not even bothering to deny the shooting, and the New China News Agency crowed that Padong was "the Dienbienphu in 1961 of the United States."

We went back to the diplomatic table and there, as on the fighting front, we lost ground steadily. At the outset Harriman found there were only two nations he could count on for support—South Vietnam and Thailand. Britain, France and Canada, as well as neutral India, Burma and Cambodia refused, time after time, to go along with the United States.

Our allies saw how uncertain was the guidance from Washington. Before long, British, French and Canadian negotiations were going on with Russia, Poland, Red China and North Vietnam over Harriman's head and behind his back. One British-Russian compromise gave Russia's Gromyko his own way in seating Pathet Lao Communists as equals of the Royal Laotian government at the conference table. That planted the seeds of the Troika solution. The Royal Laotian delegation reacted bitterly. It refused to attend further sessions. But the President said he had to agree rather than be accused of breaking up the convention.

Under the terms of a cease-fire agreement, the conference had endorsed the British proposal to name a Control Commission composed of Canada, India and Poland to supervise the truce. It was supposedly impartial.

But it came in for bitter comment from members of the American delegation who clearly saw what was happening. Said one American aide, "Instead of one Western, one Communist and one neutral country, we are confronted with a Central Commission of two neutrals and a Communist." In other words it was a forerunner of the very troika arrangement the convention would adopt for Laos.

In late June, Laotian Premier Boun Oum, whom the United States had formerly backed, gave up the ghost. The three key Laotian Princes met at Zurich's Dolder Grand Hotel, and, after five days of talk, greying Prince Boun Oum signed, "All I want is tranquillity," and went off to the Riviera for an indefinite vacation.

What he really saw was the handwriting on the wall, and the handwriting spelled 'troika.'

Prince Boun Oum's retirement automatically put Prince Souvanna Phouma in charge. He lost no time in revealing his true colors. "Boun Oum," he said pointedly, "is a patriot, but he has let himself be used by the Americans. He wants to get out of politics. I would like to do the same thing but the people are behind me, and I cannot let them down."

Souvanna suffered from a boil which he used as an excuse to withdraw early and let many of his points be driven home by his half-brother, the Red Prince Souphanouvong, top man of the communist Pathet Lao.

In commenting on the situation, Prince Norodom Sihanouk of Cambodia said: "Laos is finished. It will be completely lost in a week." He rated the chance of saving it from communism "one in a thousand," and took himself off for a rest on the Riviera to ponder the future.

Even though defeat was a foregone conclusion, loyal General Phoumi resisted the troika to the bitter end. The President finally whipped the Laotian general into line by suspending the U.S. monthly grant of $3,000,000 which he needed to meet his military and civilian payrolls.

Then came the final disaster—the climax of the policies carried out at the conference table. The decision had been to place Laos under a troika government—one man loyal to the western powers, one communist, one neutral. But in the end Laos did not get a troika government because General Phoumi, the one man who had fought the communists, was forced to flee the country. That wily Asian, Prince Souvanna Phouma, who talked out of both sides of his mouth and bemused both Averell Harriman and John F. Kennedy, became Premier. Souphanouvong, the communist leader, was named Vice President, and the Pathet Lao continued to hold all the country they had seized, refusing entry to government troops.

William Sullivan, the instrument of the Kennedy-Harriman mistakes at Geneva, became the United States Ambassador to Laos.

The upshot of the errors generated by Averell Harriman's willful stubbornness. and Kennedy's naive reliance on communist agreements, was that the communists achieved virtually all they had set out to gain. They won control of much of Laos. They turned the left flank of South Vietnam and were able to pour men and materials through Laos along the Ho Chi Minh Trail into the next country on their timetable—South Vietnam.

As late as December 19, 1967, *The New York Times* Washington correspondent, Tom Wicker, wrote that, "although the Laotian troika is still functioning, its writ does not run to a large part of the country where North Vietnamese forces operate openly in support of the communist Pathet Lao, and keep supply trails open in South Vietnam."

In November 1967, correspondents were told in North Vietnam that only 19% of the invading North Vietnamese troops filtered through the DMZ. One percent got in by sea. The other 80% made an end run through Northern Laos and seeped into South Vietnam over dozens of big and little passes through the mountains.

And it was impossible then for us to seal it off.

That is the sorry story of the big U.S. mistake in Laos which began with the President's vowing to preserve an independent Laos. He failed to act with strength and conviction. He was out-talked by Khrushchev, out-maneuvered by the Russian diplomats and out-bargained at the conference table in Geneva, with the result that two million Laotians lost their freedom, and the consequences were almost incalculable, the most terrible being the tragedy of Vietnam which would follow.

2

Getting America Into The Vietnam War

THE LARGE AUDIENCE in the ballroom of New York's Waldorf-Astoria grew quiet and expectant as former Governor Thomas E. Dewey spoke of his visit to the South Vietnamese capital of Saigon.

"It was the one beleagured capital in the world," he said, "and a person could get there only by air."

His description of his arrival was graphic. One could almost smell the lush, tropic undergrowth and feel the close embrace of the warm, moist air.

Looking around at the airport Dewey counted eighteen gun emplacements and as they drove into Saigon itself the American Ambassador pointed out why the brush was cut far back from the road.

"The reason is so the Communist snipers will have a poor chance of hitting us as we go along," Dewey quoted the Ambassador as saying. "The land mines they plant every night are cleared in the morning before we go out to the airport."

That night, four blocks away from Dewey's hotel, in the center of Saigon, a grenade was thrown, killing two soldiers.

It was a dramatic and compelling talk, not so much because Dewey's experiences were unique, but because he suddenly startled his audience by saying that the events he described took place, not this year, not last—but in 1951.

The talk illustrated just how old a problem Vietnam is, not one merely going back to the Eisenhower era, but well back into the period of Harry S. Truman and beyond.

Ignoring that fact, historians of the Kennedy Administration frequently try to explain the United States involvement in the war in South Vietnam by asserting it is an evil first caused by the Eisenhower Administration. But the truth of the matter is that Eisenhower's Vietnam bequest to Kennedy was just about what Truman's bequest to Eisenhower had been.

Appearing before the Senate Foreign Relations Committee on May 9, 1966, Secretary of State Dean Rusk traced our Vietnam policy back as far as 1947, when the United States leaders first commenced uttering expressions of support for the French in Indochina.

Six years before that time, in 1941, President Roosevelt had judged the Japanese occupation of Indochina a threat to vital United States' interests in the Far East. And some might argue that our involvement in Southeast Asia goes back more than one hundred years, to 1833, when we first entered into a trade agreement with the King of Siam.

So our ties to Southeast Asia were already ancient and honorable when, as creatures of the Geneva Conference, North and South Vietnam came into existence in 1954. That same year we signed the SEATO agreement, guaranteeing South Vietnam and the other countries of Southeast Asia against aggression. And when Ngo Dinh Diem was elected president of South Vietnam in October, 1955, the Eisenhower Administration promptly recognized his government. There was valid reasoning behind the Eisenhower decision in doing this. He realized the importance of a buffer against Red North Vietnam. South Vietnam must remain strong. At the same time, we must stay out of the war. Eisenhower thought that the best way to accomplish both objectives was to send Saigon substantial aid and a limited number of advisors to help the Vietnamese train their troops. This, he felt, would achieve our ends without getting the United States militarily involved.

Shortly after reaching his decision, President Eisenhower, recuperating from a heart attack in a Denver hospital, asked Senator

Thruston Morton, the Kentucky Republican, to take a message to the Senate Armed Forces Chairman, Richard Russell of Georgia.

The purpose of Morton's mission was to tell Russell that Eisenhower wished to send 200 military advisors to South Vietnam to assist Diem's generals. President Eisenhower believed, Morton said, that Diem's regime had to be strengthened if it was to stand firm against Communism.

Russell objected. He said it would be impossible to commit 200 without starting a manpower spiral.

In the next five years Eisenhower proved Russell wrong. He kept a firm hand on the number of men we committed to South Vietnam and did not allow the number to spiral. On January 20, 1961, when he turned the government over to President Kennedy, our advisors in the Southeast Asian country still were in the hundreds, and Diem had the situation under control.

Soon after his inauguration, President Kennedy was faced with complex and unfamiliar problems in many parts of the world. He had desperately tried to cope with the situation in the neighboring state of Laos. He had made his great mistake at the Bay of Pigs. At Vienna he had confronted Russia's Nikita Khrushchev in their well-publicized summit meeting.

Khrushchev quickly took the offensive, launching a bitter attack upon the United States and its "international imperialism." He threatened Kennedy over Berlin, saying that the missiles would fly, the tanks would roll.

Later, Kennedy told *New York Times* columnist James Reston, "I've got two problems. First, to figure out why he did it, and in such a hostile way. And second, to figure out what we can do about it. I think the first part is pretty easy to explain. I think he did it because of the Bay of Pigs. I think he thought that anyone who was so young and inexperienced as to get into that mess could be taken, and anyone who got into it, and didn't see it through, had no guts. So he just beat hell out of me. So I've got a terrible problem. If he thinks I'm inexperienced and have no guts, until we remove those ideas we won't get anywhere with him. So we have to act."

Kennedy turned to Reston and said that the only place in the world where there was a real challenge was in Vietnam, and "now we have a problem in trying to make our power credible, and Vietnam looks like the place."

What the new President assumed was that a show of force would fill the bill, and he decided to make a show in South Vietnam. During the month of April, 1961, a Vietnam Task Force was set up and the President chose Frederick Nolting as Ambassador to South Vietnam. Nolting, a Virginia gentleman, with scholarly degrees, a soft voice and a tough mind, had served in many high government posts. Kennedy knew Nolting could work with him and Diem.

Kennedy was aware also of his Ambassador's complete understanding of President Diem's determination to preserve his conception of nationalism in Saigon. Diem did not want United States combat forces and said so time and time again. This was so well known that Diem's attitude to American aid was likened to Churchill's famous challenge when Britain's sovereignty was threatened by Hitler . . . "Give us the ships and we'll finish the job!"

Diem's public utterances that he did not want or need U.S. troops was soon going to make things awkward for President Kennedy. He dispatched Vice President Lyndon B. Johnson on a tour of Southeast Asia. Part of Johnson's mission was to assure Chiang-Kai-shek in Taiwan and Larshal Thanarat Sarit in Thailand that the Administration's handling of Laos did not mean a general withdrawal from Southeast Asia.

Diem, too, was concerned about this. He wanted a treaty with the U.S. To mollify him Johnson, while in Taipei, hailed Diem as the Winston Churchill of South Asia. When he met with Diem in person he passed on Kennedy's instructions to him to "encourage" Diem to request U.S. ground troops. Diem's response was, once again, that he did not want U.S. ground troops. It would be a violation of the 1954 Geneva accords that had ended the French war in Indochina.

On his arrival back in Washington, Johnson reported to the President, "we must decide whether to help these countries to the best of our ability or throw in the towel in the area and pull back our defenses to San Francisco and a 'fortress America' concept . . . I recommend that we move forward promptly with a major effort to help these countries defend themselves."

Johnson said nothing about sending U.S. soldiers and marines to fight in Asia. In September, 1961, the Viet Cong seized a provincial capital and beheaded the governor. The Kennedy Administration decided this was a pretext for action. However, there still was opposition among Kennedy's advisors. The alternatives ranged all the way from Johnson's recommendation to Chester Bowles' idea of enlarging the concept of a neutral and independent Laos to include Burma, Thailand, South Vietnam, Cambodia and Malaya.

To overcome some of the opposition, Kennedy sent a new investigating group to Saigon. One commentator has said its very composition indicated a readiness on the President's part to concede the problem of South Vietnam to the Defense Department. Indeed, all through this period, the President relied heavily on McNamara in preference to the Secretary of State, Dean Rusk.

The task force was made up of General Maxwell Taylor and White House Aide Walt Rostow, who, after the shuttle run to Saigon and return, issued a report recommending a shift from economic aid to increased intervention and a limited partnership in the war effort. General Taylor envisioned sending as many as ten thousand men across the Pacific. Walt Rostow urged the President to send 18,000 troops and recommended that they be disguised as engineers since the Geneva Treaty called for a limitation of 1,000 troops.

In a section of the report, Taylor raised the question of how long Saigon could be expected to confine its activities to the existing ground rules which permitted North Vietnam to train guerrillas and send them across the border while denying South Vietnam, as we long denied Chiang on Taiwan, the right to strike back at the real source of aggression.

Continued pressure was exerted on Diem to cooperate with the U.S. Diem had sent a letter to Kennedy arguing that U.S. aid should be limited to material support, not troops, because the presence of U.S. soldiers in Vietnam would give some credibility to the charges from the Communists that he was a front for the colonialists. But finally, in October, Diem did make the solicited request for U.S. troops. Then, on the strength of the Taylor-Rostow report, President Kennedy made the final decision to go ahead. In December, 1961, he detailed General Paul Harkins to South Vietnam and ordered the American buildup to begin.

Actually, it had already secretly commenced. As early as November 17, several hundred more American specialists had been sent to train Vietnamese forces, but the American people were told nothing about the shipment of these men. More soon followed, and again no announcement was made to the American people of what was a major decision of gigantic import to the nation.

Soon rumors of the movements of men began to sift through
informed sources in Washington and travelled by grapevine to cities
throughout the nation. On December 20, *The New York Times*
reported 2,000 American troops and civilians in Vietnam. Still little
publicity was given to the troop movements, although by February
there were more than 9,000 Americans in the Southeast Asian
country.

The American people began to ask, "Are we at war?" The
Administration denied it. On February 14, 1962, the President
announced in a speech, "We have not sent combat troops there,
although the training missions we have there have been instructed, if
they are fired upon, they would of course fire back to protect
themselves."

The very next day, UPI managed to get a dispatch through
censorship, datelined Saigon: "U.S. pilots, flying American-made
planes, spearheaded a major counterattack last week, which resulted
in one of South Vietnam's greatest victories to date against Communist guerrillas."

As of March 25, 1962, about five short weeks after the President's
denial that he had sent "combat" troops, the Department of the
Army officially listed 153 American casualties, dead, wounded and
missing.

Thus was the United States thrust deeply into the tragedy on the
Asian continent. The President planned a show of force to "make our
power credible." Yet before he had even carried the plan to
completion the U.S. found itself fighting in the air and on the
ground.

In deference to the memory of President Kennedy, little has been
written about this great mistake in American foreign policy. Furthermore, the entire episode was purposefully shrouded in confusion by
the President himself. A clear description of this has been given by
Kennedy's Press Secretary at the time, Pierre Salinger. In his book
With Kennedy he confirms that the U.S. manpower commitment in
Vietnam when Kennedy came into office was solely in an advisory
capacity. Then Kennedy began the gradual build-up of U.S. troops.
This would amount, according to Salinger, to over 20,000 at the time
of the President's death. This build-up of troops was in violation of
the terms of the Geneva Conference of 1954. In addition, wrote
Salinger, it involved the United States in a land war in Asia and the

President did not wish to acknowledge this so soon after the Bay of Pigs and the Berlin Wall crisis. Salinger's exact words were even more blunt. He said that Kennedy "was not anxious to admit the existence of a real war." Accordingly, in State Department cable 1006 sent to Saigon on February 21, 1962, the Administration asked for "co-operation with the press" and requested Vietnam correspondents to use "restraint" in handling matters affecting national security.

This was about the time when American news media were beginning to carry stories describing U.S. military involvement in the Vietnam war. Some stories even told of the shooting down of U.S. helicopters. This was a picture which the Administration did not want to present. Salinger tells of the President being extremely sensitive about these stories. He tried to tighten the rules under which news representatives would be able to observe actual operations in the field in Vietnam.

However, on the scene in Vietnam, correspondents were anxious to tell the whole story to the American people. Back in Washington, wrote Salinger, it was the intention of the President to downplay the war for many different reasons, some of which were purely political. Accordingly, guidelines were laid down to help control news stories coming back from Vietnam. Salinger reveals that the President eventually authorized a new press policy and its execution was implemented by means of a "secret memorandum" which was hand carried by Assistant Secretary of Defense Arthur Sylvester to a strategy conference in Honolulu to which had been summoned U.S. officials from Vietnam. Later, the then Assistant Secretary of State, Robert Manning, also reported this desire of the U.S. Government to see U.S. involvement in Vietnam minimized, even "represented as something less in reality than it is." Pierre Salinger added emphasis to this in remarks on the CBS television program, "Face the Nation" when he said the start of the growing U.S. involvement in the Vietnam war came during Kennedy's term.

Others have expressed the same view. In *The New York Times* of August 28, 1966, Arthur Krock wrote: "President Kennedy expanded United States involvement in South Vietnam from the handful of military advisors dispatched by President Eisenhower to a strong American military presence in the country. He did this without Congressional affirmation on the basis of actions by Presidents

Eisenhower and Truman, which Congress had either directly or indirectly endorsed in going to the aid of nations threatened by Communist aggression."

Eisenhower himself agreed with this appraisal. In an exclusive interview in *U.S. News & World Report* on November 7, 1966 his views are reported as follows: "Looking back over growing U.S. military involvement in Southeast Asia, General Eisenhower notes that former President Kennedy made the decision to send in the first 15,000 combat troops in 1961-1962."

In his widely syndicated column Drew Pearson wrote under a headline "How We First Got Involved In Vietnam" in the Long Island Press, "Friends of President Kennedy say that after the Bay of Pigs fiasco he felt compelled to demonstrate his strength."

Kennedy decided to throw the military of the United States behind the small Catholic minority in South Vietnam. And from Eisenhower's total of only one thousand military advisors, Kennedy rapidly escalated American troops. By the end of 1961, his first year in office, there were 33,000 Americans in South Vietnam."

In 1979 James Reston wrote further about the fateful meeting between Kennedy and Khrushchev in Vienna. In *The New York Times* of June 10, Reston reported that Kennedy had told him, "We have to demonstrate to the Russians that we have the will and the power to defend our national interests." And, wrote Reston, "Shortly thereafter, he increased the defense budget, sent another division to Europe and increased our small contingent of observers and advisors in Vietnam to over 16,000 . . . the Kennedy people have always denied that there was any connection between Khrushchev's threat in Vienna and Kennedy's decision to confront the Communist threat to South Vietnam. But I know what I heard from Kennedy in Vienna 17 years ago, and have reflected on the accidents of summit meetings ever since."

In his book, *The Best and The Brightest*, David Halberstam notes that, "In retrospect, Reston became convinced that the Vienna bullying became a crucial factor in the subsequent decision to send 18,000 advisory and support troops in Vietnam, and though others around Kennedy retained some doubts about this, it appeared to be part of a derivative link, one more in a chain of events which saw the escalation of the Cold War in Kennedy's first year. Reston in particular would see these events as a study in irony, believing that by October, 1962, after the Cuban Missile crisis, Kennedy had made good his need to show Khrushchev his fiber, but by that time it was too late as far as Southeast Asia was concerned; there were already more than 15,000 Americans in South Vietnam."

It is probably true that Kennedy himself agreed that he had made a Great Mistake. In an AP story in the *Chicago Sun* of April 16, 1966, there appeared the headline, "J.F.K. Planned Full Viet Policy Review—Morse." The lead paragraph read, "Sen. Wayne Morse (D-Ore.) said Monday that President John F. Kennedy told him about 10 days before Kennedy was assassinated that he had ordered an intense review of U.S. policy in Vietnam.

Six paragraphs later the story continued, "Morse, who said he was then speaking out in the Senate against U.S. involvement in Vietnam, quoted the late President as having said the criticism might be correct."

"He said he was making an intense study and re-examination of those policies, Morse reported."

By this time the policies which President Kennedy was reviewing only partially involved the initial mistake of committing the increased U.S. force. By then, a second mistake had been made in Vietnam.

3

The Second Great
Vietnam Mistake

FOLLOWING THE ARRIVAL of the U.S. men on the ground and
in the air of Southeast Asia, the Vietnam war went well. At the head
of the South Vietnamese government was an avowed enemy of the
Communists. Ngo Dinh Diem was a strong leader. He came from a
Mandarin family long accustomed to rule. Even those who condemned him for his aristocratic pride had to admire him for his
Vietnamese patriotism. Because he distrusted their motives, Diem
had refused support from French colonists, Japanese invaders and
local Communists alike. Instead of accepting office from their hands,
he went into exile in the United States and Belgium living in Roman
Catholic monasteries, for a long time with the Maryknoll Fathers in
America.

In 1954, the French, seeking a scapegoat for their collapse in Asia,
offered Diem the premiership of South Vietnam. When he accepted,
few gave him a chance of lasting nine months, let alone nine years.
But Diem proved himself amazingly strong. When playboy Emperor
Bao Dai challenged him at the polls, his majesty found his throne out
of existence.

As President, Diem smashed the gangsters who ran the opium
dens and houses of prostitution in Saigon. Launching a comprehen-

sive land reform program, he toured central Vietnam and was nearly trampled by thousands of wildly cheering peasants.

However, he also made many enemies. He has been accused of ruling like a dictator and charged with many crimes against the people. Writing in the New York *World Journal Tribune* columnist Bob Considine wrote that Diem, "was as touchy as a tarantula, ornery as a wet mule, hard to budge from his own 'Mandarin's road' to democracy, or a reasonable facsimile of same."

Yet even Diem's enemies admitted that he kept his country together in difficult circumstances. He subdued the religious sects which were constantly at one another's throats and with the $300 million a year he got from the Eisenhower Administration he brought about a measure of economic growth and social improvement. Every authority agreed living standards rose more rapidly in South Vietnam than in Communist North Vietnam.

Things continued to go well for the Diem regime throughout 1962. South Vietnamese soldiers killed 30,000 Communist guerrillas in battle. That could be considered little short of miraculous because authorities had previously estimated only 15,000 guerrillas were terrorizing the countryside.

A strategic hamlet program, borrowed from the war in Malaya and designed to create in each village an armed camp that would defend itself against local guerrillas, appeared to be working. Ambassador Nolting and General Paul Harkins reported it was bringing the countryside into closer alliance with Saigon and the government. Encouraged, the Kennedy Administration made the first of its many forecasts of the conduct of the war. Secretary of Defense McNamara, speaking for the President following a trip to South Vietnam in 1962, said, "Every quantitative measurement we have shows we're winning the war." In his 1963 State of the Union message, a few weeks later, President Kennedy declared, "The spearpoint of aggression has been blunted in South Vietnam."

Not long afterwards, the Defense Department reported that "we have turned the corner in Vietnam." General Harkins said the war would be won within a year.

And, in fact, there was much truth in these forecasts. Even in Communist writings such as W.T. Burchett's *Vietnam: Inside Story of the Guerrilla War*, the Viet Cong were said not only to have acknowledged that 1962 was Diem's year, but admitted that their losses were so great that they were on the verge of pulling out of the Mekong Delta and withdrawing to the fastnesses of the mountains.

Unfortunately, there were those in both governments and the press corps who hated Diem and resented his success, and as his victories grew more impressive, they increased their censure and vituperation.

Furthermore, a certain wing of the State Department resented the domination of the war by the Department of Defense to which President Kennedy had grown very partial after Laos and the Bay of Pigs. They trained their guns on Diem with such determination that they became known as the Gung-ho boys who wanted to give the South Vietnamese president the heave-ho.

This segment was dominated by Averell Harriman, the man who had helped engineer the mistakes in Laos, as well as Ambassador to India, J. Kenneth Galbraith, and Roger Hilsman, Director of Intelligence and Research in the State Department. Day after day they insisted we were on the wrong course in Vietnam. They were, in effect, criticizing the President's decision to fight a war on the Asian mainland with American soldiers. As they expressed it, "fighting a guerrilla war in an undeveloped nation requires as much political and civil action as it does military action."

Once former CIA Director Allen Dulles remarked, "there are lots of governments around the world that are not all we would wish them to be—all over Latin America, for instance. The idea that the United States can be or should try to be a kingmaker all over the world is fantastic. We can't do that."

But Harriman, Hilsman and Galbraith had little sympathy for the Dulles philosophy. They resented Diem, and in making their resentment known, they gave comfort to Diem's political enemies, who became more aggressive and vocal. Newsmen raised their voices against what they termed his unfair censorship.

Schlesinger has told the story of the famous dinner meeting of Galbraith, Harriman and himself which took place at this time. When the talk got around to Vietnam someone, he does not say who, wondered aloud if the removal of Diem might not be the solution. Galbraith spoke there, as he spoke everywhere, of the ineffectuality of the Diem government.

The President listened to these words spoken so authoritatively by a fellow Harvard intellectual and was impressed. His second great mistake in South Vietnam was taking shape.

Looking back today, one finds it difficult to believe that President Kennedy, with the South Vietnamese seemingly near victory, would listen to these prophets of gloom and doom, and jeopardize the interests of the United States in Southeast Asia.

Yet the record is clear. That is precisely what he did. He was impressed with their advice to eliminate Diem.

As Washington's course of action shaped itself, more and more anti-Diem stories came back from Saigon. Newsmen saw Diem as a despot, the last of the Mandarins. They breathed hatred of Ngo Dinh Nhu, Diem's brother and right-hand man, and of Madame Nhu, his wife. They branded the strategic hamlet program as fraudulent. They wrote of villages so hastily fenced in that the Communists were on the inside; of villagers forced into stockades at bayonet point.

Ambassador Nolting and General Harkins, who had been left out of the thinking in Washington, were up in arms at this turn of events. As they saw it, the reporters were damaging the war effort. There were bitter encounters. One reporter wrote, "The U.S. Embassy has turned into an adjunct for dictatorship," and, in so writing, he expressed the feeling of many correspondents.

One outstanding correspondent, who really gave her life covering the Vietnam war, the late Marguerite Higgins, excused her colleagues. She wrote, "There is no doubt that the overwhelming majority of the American press corps in Saigon thought—out of the most idealistic and patriotic motives—that they were serving a good cause in arousing world opinion against Diem."

Then occurred an event which immeasurably aided the efforts of Diem's opponents. In May, 1963, a group of Buddhists gathered in Hue to protest a Diem order forbidding them to display political banners on Buddha's 2587th birthday.

The Buddhists expressed doubt about the intent of the Diem order. The press picked up their cry. But Miss Higgins wrote that "this writer was never able to find an instance of repression on religious grounds. Under Diem there was repression of Buddhists, Catholics, Confucianists, et cetera, when—in defiance of clearly stated laws—they took to the streets to demonstrate against the government." To fair minded persons it was apparent that parading with political banners to celebrate a religious event was in defiance of the government edict.

Diem's order forbidding the demonstration on Buddha's birthday was aimed at followers of Thich Tri Quang, a Buddhist leader who had twice been arrested during the post war French occupation of French Indochina for dealings with the Communist overlord Ho Chi Minh. By his own admission Thich Tri Quang had been a member of the Vietminh Communist Liberation Front.

He favored "Neutralism" in South Vietnam, the same formula that had resulted in the loss of much of Laos as well as other countries, and once insisted at an interview with Miss Higgins, "We cannot get an arrangement with the North until we get rid of Diem and Nhu."

Thich Tri Quang refused to obey Diem's order. The "religious" parade was ordered to proceed. And Diem sent his troops to the scene to stop it.

Later the charge was made, and denied by the State Department, that the Vietnamese troops which went out to prevent the Buddhist demonstration were in the pay of the American Central Intelligence Agency.

Whatever their allegiance, the troops fired into the parade, killing some and wounding others, and much of the onus for the incident fell upon Diem.

When Diem ignored protests, fanatical Buddhist bonzes doused themselves with gasoline and died in fiery self-immolation. Washington's reaction was to instruct the Embassy to bring pressure on Diem to compose the Buddhist quarrel. Nolting promptly replied that the quarrel had a political, not a religious motif. He was relieved as Ambassador by President Kennedy.

In Nolting's place Kennedy appointed Henry Cabot Lodge, a choice which was prompted, unbelievable as it may sound, because, as Schlesinger says in *A Thousand Days,* "the thought of implicating a leading Republican in the Vietnam mess appealed to his (Kennedy's) instinct for politics."

Reporter Jay G. Hayden of the North American Newspaper Alliance reported: "From the day Lodge arrived as ambassador, events began building toward the overthrow of Diem."

Replacing Frederick Nolting, who was considered "friendly" to Diem, Lodge provided the "public disassociation" necessary to produce action against Diem. He placed American prestige clearly on the side of the Buddhists, visiting with their leaders even before presenting his credentials to Diem.

Obviously, Lodge had his instructions from the President. In his eyes Diem, who had run the country for nine years, could do nothing right and in a long letter to the South Vietnamese President Kennedy himself reviewed what he termed troubled ties between the two countries, declaring that "unless there can be important changes and improvements in the apparent relations between the government and the people in your country, American public and Congressional opinion will make it impossible to continue, without change, our joint efforts."

Having won sympathy in Washington, the Buddhist opposition became bolder, and Diem retaliated by raiding Buddhist pagodas, behind whose walls Thich Tri Quang and other Buddhist leaders were directing the opposition. Hundreds of Bonzes were seized before they could commit further acts of defiance. This action was reported to the world as a massive action of Diem's forces. What the press corps did not make clear was that Diem's special forces attacked only 12 out of 4,000 pagodas in South Vietnam.

Lodge now cabled Washington for instructions. It was Saturday, August 24, and McNamara and Rusk were out of town. But the anti Diem forces were on the job. Roger Hilsman drafted the reply to Lodge. The United States could not tolerate "systematic repression" of the Buddhists. The Generals of the Vietnamese Army could be told that America could not support Diem unless the problems were solved. If Diem declined to solve them, then we would face the inevitable. Perhaps Diem himself could not be saved. We would not take part, but if anything happened, a military regime could expect American support.

Probably in all American history there has been no document like this open invitation to Vietnamese generals to topple the Diem government if they could. As one observer commented, "Plotting among educated Vietnamese, including the generals, is a kind of national pastime, as is chess to the Russians. Until lately it has been a pretty harmless pastime, because everybody knew that real action was dependent on an American green light—and until August such a green light had been withheld."

The cable giving that green light was cleared, but not by the top brass because they were not available. Neither McNamara nor Rusk could have seen it, nor could John McCone, head of the CIA, who was on vacation.

But Harriman saw it, and at Hyannis Port, President Kennedy reviewed and approved it.

Without delay, the cable was fired off to Saigon, and the next day, Sunday the 25th, a United States Information Agency broadcast practically called upon the Vietnamese generals to rise up and seize the government. Lodge supported the broadcast with a request of the CIA to poll the generals and see if and when they were prepared to translate revolt talk into open rebellion.

Then, on September 3, in a television interview which minced no words, President Kennedy called for "changes of policy and maybe personnel," in Vietnam. It was the first time in history an American president had publicly made such a suggestion.

Washington quickly followed up the Kennedy statement with an announcement that 1,000 American soldiers would be withdrawn by the end of 1963, and possibly a total withdrawal would take place by 1965.

Such a threat frightened the Vietnamese generals. One said, "That convinced us that, unless we got rid of Diem, you would abandon us."

Then, to force Diem to comply, President Kennedy decided to cut off the United States flow of gold to pay the South Vietnamese army that was fighting the Communists. This was the same tactic he had previously used in Laos.

In Saigon, Lodge, who had stopped calling on Diem, dutifully recommended the suspension of aid. In Washington the President issued the order. The aid was cut off. Many Vietnamese generals fell into line. "It convinced us," one admitted to Miss Higgins, the United States was serious this time about getting rid of Diem."

The last straw was then added to the camel's breaking back when the President shut off support of the special forces Palace Guard which would try to protect Diem in the case of a coup.

In the middle of September, President Diem agreed to every point put forward by the United States in a program to reform and consolidate the strategic hamlet operation in the Mekong Delta.

But he could not satisfy those who wanted his removal. Marguerite Higgins reported in *The New York Herald Tribune* that Secretary McNamara and C.I.A. Director John McCone had not wanted him overthrown, "But they were overruled by the pro-coup d'etat faction led by Ambassador Henry Cabot Lodge, Under Secretary of State Averell Harriman and Assistant Secretary of State for Far Eastern Affairs Roger Hilsman . . . On August 24 the State Department sent out word—without the knowledge of Secretary McNamara or C.I.A. Director McCone—instructing Ambassador Lodge to 'unleash' the Vietnamese generals with a view to toppling the Diem Government if they could . . . on Sunday, August 25, Washington gave the generals a green light in a Voice of America broadcast that virtually called on the Vietnamese military to take over."

Apparently with that very objective in view, President Kennedy sent McNamara and General Taylor on another mission, and along with them as watchdog went William Sullivan of Harriman's staff, who had played an important role in the mistakes of Laos.

McNamara reported that he doubted Diem could last even if he took corrective measures. The political had not effected the military yet, McNamara said, and the major goals of the American mission would be reached by the end of 1965.

Diem stubbornly stuck to his guns to the very end. On October 31, Lodge and he went to Dalat to dedicate an experimental reactor. Seeing a chance to talk to Lodge, Diem indicated a willingness to compromise and asked what he should do. Lodge coldly told him to send his brother Nhu out of the country.

The very next day the rebellion broke.

Theodore Sorensen says in his biography *Kennedy*—". . . on November 1, 1963 . . . a new effort by the Vietnamese military to take command of the government was launched and succeeded. It received no assistance from the United States nor did this country do anything to prevent or defeat it."

The correspondent of the London *Daily Telegraph*, who covered the coup first hand, thought otherwise. "The Americans, at the very least, were tacit partners in the coup, with the British happily running behind. Almost every unit that moved up to fire at the Presidential Palace automatically had American officers and NCO's attached. The Americans, at least in an advisory capacity, assisted in the attack on the Palace simply because they were so attached."

The *Daily Telegraph* reporter continued: "It was indeed on American advice that the Vietnamese corps were alerted, thus making it possible for the Third Corps to take part in the revolt."

Further confirmation of this came from the Pentagon itself when Daniel Ellsberg of 'Pentagon Papers' fame handed Rep. Paul N. McCloskey, Jr. (R-Calif.) material revealing that the U.S. "encouraged and authorized" the 1963 overthrow of Diem. The papers showed, according to McCloskey, that at the very time Lodge was working with Diem, he also was discussing the advisability of the pending coup with a key U.S. military aide.

When the blow was about to fall on All Saints Day, all of Saigon was preparing for lunch. Shutters fell over store windows. Motor bikes, pedicabs and Renault taxis choked the tree-lined boulevards. Everyone sought shade and repose to escape, for two hours, the stupefying heat.

While Saigon napped, thousands of men in combat garb gathered outside the city. Roadblocks were thrown across the road to the airport. Units of the Palace Guard were won over.

Then truckloads of red-kerchiefed Marines raced for the heart of Saigon. They rushed police headquarters, gained entry without firing a shot and put officials under arrest. Other units seized Navy headquarters on the Saigon river, the telegraph office and radio station.

Soon a message flashed out. "Soldiers of the army, security service, civil defense force and people's force, the Ngo Dinh Diem government, abusing power, has thought only of personal ambition and slighted the fatherland's interests . . . The Army has swung into action. The task of all of you is to unite."

Fourteen generals, seven colonels and a major signed the declaration.

Now the pro-Diem forces were alerted, and gunfire began to crackle along the shady avenues around the Gia Long Palace.

Throughout the day the desultory fighting went on, and at 9:45 p.m., as a grey rain began falling, mortars and artillery opened a bombardment on the Palace itself.

A force of eighteen tanks supported by armored cars and 600 troops attacked the walls and barriers surrounding the Palace. Point-blank fire opened holes in the walls and the defenders scattered over the grounds.

Rebel generals had been in constant touch with Diem's office—

and the American Embassy—by telephone. At 6:16 a.m., over the Palace phone, they arranged a five minute truce to give Diem and Nhu a chance to surrender.

But Diem was no longer there. Earlier Nhu and he had simply walked out of the Palace and driven off in inconspicuous sedans. Going to suburban Cholon, they sought refuge in the house of a Chinese businessman, where they took calls through the Palace switchboard so the insurgent generals would think they were still there. Early the next morning, they went to Mass in Cholon's St. Francis Xavier Church. An informer saw them kneeling and taking Communion. Minutes later the generals' junta was told where they were. An M-113 armored personnel carrier roared up to the church and captured them.

For months Saigon hummed with rumors that Diem and Nhu were killed in the armored car. According to Marguerite Higgins, the only certain thing about the murder was that they were shot in the back; Diem in the neck, Nhu in the right side, with their hands tied behind them. Nhu also had a dagger or bayonet wound in the chest.

"The news of Diem's overthrow," said *Newsweek*, "was received in Washington with a blandness that Joseph Surface—that splendid stock character from Sheridan's "School for Scandal"—might have envied when faced with an embarrassing situation."

Awakened at 3 a.m., when the issue was still in doubt, the President expressed the hope Diem might survive. "Let me know if I can do anything," he said.

When McGeorge Bundy reappeared at 6 a.m., with a stack of cablegrams, the President rifled through them remarking, "Events have overtaken Diem."

The fall of Diem was the signal for unbridled license in Saigon. Looters smashed windows and rifled stores. Vietnamese soldiers munched oranges, bananas and candy showered on them. Pretty girls embraced GI's, draped tank turrets with garlands, scrambled, squealing, aboard jeeps. In bars and cabarets, B-girls shucked the white, hospital-like smocks imposed on them by law and wiggled into slacks or their traditional slit skirts.

But even while the Vietnamese danced, the result of the great mistake just committed began to be felt. The Viet Cong seized the initiative. They came sweeping back across the country, recapturing one village after another and regaining in a few weeks more than they had lost in the last year.

As Marguerite Higgins reported . . . "After the coup d'etat . . . the Vietnamese war took a decidedly downward turn. The military junta with its uncertain leadership, after purges of key (and scarce) officials, finally plunged much of the countryside into the confusion from which it purportedly was trying to save Vietnam.

"No wonder the Viet Cong took advantage of the situation to seize the military initiative for the first time in many months. No wonder that in two months after the coup d'etat the military junta lost more real estate, lives and weapons to the Viet Cong than at any previous time in the war."

In Washington the deaths of Diem and Nhu started a fight among government agencies as to who had been responsible for killing Cock Robin. The Pentagon blamed the State Department for ousting Diem before a stronger regime was ready to take over.

The CIA charged the State Department with trying to pass the buck for the collapse of the Diem government. As we have seen, what incensed the CIA most was the charge that Vietnamese troops on its payroll were responsible for the attacks on Buddhists, which were the incidents cited as justification for the coup. Seeking to avoid blame, the State Department hit out in all directions. Defense Secretary McNamara was held just as responsible as anybody for the Diem ouster and the mounting troubles that occurred afterwards.

But it is clear that the responsibility must lie with the President. His were the final decisions. And with insufficient experience and training, his judgments had erred again. They opened the door to Diem's assassins. With Diem dead, the military gains of 1962 were dissipated.

"In the cold misery of hindsight," wrote Bob Considine in his column of October 10, 1966, "the feeling is widespread in Saigon today, that we should have gone along with him (Diem) a bit longer."

"We let him slip through our fingers and be killed. Seven Saigon governments later, we have found a measure of soundness in Ky's group. But irreplaceable lives and fortunes were blown to kingdom come in the terrible interim."

After President Johnson had taken office, columnist Ted Lewis wrote in the *New York Daily News*, "What Johnson wants to do is to extricate the Administration from this confused policy horror. It is a nightmarish situation which has confused the nation and the world over just what our policy is in Southeast Asia."

Columnist Edgar Ansel Mowrer wrote in the *Long Island Press*, "In Washington, many of the same people who applauded when Ambassador Lodge refused to protect former President Diem (thus permitting his murder) and gave asylum to the "pink" Buddhist Thich Tri Quang, now wish we had done just the opposite.

"For under the Diem rule the people had a constitution and a voice, something they have never had since . . ."

"Another opinion," declared Mowrer, "expressed by an American of great international experience, is deeply pessimistic. It goes like this:

"'As for Vietnam, I have found no reason as yet to change my opinion that when we conspired to overthrow the Diem regime, and did nothing to prevent the murders, we lost the war. In this I blame most Cabot Lodge and Kennedy."

In encouraging the coup, President Kennedy rejected the advice of the Pentagon. The basis upon which he decided to overthrow President Diem turned out to be completely false, as many critics understood at the time. Cries of "persecution" of the Buddhists were propaganda. In fact, a United Nations fact-finding commission on October 11, 1963 had gone to Vietnam to investigate the charges of persecution and discovered that the Buddhist agitation was the work of a small, politically extreme element, and that the "repressions" carried out by Diem were exactly the same things which would have been done against Catholics or others who had perpetrated similar actions.

Ambassador Fernando Volio Jiminez of Costa Rica, whose motion led to the U.N. inquiry, said: "It is my personal feeling that there was no policy of discrimination, oppression or persecution of the Buddhists on any basis of religion. Testimony to this effect was usually hearsay, and was expressed in vague and general terms. When a witness tried to give some concrete proof to the mission, the incident he cited came down to individuals or personal actions. On the basis of the evidence, there was not a governmental policy against the Buddhists on religious grounds."

The basic reason behind President Kennedy's decision to overthrow Diem, the alleged religious persecution, was a propaganda hoax. Yet, Kennedy premised the overthrow of a loyal anti-Communist ally on these grounds. Thich Tri Quang commented in *The Saigon Post:* "With the Americans it is not so interesting any more. They are too easy to outwit . . . We will use the Americans to help us get rid of the Americans."

The defeatist nature of the Vietnam War which was to proceed through the Johnson and Nixon administrations began with Kennedy. From the beginning, initiatives against the North Vietnamese were strictly forbidden by the Kennedy Administration. They did not begin until 1965, and even then continued to be circumscribed.

Today we can see starkly etched the tragedy of Kennedy's inexperience. The President blundered in committing American men as a "show of force." The blunder was compounded when we consented in advance to the overthrow of the successful leader Diem.

Kennedy saw too late what he had done. When President Kennedy died, America's Vietnam tragedy was only beginning to unfold. But the mistakes which had already been made led to one of the greatest tragedies in American history.

4

Why Castro Is Still
In Power Today

AT 5:15 A.M., Monday, April 17, 1961, the telephone by General Chester Clifton's elbow jangled, awakening him from a catnap.

Despite the early hour, the President's military aide was expecting the call. Wide awake now, he took the crisp message, hung up, and a few minutes later the phone rang in President Kennedy's weekend retreat at Glen Ora in Virginia.

The President, in pajamas, his touseled head bent over the phone, was also expecting the call. For four days the invasion force had been steaming north from its base in Nicaragua, and less than eighteen hours before, the last "no go" point, he had authorized the fighting men to proceed to the beaches.

The news was dramatic. At that very moment, anti-Castro patriots were storming ashore on Cuban soil.

Hopes ran high. Everything seemed favorable for the expedition. The crescent moon had set not long after sundown the previous evening. The tides were right. The fresh winds caused no problems. Approaching the southern coast of Cuba, the tiny flotilla of small, hulking cargo ships, converted fishing boats, battered one-time sub-chasers and rusty landing craft pushed through gentle swells and occasional rain squalls.

Cuban refugees, all armed, all excited and all eager for what lay ahead, jammed the ships to the gunwales. With mounting emotions they stared at the shoreline lying dark and ominous to the north. Within an hour they would be back in their beloved homeland, fighting to overthrow the tyranny of the hated Fidel Castro.

In the moonless Bay of Pigs, the men scrambled down cargo nets into landing boats. When a boat was filled the captain pulled back on the throttle and started the run to Playa Larga or Playa Giron.

As the first men splashed ashore in ragged platoons, Radio Swan, a station operated by the Central Intelligence Agency on Swan Island, 360 miles southwest of the action, sent out a crackling message in the name of Jose Miro Cardona, head of the Cuban Revolutionary Council.

"Before dawn, Cuban patriots in the cities and in the hills began the battle to liberate our homeland from the despotic rule of Fidel Castro . . ."

In the first gray of morning the Late City Edition of *The New York Times* hit the street with the story of the invasion. Before long newspapers were making extravagant claims. The Isle of Pines had been shelled and bombed. There were landings in Oriente Province. Raoul Castro was a captive. The Isle of Pines had fallen. Thousands of political prisoners were free men. The invaders had driven inland, almost splitting Cuba in two. The Cuban Navy was in revolt.

These fancies were far from the grim truth. Actually, the landings in the limited area of the Bay of Pigs ran into almost immediate difficulties. The first frogman ashore to mark the beach, an American named Gary, encountered a militia patrol in a jeep. Shots were exchanged and any element of surprise evaporated.

They came upon workmen building resort houses in what the invaders thought would be an isolated area. The landing boats did not find the sandy beaches they were expecting. Instead there were sharp reefs which upset some of the boats and threw their occupants into the surf. The LCU's were unable to bring the tanks ashore until dawn when the frogmen had found channels through the reefs.

Worst of all, Castro's men were waiting for the invaders north of the Zapata Swamps which ran parallel to the shore line for sixty-five miles. The men in the vanguard were met by murderous fire from Czech machine guns and automatic rifles. They were pinned down along the roads and tracks through the swampland, and Russian built tanks were reported coming up.

As dawn broke over the Bay of Pigs, Castro ordered his air force into action. American-built T-33 jets and British built Sea Furies roared down over the beaches and mangrove swamps and swept out into the bay. A Sea Fury hit the 'Houston' with a rocket. It went down carrying reserve ammunition and vital radios. A second ship was blown up. The five other ships scattered under heavy attack and hurriedly put out to sea.

After that, news from the beach became confused and fragmentary. The invaders knew they had run into a trap. Undaunted, they refused to pull out. Instead they fought their way through the swampland, their objective the road that was Castro's supply line. To aid them they called for air support and B-26's, patched together by the anti-Castro rebels, bombed Boca de la Zanza and the militia station at Jaguey Grande. Their triumph was short lived. Castro's fast T-33's swept in again, shot down four of the planes and drove off the others. By that time, Russian tanks and Czech trucks with Castro reinforcements were rolling down two roads into the Zapata Swamps. The fighting raged through a clear, hot day. The invaders dug in behind their tanks, bazookas and mortars.

During that long Monday, the Revolutionary Council had only intermittent contact with the landing force. As the hours stole by communications became even worse and on the beach the situation was grave. Cut off from their supply ships, the men ran out of ammunition, food, water and medical supplies. The two ships with guns that could have bombarded the shore had pulled out with the others. Castro's fast jets, ruling the air, bombed and strafed the huddled invaders at will. By dusk of the first day many of the guerrillas had been killed, wounded or taken prisoner.

Still the survivors fought on for forty-eight hours despite the knowledge that their boats had been sunk or driven off, their planes shot out of the skies. The remnants tried to slip by the main concentration of Castro units to join other rebels in the Escambray Mountains. By moving stealthily through the peat bogs and canebrakes at night, avoiding the villages, skirting Castro patrols, a few men finally made it into the hills.

In the waning hours, as Castro's forces took hundreds of prisoners, a New Jersey radio ham picked up a faint signal: "This is Cuba calling. Where will help come from? This is Cuba calling the free world. We need help in Cuba."

The battle that had begun with such high hopes before dawn of Monday, April 17, ended in black defeat about sundown of Wednesday, April 19. Then came the humiliation of the Roman circus in Havana. Castro was enraptured and exultant. On street corners, while prisoners trooped by in melancholy procession, prancing militiamen fired their burp guns into the air. Jeeps draped with hot-eyed youths careened along boulevards. Some of the captured invaders were shown on TV. Correspondents from communist countries were hustled off to the shell-pocked beach-head to view the litter of American-made mortars, recoilless rifles, trucks, machine-guns and medium tanks.

What had happened? The United States had trained these Cuban patriots. It had transported them to Cuba. It had undertaken to put them ashore to fight an enemy of the American people. Ostensibly, it was behind them all the way. How could anything conceivably go wrong? And yet obviously, everything had gone wrong.

Certainly the fault did not lie with the plan. That was fundamentally sound, based on American experience in a hundred amphibious operations and initiated by a man who had commanded the greatest amphibious operation of all, the landing on the Normandy Coast in World War II.

However, the man under whose eye the plan took shape would not remain in office to supervise its execution. President Eisenhower's second term was coming to an end and 1960 was an election year to name his successor.

That year saw John F. Kennedy, the junior Senator from Massachusetts, pitted against Richard Nixon, Eisenhower's Vice President.

Once in office, a command decision on Cuba was forced upon Kennedy. It was then, in January, that he was briefed thoroughly on the CIA's project to invade Cuba with U.S.-trained Cuban refugees, the United States to provide air cover and logistical support.

One of the first things President Kennedy did, on assuming office, was to call for all the facts of the operation and to ask the Joint Chiefs of Staff for an evaluation, for what was called "an appreciation of its validity."

Already living in the United States were thousands of Cuban defectors, many of them professional soldiers. The CIA inherited the job of organizing and training them. The direct responsibility centered in Richard M. Bissell, the man who master-minded the U-2 flights over Russia.

Piece by piece, the mosaic had been put together. On December 14, 1959, Manuel Artime, who would be the civilian leader of the expedition, was spirited out of Cuba by the CIA. On March 17, 1960, President Eisenhower officially authorized the CIA to organize, train and equip Cuban refugees as a guerrilla force to overthrow Castro. And two months later, Jose Perez San Roman, who would become the military commander of the expedition, was first told about the prospect of secret training camps to whip a liberation army into shape.

For months, the U.S. government had been negotiating with Guatemala to mass and train anti-Castro recruits on Guatemalan soil. Finally, a deal was made with Roberto Alejo, whose brother was Guatemalan ambassador to the United States. The agreement permitted the CIA to take over part of Senor Alejo's vast coffee plantation in the Sierra Madre Mountains.

The plantation was a self-contained city, named Helvetia, carved out of the jungle-clad mountains at a height of 5,000 feet. An airstrip was leveled next to the town of Retalhuleu. Afterwards, a camp was built on a farm. The recruits had trouble with cattle ticks which got into their sleeping bags, and the camp was soon christened Garrapatanango, or Tick Base. There was even a prison camp located in the Peten Jungles which could be reached only by helicopter.

Originally there was some vague idea of feeding the recruits back into Cuba to reinforce the anti-Castro forces fighting guerrilla actions in the mountains. By early autumn a more ambitious project was beginning to take shape. There must be an early, sharp, decisive blow because Castro was rapidly building up his militia, and the patriots must strike before it became too strong.

At various times President Eisenhower personally went over the blueprint. Gradually the structure of the invasion grew. As a veteran military commander, Eisenhower knew the necessity of dominating the air, and the plan included a recommendation for an "air cap" by U.S. Navy jets, "air cap" in Navy parlance meaning limited air cover for ships and landing craft.

While the Eisenhower government still retained control, certain alarming facts developed. Fears arose that Russia was sending Cuba jet planes, and in Czechoslovakia Cuban pilots were being trained to fly them. Castro had guerrilla forces in the mountains under heavy pressure and they might be snuffed out unless aid reached them soon.

As the project grew, thirty U.S. Army instructors were assigned to train the Cuban patriots in Guatemala, and in smaller camps in Louisiana and Florida. Paratroopers made practice jumps in Florida and Guatemala. Cuban sailors learned landing operations at Vieques Island, off the eastern tip of Puerto Rico, where frogmen also acquired the latest techniques in marking beaches and blowing up underwater obstacles.

Still fluid in early 1961, but beginning to jell, the plans called for a landing near Trinidad, a town of some 20,000 on the south-east coast. It lay in open country, with good roads leading up into the Escambray Mountains where there was an active group of guerrillas.

The blueprint still assumed U.S. military help would be on call during the landing. Fidel Castro's air force had a dozen or so obsolete B-26's, about the same number of British prop-driven Sea Furies, and eight T-33 trainers which the United States had sold to Cuba while Batista was in power.

To match that air strength, the rebels were given sixteen patched up B-26's, which would have little chance against the Castro jets if the latter were armed with rockets. This disparity in force was known to CIA and Pentagon strategists and weighed by them early in the drafting stage. It was decided to destroy the Castro jets on the ground in a surprise raid. If they escaped that first strike, then they would be caught on the ground when they refueled. As a last resort, as Charles V.J. Murphy, in *Fortune Magazine*, and others have pointed out, two United States carriers would be close by, below the horizon, and one or two tactical jets, without markings, could be dispatched to scrub the Castro T-33s.

The entire scheme turned on destroying Castro's air force so that the B-26s could control the beach-head. During the invasion they would have to operate from a base 500 miles from Cuba. The roundtrip would take six hours, leaving less than an hour for bombing and air cover. So the invaders must push inland fast and seize an airfield from which the B-26 planes could operate.

In essence, this was the plan President Kennedy asked the Joint Chiefs of Staff to evaluate. They sent a team of officers to Guatemala to observe training conditions and, satisfied, gave the operation their approval.

Late in January, only a few days in office, Kennedy authorized the CIA to go ahead, reserving the right to rescind up to the last minute. D-Day was fixed for March 1, 1961.

It did not come off as planned. Washington failed to take into account the discord among invasion leaders and, before the attack could take place, their differences had to be resolved and a provisional government formed. Political harmony was not achieved until March 22, the day the Cuban Revolutionary Council was formed. By that time it was too late to meet that deadline—twenty-one days too late.

Unfortunately, the President also felt it was too late to carry out the invasion in the Trinidad sector. One day after the formation of the Cuban Revolutionary Council, Captain Enrique Llanso picked up the twelve last survivors of the Escambray, who had fought their way out of the mountains, bloody, broken and beaten.

Partly because a link-up with the guerrillas was now impossible, the President scratched Trinidad and picked the more remote Bay of Pigs as the target. The latter had its advantages. An airstrip was located there. The swamps eliminated the chance of flanking maneuvers. It also had its disadvantages. True, the brigade could not be outflanked, but it could be easily stopped by a frontal counterattack on the tracks and roads across the swamps. The CIA and the Chiefs of Staff opposed the change of location.

In his *Fortune* article, Murphy gives another reason for the switch from Trinidad to the Bay of Pigs. Kennedy, listening to Secretary of State, Dean Rusk, became obsessed with world opinion. Only a week before the embarkation, he let Rusk prevail upon him to eliminate Trinidad because the operation had to be kept "unspectacular." Besides, an invasion so close to a large populated area might give away the fact that it was supported by the United States. To court a favorable international impression the soundness of the invasion plan was sacrificed and the attack was shifted to a less populated and less accessible site.

That was not all; one more change was made. Instead of landing at daybreak, as originally planned, the invaders would go in at night, and as Haynes Johnson, author of *Bay of Pigs*, wrote, "present the world with a fait accompli by dawn."

April 5 was the new date. Later it was postponed to April 10, and finally to April 17.

Kennedy, who had approved developments each step of the way, was to give the final go-ahead to the invasion on April 5. The previous day, on the 4th, the President met for a last review with White House insiders.

At least a dozen meetings, conferences and briefings on the invasion had been held in Washington since November 29, 1960. None was of the magnitude of the April 4 session. Present at the meeting were: Secretary of State, Dean Rusk; Secretary of Defense, Robert S. McNamara, and Secretary of the Treasury, Douglas Dillon; General Lyman L. Lemnitzer, Chairman of the Joint Chiefs of Staff; Allen Dulles, Director of the CIA and his Assistant, Richard Bissell; Presidential Assistant, McGeorge Bundy; Paul Nitze, Kennedy's specialist on strategic planning at the Pentagon; Thomas Mann, Assistant Secretary of State on Latin-American Affairs; Adolf A. Berle, Jr., Arthur M. Schlesinger, Jr., and Richard Goodwin, three Kennedy specialists on Latin America, and one outsider, Senator William Fulbright, Chairman of the Senate Foreign Relations Committee on which the President himself had served while a member of the U.S. Senate.

Bissell was the first to speak. He gave his final view of the Cuban operation. Castro's whole air force would be wiped out. This was vital. The Cuban contingent would land under air cover, drive inland and hold its beach-head until the Cuban Revolutionary Council declared itself a "government in arms," rallied internal support to it and made itself eligible for foreign recognition and assistance.

The CIA Aide told the Presidential advisers that the situation inside Cuba was ripe for rebellion. The rebel air force would control the skies and, as the invasion force drove inland, operate from the captured field near the Bay of Pigs. He cited the fighting quality of the Cuban Brigade and listed the arms it would have.

The CIA Aide told the Presidential advisers that the situation inside Cuba was ripe for rebellion. The rebel air force would control the skies and, as the invasion force drove inland, operate from the captured field near the Bay of Pigs. He cited the fighting quality of the Cuban Brigade and listed the arms it would have.

The history of Latin America, Bissell pointed out, was a history of revolutions and coups d'etat. Small forces had frequently won over larger ones. On more than one occasion the populace had risen and joined the liberators.

There was a question from one of the men around the big conference table: What would happen if the invasion failed to bring down the Castro government?

In the event of a total disaster, Bissell said, the invaders would move inland to the Escambray Mountains. A total of almost 1,500 men, operating as a guerrilla force would be more than a thorn in Castro's side.

But Cuban leaders to whom Haynes Johnson talked, said the invaders were never told of this. "What we were told was, 'If you failed, we will go in,'" he quoted San Romas as saying.

After hearing Bissell, Rusk voiced no objections. Nor did McNamara, Dillon, Lemnitzer, Bundy, Dulles, Paul Nitze, Thomas Mann, and the three specialists on Latin American affairs, Berle, Schlesinger and Goodwin. Indeed, it is a matter of record that Berle argued with some passion that "a power confrontation" with communism in the Western Hemisphere was inevitable anyhow, and the sooner the President faced up to it the better it would be.

Much has been written about the objections raised by Senator Fulbright. Some people feel he did not express himself at all during the conference but waited until he had the President's private ear. However, there is no disagreement on what he said when he did talk. Fulbright was violently against the invasion. The wise course, he contended, was not to overthrow Castro but to work constructively in other Latin American countries. He repeated Kennedy's own philosophy expressed during the campaign . . . "the road to freedom runs through Rio and Buenos Aires and Mexico City." He argued vehemently about the immorality of an act which, he said, would only arouse the African and Asian blocs; it was the sort of thing the United States always fumbled or mishandled.

Except for Fulbright's, not a dissenting voice was raised. On that April 4, the President went from man to man around that big conference table and put the question to each one. Rusk, McNamara, Schlesinger—all agreed. The vote for the invasion was unanimous.

Still Kennedy hesitated. He was young; he was wholly inex-

perienced in these matters and, some say, he had had strong doubts
about the operation from the beginning. Now he was torn between
two opposite points of view—to invade or not to invade. In his
quandary he made a fatal mistake; he tried to straddle both horses
and fell between them.

He gave his consent grudgingly for the operation, but he imposed
ruinous conditions and, once again, still vacillating and indecisive, he
reserved the right to cancel the invasion at the last minute.

The conditions the President imposed made changes in the
original Eisenhower concept which considerably weakened the
effort. In no circumstances whatsoever were United States forces to
become involved in the landing. The air strikes against the Castro air
force were to be conducted only by Cuban pilots flying B-26s from
bases in Guatemala. The sorties were to be publicized as the work of
defectors from the Cuban Air Force.

Shocked by the President's position, the Joint Chiefs are reported
to have advised the President that without American air support the
rebels might not be able to hold the beachhead.

The President overruled them.

As D-Day approached, preparations were stepped up. Just before
the invasion fifty freight carloads of aerial bombs, rockets, ammunition and firearms were airlifted into the Nicaraguan port city of
Puerto Cabezas by unmarked C-54s, C-46s and C-47s so fast that on
some days the planes were stacked up over the airstrip.

During Easter week, 27 American C-124 Globemasters roared in,
three or four at a time, and unloaded full cargoes of rations, blankets,
ammunition and medical supplies at the U.S.-built airstrip at
Retalhuleu, at Guatemala City and at San Jose air base.

Five thousand to six thousand men were standing by who could be
committed to the invasion. Some waited at airports in Florida. On a
Miami airstrip were several unmarked C-26s and C-47s ready to
carry airborne forces. Included was a press plane to fly newsmen
over the battle area.

On April 19, the assault brigade of 1,350 men received the
mobilization order at Base Trax in Guatemala. The following day the
men were flown to Retalhuleu, where they boarded transport planes
for the flight to Puerto Cabezas, which in their orders was known as
Trampoline, the launching site.

The invasion fleet of seven ships was outfitted, equipped with guns and radar, and painted black in New Orleans. The cargoes loaded aboard the ships in Puerto Cabezas were enough to supply the landing force through ten days of battle, and also to equip the thousands of guerrillas expected to be recruited after the beachhead was gained.

As the flotilla of seven small ships waited in the Nicaraguan port, Louis Somoza, President of that country, appeared on the dock and shouted up to the men, "Bring me a couple of hairs from Castro's beard."

But, by now, one of the most important factors in the entire operation, the factor of surprise, had been lost. So poorly had the secrecy been kept by the Administration that rumors were circulating all over Washington that the United States was about to overthrow Castro. The rumors were even actively supported by one member of the Administration, Undersecretary of State, Chester Bowles. He happened to be sitting in as Acting Secretary the day documents about the project crossed Dean Rusk's desk. Angry at not having been let in on the secret, and 'horrified,' as he told friends, he retaliated by quietly leaking the information to the press.

Although these developments worried the President, he still believed he could deceive the world on American participation in the plan. On April 12, when the fleet was steaming north under escort of American destroyers and an aircraft carrier, President Kennedy held a press conference. Naturally, the press corps had been primed by the rumors and the Bowles tip. The very first question involved Cuba.

Kennedy's reply was prompt—but it was a deliberate deception for he ruled out "under any condition, an intervention in Cuba by the United States armed forces."

The President went on, "The basic issue in Cuba is not one between the United States and Cuba. It is between the Cubans themselves. And I intend to see that we adhere to that principle, and as I understand it, this Administration's attitude is so understood and shared by the anti-Castro exiles from Cuba in this country."

On Monday morning, the day of the invasion, Dean Rusk was to make sure that the message struck home by repeating the same solemn promises.

It was all good propaganda for world consumption, but it would not be long before the world would see through the ill-conceived ruse. Furthermore, there was a devastating consequence. As one commentator pointed out, the net "effect was to serve notice on Cubans in Cuba, who were waiting for an encouraging signal from the United States, that if they rose up against the Castro tyranny, it would be at their own risk."

This press conference effectively eliminated one vital premise on which the entire success of the attack rested. How could President Kennedy expect the Cuban people to rise against Castro when he told them in so many words the United States assistance they had been promised now was being denied? The proof of the pudding was, when the time came to rise, they did not rise.

What crippled the plan even more, our hand was tipped. Kennedy protested so much that Castro, as the bearded dictator revealed later, was sure an invasion was coming. And when it struck, the Cuban army was mobilized and waiting to smash it.

On Saturday morning, April 15, the anti-Castro B-26s attacked Castro's air force. But instead of all sixteen rebel planes joining in the attack as called for in the original plan, only eight took part. The White House had ordered the change. It was to prove to be a fatal error.

Four of the eight planes bombed and strafed Ciudad Libertad, adjoining Camp Columbia, the main base for Castro's planes. Two others hit at San Antonio de los Banos and two at Santiago. But the B-26 attack was only partly successful. Only half of Castro's B-26 and Sea Fury force and four of the T-33s were destroyed on the ground. It had been vital that they all be destroyed.

The rebel planes had Cuban Air Force markings painted on them, and the story was put out that Castro's own pilots, in the act of defecting, had attacked their own airfields. To lend credence to this story, one plane flew directly to Miami International Airport and made a landing with one prop feathered. A dozen machinegun bullets had been fired through the fuselage. The Cuban pilot, jauntily wearing a baseball cap, dark glasses and a T-shirt, and nonchalantly smoking a cigarette, was hustled away by United States Immigration authorities.

About the same time another bullet-riddled B-26, bearing the markings of Castro's air force, made an emergency landing at the Boca Chica Naval Air Station, Key West. And the Administration's "deception" fell apart.

In the United Nations Political Committee that morning, the Cuban Ambassador, Dr. Raul Roa rose to say, "At 6:30 this morning, North American aircraft . . ."

Frederick H. Boland of Ireland gavelled Dr. Roa to order. The business before the assembly was the Congo, not Cuba. But Russia's Valerian A. Zorin rose and demanded that the debate on the Congo be shelved. A two-thirds vote implemented the motion, and Dr. Roa was given the floor to voice his charges against the United States.

"I have been instructed by my government," Roa said, "to denounce before this Committee the vandalistic aggression carried out at dawn today against the territorial integrity of Cuba, with the most grave implications. The responsibility for this act of imperialistic piracy falls squarely on the government of the United States."

There was a buzzing in the crowded room as Roa charged that the aerial bombings were "undoubtedly the prelude to a large-scale invasion attempt, organized, supplied and financed by the United States with the complicity of satellite dictatorships of the Western Hemisphere."

To make matters worse, the President had committed an embarrassing oversight. He had neglected to forewarn and forearm our UN representative.

Not knowing all the facts, Ambassador Adlai Stevenson had only appearances to go on, and the charges aroused his most righteous indignation. He emphatically denied that United States planes had bombed the Cuban airfields. He held up a photograph of one of the planes that had landed in Florida and pointed out the markings of Castro's air force on its tail. The Cuban star and the initials FAR Fuerze Aerea Revoluncianaria, he said, were clearly visible.

Meanwhile, skeptical reporters had been going over the B-26 plane that landed in Miami. One noticed the undisturbed dust and grease covering the bomb-bay fittings, the corroded electrical connections to rocket mounts, the uncocked guns. Obviously the plane had not been in combat, but had flown direct from its point of origin to Miami.

The newsmen began asking embarrassing questions. Why did authorities withhold the name of the pilot after it had published photographs showing the serial number of his plane? What about rocket fragments recovered near Havana bearing the inscription U.S.A.? How about the two auxiliary fuel tanks recovered twelve miles off the northern coast of Cuba? Didn't that show the planes had come from a distant point?

The cover story collapsed like a house of cards and Adlai Stevenson was caught in the tangle of his own unconscious misstatements of fact.

"When Stevenson learned," said Andrew Tully in *CIA: The Inside Story,* "that the story about the strike being the work of defectors was a lie and that the American Ambassador to the UN had had his credibility impaired before the world, he hit the roof. He demanded of Kennedy that there be no more air strikes and Rusk supported him. Thereupon, Kennedy canceled the second strike."

Murphy wrote a different version in *Fortune,* but the effect was the same. "Stevenson has flatly denied," he said, "and continues to deny (late in 1961) that he even knew about the second strike, let alone that he demanded that it be called off. But there was little doubt about his unhappiness over the course of events in the Caribbean. Before Sunday was over, McGeorge Bundy was to fly to New York to see Stevenson, still wearing—in his haste to be off— sneakers and sports clothes. This sudden errand followed a shattering order that went out to Bissell."

The order came from the President. It did not mince words. There was to be no second air strike that morning. The B-26s were to stand down. The rest of Castro's planes were not to be attacked and the men fighting for their lives on the ground were to be left without air support that had been promised them.

In *A Thousand Days,* Arthur Schlesinger says that "the collapse of the cover story brought the question of the second air strike into new focus. The President and the Secretary understood this strike as one which would take place simultaneously with the landings and have the appearance of coming from the airstrip on the beach. It had slid by in the briefings, everyone assuming it would be masked by the cover story. But there could be no easy attribution to defectors now. Nor did the fact that the planes were B-26s flown by Cuban pilots save the situation; despite the great to-do about "Cubanizing" the operation, they would still be United States planes in the eyes of the UN. Rusk, after his talks with Stevenson, concluded that a second Nicaraguan strike would put the United States in an untenable position internationally and that no further strikes would be launched until the planes could fly—or appear to fly—from the beachhead. Bundy agreed, and they called the President at Glen Ora.

Schlesinger tells it this way:

"It was now Sunday afternoon . . . when Rusk said that the projected strike was one which could only appear to come from Nicaragua, Kennedy said, 'I'm not signed on to this:' the strike he knew about was one coming ostensibly from the beachhead."

When Rusk called the President, Bissell and General Charles Cabell, Deputy Director of the CIA, were standing at his elbow. While talking, Rusk turned his head and asked Cabell if he wished to talk to the President. Cabell shook his head 'no.'

After a long conversation the President directed that the strike be cancelled. The invaders' doom was sealed.

When he put down the phone, Kennedy sat on in silence for a moment, shook his head and began to pace the room in evident concern, worried about the decision he had made.

About 4:00 A.M., Monday morning, when the Cuban brigade was fighting for a foothold in the Bay of Pigs, General Cabell, an experienced airman, reconsidered. He went back to Rusk with another proposal. The carrier *Essex* was standing by, just over the horizon. Could Navy airmen on it fly cover for the landing operation?

The President was awakened and the question was put to him. His answer was 'no.'

By this time the brigade was fully committed to the landing attempt. Naturally, it had little chance of success. The anti-Castro Cubans were without the ranging fire power that the B-26s with their bombs and machineguns would have applied against Castro's tanks and artillery pieces as they wheeled up into line.

Most important, Castro had four T-33 jets left as a result of the mistake of reducing the number of B-26s permitted to attack the Castro planes. And these planes, armed with powerful rockets, had a field day. Before the sun had touched its meridian they had sunk two ships in the Bay and scattered the others. One ship fled as far as 218 miles south before its captain felt safe from the terror of the skies.

By mid-afternoon of Monday, President Kennedy became alarmed at the adverse reports that filtered out of Cuba. When he realized fully that he had set the seal of doom on the expedition, he belatedly

issued orders for the B-26s to attack Castro's airfields at will. They
arrived over their targets to find the fields hidden by low, impenetra-
ble fog.

On Tuesday, Castro launched a counter-attack which drove the
invaders back to Playa Giron where they dug in for a last ditch stand.

That evening the President held his first big reception—a traditional white tie affair for Congressmen, cabinet members and their
wives. Nearly 450 VIPs showed up for the gala occasion. At 10:15
P.M., the President and Mrs. Kennedy descended the grand stairway
to ruffles and flourishes. The First Lady had on a sleeveless, floor
length sheath of pink and white straw lace. She wore a feather-
shaped diamond clip in her hair.

The Marine Band played "Hail to the Chief" and then, at a signal,
struck up "Mr. Wonderful," and the President and his lady whirled
around the East Room, with the Vice President and Mrs. Johnson
right behind them.

What White House retainer John Pye called the most elaborate
buffet since 1920 was set up in the State Dining Room—chicken a la
king, roast beef, pheasant, tongue, turkey and ham, dainty sand-
wiches, breads, French pastry and champagne punch.

At the height of the festivities, an aide informed the President that
Bissell wished to see him. Bissell was asked to come to the White
House. Rusk was called from a formal dinner party for the Greek
Premier. He arrived at the President's office with McNamara,
General Lemnitzer and Admiral Arleigh Burke, the Chief of Naval
Operations.

Bissell gave the conferees the grim facts. A remnant of the anti-
Castro force was fighting desperately without adequate ammunition,
food and water. Bissell asked for air support from the *Essex* in a
desperate effort to save the operation. Admiral Burke vigorously
supported Bissell. Rusk, pointing out that the President had pledged
no intervention, just as vigorously opposed him.

An intense discussion lasted far into the early morning hours and
resulted in a strange change of plan. Once again the President
compromised. He would allow a flight of six unmarked jets from the
carrier. They would provide an air cap for one hour—from 6:30 to
7:30 A.M.—just long enough for the ships to run in and land
reinforcements and supplies, and for the rest of the B-26s to get in a
hard blow.

Back at the Puerto Cabezas air strip, the rebels had a hard time getting a flight of B-26s into the air. Nine of the sixteen B-26s had been shot down and many of the remaining planes were in poor flying condition. In the briefing room most of the Cuban pilots refused to fly again without the assurance of air support.

In this emergency four American advisers, under contract to the CIA, knowing that an order had been received pledging Navy jet support, volunteered to fly for the exhausted Cubans. The pilots, Riley W. Shamburger, Jr., Wade C. Gray, Thomas Willard Ray and Lee F. Baker, took two of the planes. Oscar Vega and Gonzalo Herrera took two others. The four planes headed for the beach.

By an incredible miscalculation, the B-26s arrived over their target nearly an hour before their jet support. One B-26 was shot down on an air strip near the Central Australian sugar mill. Another fell into the sea enveloped in flames and smoke. All four Americans died in the two crashes.

Their last radio cries, "Mayday! Mayday!" were a solemn requiem for the Bay of Pigs fiasco.

At 2:30 P.M., Bissell heard from one of his men aboard a ship in the Bay of Pigs; the last ragtail of the landing force had been driven back into the water and was under fire. There was a final message from the gallant commander of the rebels—"I have nothing left to fight with and so cannot wait. Am headed for the swamp."

And so ended the disastrous attempt to overthrow the "communist dictatorship just ninety miles off our coast." It was a blunder of the highest magnitude, and one which would have repercussions of the most serious nature for the United States.

The New York Times remarked, "the outcome of that battle was a blow to American pride and prestige which was certainly unmatched in the history of our relations with Latin America."

The politically liberal writer, Theodore Draper, said, "The ill-fated invasion of Cuba was one of those rare politico-military events—a perfect failure."

In Germany, the *Frankfurter Neue Presse* said, "Kennedy is to be regarded as politically and morally defeated. For the time being, Moscow has not only maintained but strengthened its outpost on the threshold of America."

"In one day," declared the *Corriere Della Sera* of Milan, "American prestige collapses lower than in eight years of Eisenhower timidity and lack of determination."

And Eisenhower privately told friends, "Any second lieutenant with combat experience could have done better."

Even Schlesinger, the historian of the New Frontier, wrote, "Subsequent controversy has settled on the cancellation of the second air strike as the turning point . . . Kennedy came later to feel that the cancellation of the second strike was an error." In *A Thousand Days*, Schlesinger concluded, "Once it grew into a conventional amphibious invasion, it was clearly beyond the limits of disownability. Unless we were prepared to back it to the hilt, it should have been abandoned."

Kennedy himself realized how badly he had blundered. Although he scolded Turner Catledge, managing editor of the *New York Times*, for running a premature story on the planned invasion of Cuba and risking the vital secrecy, he later said in an aside to Catledge, "If you had printed more about the operation you would have saved us from a colossal mistake."

More than a year later, he was still talking the same way. In a conversation with Orvil Dryfoos, late publisher of the *Times*, at the White House on September 13, 1962, he said, "I wish you had run everything on Cuba . . . I am just sorry that you didn't tell it at the time."

Schlesinger echoed these words when he wrote, "I have wondered whether, if the press had behaved irresponsibly, it would not have spared the country a disaster."

Not the least part of this disaster, as the *Frankfurter Neue Presse* said, was that President Kennedy had strengthened Moscow's "outpost on the threshold of America."

Today we realize the full scope of Moscow's post on our threshold. Secure in the knowledge that Cuba will never be attacked again, an assurance given by President Kennedy at the time of the Cuban Missile Crisis, Cuba and Moscow are proceeding to work together against the interests of our country not only in Africa but, to an alarming degree, in Latin America.

U.S. intelligence has verified that Cuba and Fidel Castro trained the guerilla forces which led the revolution in Nicaragua. The eventual outcome of the overthrow of the Samoza regime has ominous potential to the United States. Columnists Rowland Evans and Robert Novak reported on August 1, 1979 that "the President's most sophisticated advisers do not doubt that, sooner or later, the Sandinista regime will be overtly Communist. Present cordiality from Managua is, like Fidel Castro's smiles in 1959, an effort to shake down Uncle Sam before the true colors are shown. Nor is there any doubt about what's next on the agenda: extension of the Soviet-Cuban thrust into El Salvador, Guatemala and Honduras over an undefined but probably protracted period. However slowly, Central American dominos are falling."

Directly north of these countries lies our neighbor Mexico. Who can doubt that it, too, is on Fidel Castro's timetable.

One thing is certain: the guerrilla movement is active in Latin America and will continue so. The Kremlin considers the Cuban-based effort to export their revolution to all Latin America so important that the Soviet Union pours more than a million dollars a day into Cuba.

This is the price America and its allies to the south have paid today for the mistakes which caused the disaster at the Bay of Pigs, and the failure to overthrow Castro and return Cuba to its position of friendly alliance with the United States.

5

The Story Behind
The Berlin Wall

IMAGINE A HIGH wall bristling with wire slashing New York City's Manhattan Island around 42nd Street, running generally along the thoroughfare but, in places, passing through apartment houses, backyards, stores and churches.

Under your feet it blocks the sewers and subways. Overhead, in buildings, it severs the telephone lines.

Or imagine such a wall bisecting Chicago, dividing the heavy traffic at Madison and State, said by some to be the busiest intersection in the world.

Picture any American city or town split by a wall which denies the free passage of its inhabitants from one sector to the other.

That is the Berlin Wall today.

Like a monstrous guillotine, it has fallen across the one-time German capital, cutting the nerves and arteries of the city in two.

It slices through sewers and subways, severs bridges and thoroughfares. In one place it marches unfeelingly across a cemetery. In another it blocks the entrance to the Church of the Reconciliation.

Apartments fronting on it have been bricked and boarded up on their lower floors. Beside a green canal it becomes an ugly mass of barbed wire. Along a quiet suburban street it extends its spine glinting with broken glass.

The wall separates families, separates mothers from children, separates friends from friends.

Brave men and women have tried to climb over it, tunnel under it, smash through it in racing trucks. They have tried to circumvent it by strength and by stealth.

A few have succeeded; many more have failed. Yet some still try.

Peter Fechter was one of those who tried to escape East Germany over the barrier. He had almost succeeded when a shot rang out and he fell mortally wounded. It was not an unusual incident in Berlin. Many are fired upon as they try to climb over the wall. But Peter Fechter bled to death slowly in full view of a helpless, outraged crowd. He lay on the wall beyond their reach. East German guards refused to help him, and American soldiers on the other side of the wall could not go to his aid.

This is the story of the Berlin Wall, the living symbol of forty eight years of antagonism between the monolithic East and the free West, and how and why it was permitted to be built.

Historically, Russia, the country which built it, has long been the most aggressive nation in Europe. In his *Day of the Saxon*, written before World War I, Homer Lea traced how Czarist Russia pushed her frontiers westward all through the eighteenth and nineteenth centuries. Based on that historic record, Lea accurately predicted both world wars, and forecast that if Germany were on the losing side in both of them, Russia would rush into the vacuum and a third world war would result, with Russia on one side and the United States on the other.

That prediction, which has been alarmingly accurate so far, Homer Lea made in 1911. Not many years later, the Communist Revolution sharpened Russia's hostile attitude towards the West and Poland became the sheaf of wheat caught between the two massive millstones.

In its attempt to use Germany as a potential ally, Russia established diplomatic relations with the Reich as early as 1923. On the basis of the Rapello Treaty of 1922, it encouraged Germany to build up a war machine. From 1930 to 1933, the Soviet Union urged the German communists to help Adolf Hitler to rise to absolute power by cooperating with the Nazis in promoting lawlessness and riots.

After Hitler won power in 1933, Russia and Germany extended a neutrality pact that had its origins earlier. Altogether, over a period of years, the two countries entered into no fewer than eighteen credit and commercial agreements which helped the Nazi regime at a time when Hitler was gathering his armed strength.

Even after Hitler suppressed the German Communist Party, Russia remained friendly to Germany. After the Munich Conference, Germany, in March 1939, annexed Czechoslovakia; the French and British governments sought to block further German aggression towards the east by guaranteeing the integrity of Poland and Romania. England and France sought Soviet support as well and to that end opened negotiations with the Soviet Union in April, 1939.

Instead of joining England and France in resisting Germany, Russia encouraged the aggressor by signing the Molotov-Ribbentrop agreements of August 23, 1939, replacing the Soviet-German neutrality treaty of 1926 with a ten-year non-aggression pact. This was the green light for which Hitler had been waiting and without which he might not have started World War II. Eight days after the agreement was signed, Germany invaded Poland from the west, and less than three weeks later, Russia invaded Poland from the east.

Molotov found an excuse for this stab in the back, saying ". . . one swift blow to Poland, first by the German and then by the Red Army, and nothing was left of this ugly offspring of the Versailles Treaty which had existed by oppressing non-Polish nationalities."

On September 28, Germany and Russia presided over the partition of Poland and gave each other appropriate souvenirs of the occasion. In return for Russia's recognition of a new frontier that included half of Poland, Germany recognized Soviet influence over Lithuania.

Soviet Russia now set out on her annexation of territory. In December she attacked Finland, and the following June absorbed Lithuania, Latvia and Estonia, Bessarabia and Northern Bukovina in Romania.

Russia also entered into a mutual non-aggression pact with Japan, Germany's Axis ally.

Despite these aggressive acts, the United States tried to maintain friendly relations with Russia. Several times in 1941 Washington warned Moscow that Hitler could not be trusted; that he planned to send his legions against Russia.

The Soviet Union not only turned a deaf ear to this, but gave recognition to Nazi aggression by breaking off diplomatic relations with Yugoslavia, Greece, Norway and Belgium after Germany occupied these countries.

In June 1941, Hitler acted as had been predicted, turned on his ally and invaded Russia. Then, hoist on his own petard, Stalin sought Western cooperation in resisting Nazi Germany. In spite of the Soviet record of collaboration with the Reich, the Western powers immediately gave aid to the Soviet Union.

So long as the Allies were helping Stalin by fighting Hitler, there was a truce between Russia and the West. Once Hitler was dead and Nazi Germany defeated, war was declared again between the East and the West. It was a "cold" war, but it was war to the death, a fulfillment of Homer Lea's prediction of thirty-five years earlier.

Stalin didn't waste much time in announcing the "cold war." In a speech in Moscow, on February 8, 1946, he made clear to the world that the war-time alliance with the Western powers had been a marriage of convenience. They had never intended the cooperation to be permanent. He reminded his listeners communist doctrine was dedicated to destruction of capitalism. War was inevitable until all capitalist countries had been taken over by communists. He then outlined the economic plans by which the Soviet Union should lay the foundations to defeat the West. Years later, when Khrushchev succeeded Stalin, his coarse boast that "we will bury you" was merely an extension of the old Stalin philosophy of war to the death between the two ideologies.

In the field of practical politics, Russia demonstrated there was no real change in the old Czarist policy of expansion by usurping power in Romania, Bulgaria, Hungary, Albania, Czechoslovakia, Poland and East Germany. A man who understood the duplicity of the Soviet Union better than most, Winston Churchill, pondered Stalin's oral declaration of the Soviet Union's resumption of its war against free, capitalist nations, after their military and economic assistance in defeating Hitler was no longer required. Less than a month later, Churchill, in a speech at Westminster College, in Fulton, Missouri, warned his audience, "An iron curtain has descended across the Continent."

The allusion was literary in 1946. It was real when the wall went up between East and West Berlin on that August Sunday in 1961.

Berlin was always the focal point of Russia's cold war. It was surrounded on all sides by Communist East Germany and East Berlin, as the result of an error near the close of the war.

While the fighting was still going on, and the Allied armies were striking into the heartland of Germany, we made several grave mistakes. We could have seized Berlin. Indeed, it is a matter of record that in the last weeks of the war German authorities made an offer to withdraw their forces from the western front and hold along the eastern front, thus allowing the Western allies to occupy nearly all of Germany.

Truman rejected that offer because our war aims were high. Our main objective was to destroy the German Wehrmacht so that it could never again be a threat to the peace. But even while we were deploying our forces to accomplish that military objective, the Red Army seized its political objectives—Vienna, Prague, and all of Berlin.

Harry S. Truman wrote in, "Year of Decisions," the first volume of his Memoirs, that Churchill, who never trusted Stalin, had urged that "our armies should push as far to the East as they could reach and firmly hold. Churchill, in fact, had been pressing this point for some time in messages to President Roosevelt. Churchill waged his own battle over it with the military too, particularly with our military chiefs, and had clashed on this general issue with Eisenhower when the plan for the last big offensive was prepared."

This plan called for our troops to stop at the Elbe. Churchill believed the capture of Berlin was of extreme importance.

As Mr. Truman tells it, "Eisenhower would not give in, and we supported him . . ."

"On March 30, General Eisenhower had reported to General Marshall that 'Berlin itself is no longer a particularly important objective,'" Mr. Truman writes. "Churchill was worried over Russian intentions and wanted all the territory we could get for bargaining purposes after the war."

In anticipating the victory over Germany, Churchill never underestimated the Russians. The British Prime Minister renewed his efforts to safeguard the future when Harry S. Truman succeeded to the Presidency on Roosevelt's death on April 12.

On April 24 he told the new President, in office only 12 days, that he was unhappy over Truman's proposal that Allied troops withdraw to their respective zones as soon as the military situation permitted.

President Truman notes that Churchill pointed out to him, "American troops would have to fall back some one hundred and fifty miles in the center and give up considerable territory to the Russians at a time when other questions remained unsettled.

"General Eisenhower, in his message of April 23," Mr. Truman goes on, "we gave some indication of the many problems that were developing in the matter of procedure with the Russians when they met up with our troops.

"'. . . I do not quite understand,' Eisenhower cabled, 'why the Prime Minister has been so determined to intermingle political and military considerations in attempting to establish a procedure for the conduct of our own and Russian troops when a meeting takes place . . .'" History proved Churchill right, Eisenhower wrong.

We paid for the right to occupy a part of Berlin. On the basis of the agreements of September 12, 1944, and May 1, 1945, the Western Allies withdrew from large parts of Mecklenburg, Saxony, Thuringia and Anhalt, in favor of Soviet occupation.

Concurrently, the three Western Powers occupied Western Berlin, which then was mostly rubble.

At that time, Greater Berlin was considered by the Russians and all the Western Allies as a single city to be occupied jointly by the victors. There was no "East" or "West" Berlin.

Difficulties began to arise when the Germans elected Ernst Reuter, Mayor of the City. The Russians "vetoed" his election because they thought he would install officials of his own rather than administrators of the communist persuasion. A struggle broke out over control of the police. On March 20, 1948, Soviet Union representatives walked out of the Allied Control Council for Germany. A few weeks afterwards, they quit the Allied Kommandatura for Berlin. In reprisal, the Western allies introduced a new currency and, on May 31, agreed to set up a new German state comprising the three Western zones.

On June 23, the Soviets ordered the Socialist Unity Party to carry out riots around the Berlin City Hall. Russian Army trucks transported the demonstrators to the scene. The next day the Russians imposed a full blockade to take over all of the city. But the allies defeated the scheme with a full-scale airlift, transporting food and other necessities into the German city with a never-ending stream of aircraft over a period of eleven months.

A defeated Moscow signed, on May 4, 1949, a four-power agreement to administer the city as a unit with free circulation for all Berliners.

The next crisis in Berlin did not come until 1958 when Russia handed the American ambassador in Moscow a communication on Berlin. Similar notes were given the British, French and German ambassadors.

In essence, the Soviet notes demanded that the United States, the United Kingdom and France abandon West Berlin. In short, they were to get out of the city.

Characteristically, in connection with the notes, the Russian government rewrote history so drastically that persons who had lived through the period failed to recognize events.

President Eisenhower responded stiffly that we would go to war if we had to, and the Russians knew he meant it. The crisis soon subsided.

Still, the Russians never took up their place again in the Kommandatura and the administrative division continued. Yet, in the gleaming Berlin conference room a seat was carefully saved for the Russians, even while the United States, British and French commandants held West Berlin on a tripartite basis.

When President Kennedy assumed office in January of 1961, his Administration was prepared for a Russian revival of the Berlin problem. So sure were White House aides that Khrushchev would take some sort of action involving Germany that former Secretary of State Dean Acheson was given the task of trying to anticipate them . . . when, where and in what form the blow would fall. Acheson attacked the matter with his usual bulldog pertinacity.

As events were to prove, however, he was a little too narrow in his predictions. He saw no danger, except from another blockade and felt that the West should react to that by pushing a division out of

West Germany along the Autobahn into Communist East Germany to relieve isolated Berlin, even if the action brought us to the brink of an atomic war.

In view of all the preliminary work, President Kennedy was prepared for discussion centering on Berlin when he met Khrushchev at Vienna in the spring of 1961. However, he was caught off balance when the Soviet Premier brought up the topic on the first day of their meetings.

In introducing the subject, Khrushchev said the main problem was a peace treaty. The current situation, he said, was intolerable. More than fifteen years had gone by since the end of hostilities. If the United States refused to join in a treaty, then the Soviet Union would go it alone and nothing could stop it.

The conferees then recessed for dinner on a sour note. When talks resumed the next day, the new President asked if the treaty Russia proposed would block access to Berlin.

In reply to the President's question, the foxy Russian Premier said yes, such a treaty would block Western access to Berlin, and he asked a question of his own, "Why does America want to stay there?"

Kennedy gave him a fairly blunt reply. He was not talking about his country going to Moscow, or the Russians coming to New York, but about American soldiers staying in Berlin, which they occupied by the right of conquest and where they had been garrisoned for fifteen years.

But Khrushchev insisted Berlin would be a "free city" and any continued Western presence inside East Germany after a treaty had formally ended the war would be illegal, humiliating and a violation of East Germany's borders.

On June 4, the Soviet Union directed notes to the United States, Britain and France demanding a German peace treaty by the year's end.

The Soviet Premier followed this up with what a Kennedy aide called a "testy television report" on the Vienna talks to the Russian people in which he repeated that Soviet Russia would sign a treaty with East Germany in six months and such a treaty would declare the former German capital a "free" city. In other words, the Allies could get out or face the prospect of being sealed in. Then, if the United States wanted a nuclear war, that was for the United States to choose.

Walter Ulbricht, Chairman of the East German Council of State, echoed the Soviet Premier's speech with a fist-swinging tirade. He complained about the flow of refugees from East Germany into West Berlin and forecast new restrictions.

Despite Ulbricht's tone and his mention of refugees, few anticipated what he had in mind. West Berlin planned to meet another blockade. It had stockpiled a year's supply of food, fuel and clothing. More were added.

The United States, which once saved Berlin with slow-moving C-47s and C-54s, now had five to seven times the airlift capacity of 1948.

As the crisis mounted, Kennedy flew off for a weekend at Hyannis Port. With him went some of his aides and on the sun-drenched patio and aboard the presidential cruiser *Marlin,* he talked with Secretaries Rusk and McNamara. In Hyannis Port, too, was his new military adviser, General Maxwell Taylor.

Over that Fourth of July weekend, Khrushchev was equally busy. He cited Kennedy's call for a larger American defense effort as reason enough for a summit conference to sign a German peace treaty. He announced a suspension of the partial demobilization of the Red Army and a thirty per cent increase in Russia's defense spending.

Much thought, second thought, reconsideration and revision went into the President's answer to the Soviet note of June 4, which was now being drafted. It agreed with the Soviet contention that "a peace settlement is long overdue," but blamed the delay on continuing "Soviet efforts to obtain special advantages for itself and the Soviet bloc at the expense of a lasting peace."

The note made two further points:

First, the West had a perfectly legal right to be in Berlin and its claims "derive absolutely from the unconditional surrender of Nazi Germany, and were not granted by, nor negotiated with, the Soviet Union." If rights of access were interfered with, then the Western Big Three have "the responsibility to make such dispositions with respect to the exercise of their access rights as they deem appropriate."

Second, the note hit at Russia's act of setting up a puppet East German government that was "no more than an extension of its own authority."

The note went on to say, "The United States Government

continues to believe that there will be no real solution of the German problem until the German people are reunified on the basis of the universally recognized principle of self-determination."

Cartoonist Bill Mauldin's drawing in the *St. Louis Post Dispatch* showed Kennedy and Khrushchev with pistols to their temples in a game of Russian roulette.

Kennedy is saying, a little ruefully, "Personally, I prefer touch football."

The cartoon dramatized the situation with sardonic humor as the young President went before the television cameras to give the American people, and the world, his answer to Khrushchev's challenge on Berlin.

The morning newspapers played up the military aspects of the speech. This was understandable. Not even nineteenth century Great Britain in the heyday of the empire had as many military commitments as did the United States in 1961.

On that June 26th, America's armed forces around the world included 870,000 troops at 200 army bases; 620,000 sailors and 177,000 marines manning 817 ships and 8,800 planes; and 820,000 airmen with 18,700 planes at 175 airbases. In West Germany alone, the United States had a total of 250,000 men.

The President said he proposed adding 217,000 men to the armed forces, increasing the standing army to a million men. Draft calls would be tripled and the reserve called up.

With commendable candor, the President said, "Seven weeks ago I returned from Europe to report on my meeting with Premier Khrushchev and others. His grim warnings about the future of the world, his aide-memoire on Berlin, the subsequent speeches and threats which he and his agents have launched and the increase in the Soviet military budget that he has announced have all prompted a series of decisions by the Administration in a series of consultations with the members of the NATO Organization . . .

"West Berlin has now become—as never before—the great testing place of Western courage and will. I hear it said that West Berlin is militarily untenable—and so was Bastogne, and so, in fact, was Stalingrad. Any dangerous spot is tenable if men—brave men—will make it so. We do not want to fight—but we have fought before. And others in earlier times have made the same dangerous mistake of assuming that the West was too selfish and too soft and too divided to resist invasion of freedom in other lands."

These were fine, spirited words which made Americans feel proud and led them to believe that we were determined to keep Berlin free.

There was another fine paragraph on freedom. "We shall always be prepared," the President said, "to discuss international problems with any and all nations that are willing to talk and listen with reason. We have previously indicated our readiness to remove any irritants in West Berlin. But the freedom of the city is not negotiable. We cannot negotiate with those who say, 'What's mine is mine and what's yours is negotiable.'"

The broadcast was highly dramatic. The air conditioning was turned low so that microphones would not pick up the hum, and the President perspired heavily under the klieg lights. His delivery seemed almost deliberately low-keyed, and he appeared nervous and he frequently wiped the sweat from his brow and brushed back his damp hair. The responsibilities he had sought so eagerly in the recent election campaign were bearing down with an awesome finality.

As the West resolutely girded for a showdown over Berlin, East Germany's puppet boss Walter Ulbricht displayed signs of nervousness. He ordered the 100,000 men of the People's Army alerted to maximum combat readiness. He gave them their first assignment: to use all means to try to stop the East German refugees who were pouring through Berlin to the West.

Despite this, the flow of refugees remained a steady stream. During July, 30,415 East Germans escaped to West Berlin. In the early days of August they were pouring across the line at the rate of 1,500 a day. To thwart the exodus, the People's Army patrols in camouflage uniforms stalked the spruce forests and potato fields in a twelve-mile circle around Berlin. Jackbooted People's Police combed all access roads, airports and railways leading to the city.

Within the city itself, the communists began making trouble for the 52,000 East Germans who daily commuted to jobs in West Berlin, by subway and elevated. No published order existed prohibiting East Germans from working in West Berlin, but East German soldiers and police began hauling these workers off the commuter trains both before and after they reached the East Berlin sector on their way to the Western half of the city. They invalidated or confiscated East German commuters' identification cards. They took some unfortunates off to jail.

The commandants of the United States, British and French sectors protested these new harassments. Emphasis was put on the Russian infringement of the right to circulate freely throughout the city.

In retrospect, one finds it difficult to believe that all this gave the President no inkling of what was to come. He was proceeding entirely on the supposition that the Russians intended to blockade the entire city. Indeed, it looked as if that was what they proposed when two battle-ready divisions ringed Berlin with their armor and artillery. Eighteen other Russian divisions in East Germany were put on the alert.

Then, suddenly, on August 13, in the early hours before dawn, the first part of Khrushchev's plan started to reveal itself. East German troops and police occupied most of the crossing points on the East Berlin side of the dividing line between East and West Berlin. Under their guns, workmen tore up the streets and built roadblocks. They dug post holes and strung barbed wire.

It was Sunday, and the President was boating off Hyannis Port, when word came that the communists were building barricades along the line between East and West Berlin.

He called his brother Robert and Dean Rusk, but evidently they reached no conclusion on what to do to honor the President's solemn pledge to keep Berlin free.

At dawn on Monday thirteen crossing points, including the Brandenburg Gate, still remained open and many foot pedestrians were passing through check-points both ways. But by 9 o'clock, not one of the 52,000 East Berliners with jobs in West Berlin had managed to cross the border.

Throughout the day the Russians gave every indication of their ultimate intention to divide Berlin. The barrier sneaking through the city was strengthened. Stone and cement block walls began to appear.

Emboldened by success, the East German Communists tightened their squeeze on West Berlin, even closing the Brandenburg Gate. No warnings to stop came from Washington. There was no renewed insistence that Berlin must be completely free. The White House was silent.

One by one the other gates were closed. The East German Interior Minister announced all West Berlin cars and other vehicles must have special permits to cross into East Berlin. Telephone lines were cut between the two sectors. Postal and telegraph service was interrupted.

At the Brandenburg Gate thousands of West Berliners gathered to protest. They shouted insults at the East German police and workmen. West Berlin police had to lock arms to hold back the throng and a full-blown riot seemed imminent.

Now, at last, Washington sent word the United States would protest the communist action in the strongest terms.

But the work on the Wall went on. The few check-points that remained open were closed.

On Tuesday, the 15th, the President finally got off his note of protest as workmen continued to make the Wall stronger and angry crowds demonstrated before the Brandenburg Gate. A heavy downpour of rain dispersed the protesters on the very threshold of crisis.

Then from Washington came a statement approved by the President. It was far different from the solemn assurances Kennedy had given a few weeks before when he had recognized that "West Berlin has become the great testing place of Western courage and will . . . the freedom of the city is not negotiable." Now, instead of demanding that work on the Wall stop at once, he resorted to semantics. The communist actions were a "confession of failure," he said.

Openly exasperated at this do-nothing policy, Mayor Willy Brandt of Berlin asked Kennedy that he use "not merely words but political action" against the communists.

What had happened? After the brave fighting talks given by President Kennedy, why had the United States failed to act through the several days that the communists were building a stronger and still stronger wall?

The truth of the matter was that among all the contingency plans advanced and reviewed by the new President, neither he nor anyone else had provided for a positive response to a blockade of the border between East and West Berlin.

When the communists divided Berlin, in contravention of a solemn agreement, President Kennedy and his Administration were unsure of themselves; they did not know how to react to this unprecedented situation.

Angry Berliners demonstrated for four days before a wall daily being made stronger. They jeered at the East German and Russian troops and mocked the soldiers of the Allied Powers who stood by and did nothing.

Finally, Walter Dowling, the American Ambassador to Bonn, pleaded for a swift, positive reaction to the communist shutdown.

Belatedly, when the Wall was a fait accompli, the United States, Britain and France issued brief, identically worded protsts urging the Soviet Union to "put an end to these illegal measures."

Russia rejected the protests out of hand and went on sealing off East Berlin from West Berlin.

Washington sought to recover face with a statement that Russia had suffered a terrible propaganda defeat in the eyes of the world. But the fact was that Russia had done what it set out to do without interference from us. President Kennedy had not lifted a finger to stop them as he had promised.

In the end, after more days of inaction, the President finally arrived at two decisions.

First, he ordered 1,500 troops of the Eighth Division to proceed along the Helmstadt-Berlin Autobahn in armored trucks to reinforce the 5,000 man garrison in Berlin. Over a quiet weekend in late August the troops rolled along the Autobahn and into West Berlin in a move to test the Russian pledges that the Berlin Wall had no effect on the Allied right of access to the city.

Second, Kennedy sent off Vice President Lyndon B. Johnson to shore up West German morale. Along with Johnson went retired Army General Lucius D. Clay, who had been Commander of American forces in Europe and Military Governor of the United States Zone of Germany during the 1948 Berlin airlift.

At the airport near Bonn, Johnson stood up in a misty rain to address the crowd. Then he flew on to Berlin, where his car drove down the Potsdamerstrasse to a spot where he could examine the illegal barrier put up by the communists.

"This is a time for confidence, for poise, and for faith—faith in yourselves," said his message from the President to the people of Berlin. "It is also a time for faith in your Allies, everywhere throughout the world. This island does not stand alone."

The sad truth was that the free West Berlin enclave was more than ever an island alone in a communist sea.

Sporadically, in the months that followed, crowds of 5,000 and more gathered in West Berlin to stone East German police and

Soviet buses; or merely to gape and grumble; to elbow West Berlin police and boo American soldiers.

After a year the crowds grew smaller and Berlin began to live with its shame. Now they pointed out each place where the Wall had been breached; eight celebrated holes in the ground where East-to-West tunnelers had come up to the surface and freedom.

The Wall itself ended at Schonefeld Airport in East Germany, but watch towers and barbed wire also sealed the city's 65-mile western border with the Soviet zone.

Soon the Wall would become a barrier of 830 miles traversing East Germany's western frontier all the way from the Baltic to Czechoslovakia. By 1962 that "Anti-Fascist Protection Wall," as Walter Ulbricht cynically called it, boasted 500 watch towers, 1,000 fortified bunkers and 93 miles of minefields. Throughout its length were wide, plowed strips of earth, not for crops, but so that Russian guards could see something as small as a footprint and alert guards with savage dogs to prevent another escape.

This is the story of the Berlin Wall, told in its simplest form.

Why did Russia go ahead and build the Wall when Kennedy's words on his world-wide television broadcast had promised that the freedom of the city was not negotiable?

Had not the Russian leader backed off in 1958 when Eisenhower said we would go to war if necessary rather than give in to Russia's demands? Why did he not back off in 1961?

One answer can be found in the area of credibility. By July, 1961, Khrushchev and Kennedy had already met in Vienna. The shrewd Soviet Premier had sized up his young opponent. He had heard the President's promises about Laos, and noted Kennedy's failure to follow through there. He had watched the feckless performance at the Bay of Pigs. Presumably, he felt sure that he would not be challenged in Berlin. Indeed, this was the very reason given in Germany for the confidence with which Khrushchev proceeded.

In August, 1966, *Der Spiegel*, the West German news magazine, featured a story in which it claimed President Kennedy actually gave Nikita Khrushchev the green light to build the Berlin Wall. It recounted the sequence of events and decisions which led to Khrushchev's decision, quoting from an East German Central Committee meeting of March 16, 1961; a Warsaw Pact summit meeting in Moscow, March 29, 1961; and from the famous meeting between Kennedy and Khrushchev in Vienna in June, 1961.

At the Warsaw Pact summit meeting on March 29, 1961, *Der Spiegel* said, Khrushchev is known to have told the East German leader, Walter Ulbricht, that he could make no important move until he, Khrushchev, had weighed the difference between Eisenhower and Kennedy and learned how the new President's policies would differ from those of the old President.

Then, during the Vienna confrontation, the two leaders exchanged their views on Berlin. *Der Spiegel* affirms the Kennedy-Khrushchev exchange in which Khrushchev threatened to sign a separate peace treaty with East Germany, warning of atomic war if there was any violation of East Germany's territory after the signing. It reports on Kennedy's vow that he would not accept any action by East Germany touching on West Berlin or its access routes. It goes on to report on a meeting between Presidential adviser, John J. McCloy, and Khrushchev during which a warning was given to the U.S. to the effect that atomic war might result if East Germany collapsed. And, *Der Spiegel* says, in his June 25 television address, President Kennedy failed to mention four-power rule of the whole city. This, *Der Spiegel* reports, is when Khrushchev decided to make his move and permitted Ulbricht to go ahead with the Berlin wall.

Following the *Der Spiegel* story, on August 15, 1966, the West Berlin newspaper *Morganpost* ran quotes from memoirs of men close to President Kennedy also telling how the President acquiesced in Berlin.

In November, 1966, still more emphasis was added when *U.S. News and World Report* revealed that Herbert Wehner, second to Willy Brandt in the German Socialist Party, also felt the U.S. was to blame for letting the Reds build the Berlin Wall.

When the Wall was built, the United States was the most powerful nation in the world, far stronger than its two allies in Berlin— England and France. The initiative on action in Berlin had to come from Washington, just as it had during the Truman and Eisenhower Administrations. The Russians had twice before threatened the freedom of Berlin. Prompt action by these United States Presidents had vitiated Soviet intentions. Kennedy's preoccupation with public opinion here and abroad held him back, as it had in Cuba. This is what the late German Chancellor Konrad Adenauer meant when he said that the Kennedy Administration was too sensitive to voter opinion.

Perhaps the most ironic commentary on President Kennedy's great mistake at the Berlin Wall was made a year after it was put off.

General Frank L. Howley, who had been U.S. Commandant in Berlin from 1945 to 1949, returned in the summer of 1962 as a civilian to receive a decoration. In his four years of dealing with the Russians, Howley had their measure, and he never gave them an inch. Because of his firmness and scrupulous honesty, he had little trouble with them, and he won German respect and affection. The Berliners referred to him in the press and among themselves as "Franki," in the same affectionate, informal way they spoke of their own "Willi" Brandt.

General Howley's visit was noted in all West German newspapers and one of West Germany's best political cartoonists paid the American a unique tribute.

He made a drawing for page one of the leading West Berlin newspaper, *Der Tangenspiegel,* of two Germans standing looking at the Wall. The first German says, "If Franki were here, he'd tear down that wall."

The second German's response tells a volume.

"If Franki had been here, they wouldn't have dared to put the wall up!"

But put it up they did. And the wall stands today, cruel, ugly and evil along its entire length, not only a symbol of a great mistake, but a visible monument to remind us of the consequenees of great mistakes made by a President of this country.

6

Un-Presidential Conduct
In The White House

IN THE POST-WATERGATE era there are few secrets left in public life. We are all now privy to the latest information about Wilbur Mills' high living, Wayne Hays' sex life, Margaret Trudeau's "most private" life style . . . the list gets longer every year.

During the early nineteen sixties when John F. Kennedy and his Administration held sway in Washington, however, things were far different. There was, at that time, a virtual conspiracy of silence on the part of the press concerning the real goings-on in the Kennedy White House.

"The best kept secret of the Kennedy Administration," reports Victor Lasky, "was the President's predilection for pretty girls . . . Even more significant was the way Kennedy managed to carry on without a breath of scandal reaching the public prints. It wasn't because the boys with the ballpoint pens weren't aware of what was going on. Many of them were. The media that wept copious tears about how Nixon degraded his office could never work up any moral indignation about the 'moral stain' brought to the White House by one of its heroes . . ."

"President Kennedy's public image," declares Lasky, "clashed

113

mightily with his private life. The public image, presented through an all-too-willing media, was that of the good husband, the kind family man, and the perfect father. Camelot was never sullied by stories of what really was going on behind the scenes, the sybaritic, hedonistic life led by a President who felt he could do anything and get away with it."

It was really not until December, 1975 that the nation began to learn about the swinging nature of the Kennedy White House. It was Judith Campbell Exner who told the nation at least a bit of the story.

According to Exner, she had a brief fling with singer Frank Sinatra which ended after a few months when Sinatra's sexual demands became too "kinky" for her.

Still, it was Sinatra who introduced her to Jack and Ted Kennedy at a gathering in Las Vegas early in the 1960 campaign. The party broke up after the midnight show at the Sands Hotel, but Teddy took her on a tour of the gambling tables and began "pressing" her to join a campaign trip to Denver. She turned him down . . . having already agreed to lunch with Jack the next day. Ted then became "childishly temperamental and tried to hustle her into changing her plans," even pursuing her by phone right up to the moment she left to join Jack.

The lunch between Judith Campbell Exner and Jack Kennedy took place in Frank Sinatra's hotel suite. This, she told the world in 1975, began a two year affair that included twice-a-day phone calls, a four day stay at New York's Plaza Hotel (where, she says, they began their "sexual relationship") and romantic interludes in Palm Beach, Chicago, Los Angeles, and even Kennedy's Georgetown home while Jackie was away. By her count, they rendezvoused about 20 times in the White House itself in mid-1961. Mrs. Exner says that she knew Jack Kennedy "in ways no one else did."

He told her, for instance, that his marraige was "in poor shape and that Jackie had intended to divorce him but the Kennedy family had managed to hold them together for political reasons." Before he was elected, Jack Kennedy promised to take Judy on a three month cruise if he was defeated. Once in the White House, he attempted to place her name on a list for "major state affairs," but she declined the honor. When she was recovering from an appendectomy, he sent three dozen roses a week. This may or may not have impressed her. At the same time she was visiting the White House, she was also conducting an affair with Mafia leader Sam Giancana, who was, among other things, showering her with five dozen yellow roses a day.

Judy had also met the mob boss through Frank Sinatra. Exner was then 23 and was an aspiring actress. There were many women like Judy around Sinatra at that time. "Frank was around here all the time, doing a show or shooting a picture down by the dam," recalls a Vegas associate. "There were dozens of broads like that with him."

It could do a girl some good to be around Sinatra, for being a friend of Frank's meant being a friend of Frank's friends—and they ranged from the Kennedys on down to the Giancanas, the Morettis, the Fischettis, even down to Lucky Luciano, the boss of all mob bosses.

The Kennedys knew of Sinatra's mob connections and did not seem to mind. He played an important role in Jack Kennedy's presidential campaign, thanks in part to Kennedy's brother-in-law Peter Lawford's charter membership in Sinatra's "Rat Pack," but in larger measure, according to reporter Robert Sam Anson, "to Kennedy's and Sinatra's mutual attraction to glitter and power."

"After Kennedy's election as president," writes Anson, "the new attorney general asked the F.B.I. to run a precautionary check on Sinatra's associates, and when the word came back that Sinatra's chums included some of the most notorious members of the underworld, Kennedy put some distance between himself and the singer . . . They continued to socialize, however."

Judith Exner had met Giancana only weeks after she first dined with Jack Kennedy. Giancana was well aware of Exner's close relationship with the President, and often joked about it.

By any standard, Salvatore Giancana was the boss. The silk suits, the shades, the cigars from Cuba, the pink Cadillacs and the blonde on each arm. Giancana had them all.

A product of Chicago's tough West side, Giancana began his career as a wheelman for "Machine Gun" Jake McGurn, one of the prime suspects in the St. Valentine's Day Massacre.

He did his first stretch in prison at age 15. By the time he was 20, Giancana, known as "Mooney," had 51 arrests, three of them for murder. When his draft board asked Giancana his profession, he replied: "I steal." The board granted him deferment, convinced that Giancana was a psychotic. During the war, he devoted himself to organizing the numbers operation in Chicago and after World War II, extended his reach into gambling, policy, loan sharking, juke boxes, prostitution, hijacking and labor racketeering. By 1957, he was ready to take over control of the entire 300-member Chicago family. To do so, he had Tony "Big Tuna" Accardo murdered as he entered his $500,000 suburban estate. From then on, Giancana was boss. His empire stretched from Cleveland to Kanas City and souh to Miami. The estimated yearly income was $2 billion, with $40 to $50 million going directly to Giancana.

Sam Giancana was not Judith Exner's only romantic attachment away from the White House. There was also "Don Giovanni" Roselli, another member in good standing of organized crime.

"Johnny," as everyone called Roselli, was not nearly as important in the Mafia as Giancana. His conviction in 1968 for hustling a number of prominent Hollywood figures in a card-cheating scam at the Friar's Club did little to enhance his reputation.

Earlier, in Chicago, he operated as an extortionist and strong-arm man. During the fifties and sixties he operated in Las Vegas as a "fixer," the man to see when you wanted to cut a deal. Suave, charming, a legendary ladies' man, Johnny, according to Las Vegas Sun publisher Hank Greenspun, was "the guy who made you the offers you couldn't refuse."

At the time Judith Exner was simultaneously involved with Kennedy, Giancana, and Roselli, one of the Mafia's major goals was turning off the Kennedy assault upon organized crime. This became one of Giancana's obsessions. He knew Kennedy was vulnerable, and, interestingly enough, he shared a bed with one of those vulnerabilities.

If Judy Exner played a role in Giancana's plans remains unclear. Sexual blackmail, however, was certainly a possibility. Such an approach would have been in keeping with Giancana's methods of doing business. He was repeatedly heard to boast that his organization had placed a girl with the President. It could have been a bluff, or it could have been true. This may never be known with any degree of certainty.

What brought the Exner affair into public view was the U.S. Senate Intelligence Committee. As part of its probe of the CIA, the committee investigated Roselli's and Giancana's other federal connection: a possible contract with the CIA to assassinate Cuban dictator Fidel Castro. By this time it was known that Giancana had been talking to Ruby, the man who killed Kennedy assassin Oswald, prior to the tragedy in Dallas.

Before Giancana could be questioned, he was murdered in his Oak Park, Illinois home on orders from the high command of the Mafia. There were a number of reasons for this, including the fact that the Mob bosses thought Giancana had been telling a grand jury about gangland activities.

Senate committee members did question Roselli, and committee lawyers questioned Mrs. Exner. They turned up no evidence to contradict her claim that she had never known about the plot to kill Castro. Persuaded that she the affair was irrelevant to their investigation, the committee, under the leadership of Senator Frank Church (D-Idaho) voted unanimously to describe her in their report only as a "close friend" of Kennedy's, not even disclosing her sex. Some committee staffers considered this a whitewash, and leaked the story to several newspapers.

Much of the press were true to their traditional pattern of mythologizing Jack Kennedy. *The Washington Post* quietly tucked the story away on Page 6. *The Chicago Daily News* and the Scripps-Howard Bureau in Washington, however, were more explicit. In a front page story, the *News* quoted Evelyn Lincoln, Kennedy's personal secretary, as saying of Mrs. Exner: "She got like a pest. She would call and call." As for Judy's relationship with the President, Mrs. Lincoln said: "The President was right attractive and lots of girls used to call him."

Senator Church was furious that the truth had finally come out. He ordered that every member of the committee's staff sign a statement that he or she had not been their source. No one confessed. The friends of the Kennedys refused to divulge anything. Dave Powers said that the only Campbell he ever heard of "was the kind with the chunky soup."

Charging that the Church committee had engaged in a "cover up," *New York Times* columnist William Safire declared that, "The private life of any public figure is nobody's business but his own, and salacious gossip of White House kennelkeepers and self-described intimates can be dismissed as offensive. But when the nation's Chief Executive receives even a few calls from the home telephone of a leader of the Mafia in Chicago, that crosses the line into the public's business. That is particularly the case when—of all Mafia leaders around—the one with whom the President shared a close friend turns out to be the one whom the CIA selects to handle the arrangements for the assassination of Fidel Castro, and the one who is murdered just before testifying . . . The Church Committee has attempted a cover-up from the Government's end; the Mafia, by silencing Giancana forever, has clamped down the lid from its end."

Now that the connection between Kennedy, Exner and Giancana had been revealed, Dan Thomasson and Tim Wyngaard of the Scripps-Howard Washington Bureau developed more of the story of the Kennedy-Exner affair for the American public.

Thomasson and Wyngaard found that F.B.I. documents showed that J. Edgar Hoover, whose agents were watching Giancana and Roselli as part of Attorney General Robert Kennedy's war on organized crime, discovered the link between the President and the Mafia leaders. On February 27, 1962, Hoover alerted Robert Kennedy and aide Kenneth O'Donnell to the associations of the President's friend, Judith Exner, and on March 22, the F.B.I. Director took another memo on this subject to a luncheon meeting with President Kennedy. It was after this meeting that Jack Kennedy was forced to break off his relationship with Judy Exner.

The full story has never been told. Among the unanswered questions about the entire affair are these, stated columnist William Safire:

"(1) Since gangland figures are concerned about the liaisons of their girlfriends, did Mafia figures encourage the girl's White House relationship, and if so, to what end? (2) Did Director Hoover's obvious concern with Mr. Giancana's White House connection suddenly cut off just short of knowledge of the Giancana-CIA plot to get Castro? (3) Why did Mr. Hoover check in with the CIA and then tell a Las Vegas sheriff to stop prosecuting Giancana for wiretapping an unfaithful girlfriend—right after his luncheon showdown with President Kennedy?"

There were, many believed, far too many coincidences when Mafia leaders and the President of the United States shared the same girl's attention, and when, as William Safire put it, ". . . those two Mafiosi are chosen to make the hit on a foreign leader by our CIA; when the delivery of poison pellets is made to one of them on the weekend the President is with the girl in Florida; when the F.B.I. is listening in, and cautioning the President—and when the President winds up murdered by a supporter of Castro, target of the aborted CIA assassination plot, the matter is worth a thorough public examination."

Such a thorough public examination, however, never took place. Instead, as Mr. Safire pointed out, "The Church committee has attempted a cover-up from the Government end; the Mafia, by silencing Giancana forever, has clamped down the lid from its end. Thanks to Thomasson-Wyngaard reporting, however, the story of the President's friend gives us a useful clue to a related mystery: why the Kennedy men were so ready to acquiesce in the wiretapping and bugging of Dr. Martin Luther King. The clue: After that luncheon in March, 1962, when the F.B.I. director laid out the evidence of the Mafia connections of the President's friend, the Kennedys must have been prepared to do anything and everything J. Edgar Hoover wanted."

The Exner case is, unfortunately, only the beginning of the story of Jack Kennedy's extra-marital affairs while in the White House.

Although neither it nor any other leading newspapers or magazines mentioned anything about it at the time it was taking place, *Time Magazine*, in its December 29, 1975 issue, put it this way: "When Judith Campbell Exner said . . . that she had a 'close personal' relationship with Jack Kennedy, she was only confirming what had long been a matter of open and widespread speculation: that even after he entered the White House, the handsome and fun-loving Kennedy never stopped pursuing attractive women—nor they him. His privacy guarded by discreet Secret Service agents, his wife often away on vacations, his duties affording frequent travel, and the aura of his office proving nearly irresistible, Kennedy as President found the catching all the easier."

Kennedy's attitude toward women was hardly a secret. Once he had startled two proper Englishmen, Prime Minister Harold Macmillan and Foreign Minister R.A.B. Butler, during a 1962 conference in Nassau, by casually confiding that if he went too long without a woman, he suffered severe headaches.

It was known, even at that time, that the President and his wife had separate rooms. Years later this appeared in the press when New

York Mayor Koch described a visit he had made to Jimmy Carter's White House. Carter took Koch and other guests on a tour of the living quarters, including his bedroom.

Carter said, "this is where the President sleeps. Some Presidents slept with their wives and some didn't." He added that he slept with his wife.

In telling this story Koch added, "For instance, the Kennedys had separate rooms. I'm not telling anything out of school. This is all well known."

How many women shared Kennedy's room is not known. One woman who moved in Kennedy's social circle said: "If all women who claimed privately that they had slept with Jack had really done so, he wouldn't have the strength left to lift a teacup."

Yet, beneath the smoke there appeared to be a good deal of fire. A number of women told friends about their affairs with Kennedy. One of these was actress Jayne Mansfield who, before her accidental death in 1967, claimed to have carried on a three year intimate and intermittent romance with Kennedy.

Another who was not hesitant to relate her experiences with Jack Kennedy was San Francisco socialite Joan Hitchcock Lundberg. She said that she met Kennedy when he was a U.S. Senator and carried on an occasional affair with him over a period of three years. She has been married four times, is the mother of four, and is a popular local hostess. "He was a very busy fellow," she said of Kennedy, "a wonderful guy and a lot of fun."

Mrs. Lundberg said that she was only one of a long "exclusive" list of women who had affairs with Kennedy. At the time she romanced Kennedy, Mrs. Lundberg was living at Malibu near Los Angeles and saw him whenever he visited Mr. and Mrs. Peter Lawford. She said that she was accepted socially at the Lawfords' until her relationship with Kennedy became obvious, and then "I was no longer allowed in the house."

"He was very interested in how a person looked," she said. "He liked to think he could determine a woman's intelligence by looking at her eyebrow structure and the way her eyes were spaced. He was very positive about the kind of woman he liked. It seemed he got less fussy as time went on."

Joan Lundberg finally stopped seeing Kennedy "because there didn't seem to be much future in it." Her children knew about the relationship she had with Jack Kennedy. "To the kids, he's just another one of my lovers—only he's got some prestige in the family."

Late in 1975, *Time Magazine* declared: "There is little doubt that Marilyn Monroe also had a sexual relationship with the President."

Show business columnist Earl Wilson claims without qualification in his book *Show Business Laid Bare:* "Marilyn Monroe's sexual pyrotechnics excited the President of the United States."

According to Wilson, their intimate relationship began about a year before her death and was pursued in New York's Carlyle Hotel, the Beverly Hills Hotel, Peter Lawford's Santa Monica home, the White House and even in Kennedy's private plane, *Caroline*. Once, Wilson relates, Monroe returned from a meeting with the President and confided to a friend: "I think I made his back feel better."

"Jack Kennedy probably would have approved," wrote Wilson, "of the contention that he was the sexiest, swingingest President of the century, and not have thought it disrespectful." Wilson estimates that the President's "score card," if he kept one, would probably have run into dozens, even possibly hundreds." And these were not just celebrated actresses or socialites either. Wilson reports that Kennedy's conquests included "stewardesses, secretaries, models and those strange creatures who like to offer their bodies to big names."

Wilson made the information about the romance between Jack Kennedy and Marilyn Monroe public, he said, in order to "set the record straight," because Norman Mailer, in his book on the actress, dwelled on Marilyn's relationship with Bobby Kennedy.

Another authority is Hollywood columnist Sidney Skolsky, who ended his memoirs by apologizing for having failed to report at the time about the Kennedy-Monroe affair. He wrote: "I confess that I still find it grim to speculate on what might have happened to me if I had tried to write about this romance in my column when it first came to my attention."

Discussing the mysterious death of Marilyn Monroe, Victor Lasky stated: "Whatever did happen concerning Monroe's death, the truth is that there had indeed been a massive cover-up, one designed to protect the Kennedys by hiding their relationships with the actress. And while those relationships were common gossip in press circles at the time, no major newspaper or t.v. network appeared interested enough to delve into the story."

"My own sources during the Kennedy era," Lasky reports, "were Secret Service agents assigned to guard the President. On an off-the-record basis they expressed concern about 'Lancer's' (Kennedy's code name) dalliances with women he barely knew. It wasn't so much that they were prudish. What concerned them were the security problems involved. One agent even wondered aloud whether the Russians might be 'tempted to plant a broad' in the President's bedroom."

Other celebrities linked with Kennedy in gossip columns have either denied any intimacies with him, refused to talk, or in some cases said they had never even met him. These include actresses Angie Dickinson, Kim Novak, Janet Leigh and Rhonda Fleming.

Time reported that, "Sources familiar with the Kennedy White House contend that Kennedy's liaisons were mostly with relatively unknown young women. Most often cited are two women who displayed few secretarial skills but worked on his staff. Bright and charming, they were attractive—but neither sensational beauties nor sultry playgirls. British Director Jonathan Miller, who once saw them around the White House, claimed that they looked 'like unused tennis balls—they had the fuzz still on them.'"

Reporters recall that these two often turned up in the presidential entourage when Kennedy was traveling. Although assigned no discernible duties, they were with Kennedy in Nassau when he met Harold Macmillan to discuss cancellation of the Skybolt missile program, at Yosemite Park when he was promoting conservation measures, at Palm Beach when he was vacationing. They were usually assigned quarters near the President and were code-named "Fiddle" and "Faddle" by the Secret Service.

Jack Kennedy did his best not to permit his sexual adventures to interfere with his presidential duties.

One summer afternoon, for example, when the President and a young lady he had assigned a job on the National Security Council staff, were in the Lincoln bedroom, the two were interrupted by a knock on the door. Angered, Kennedy threw the door wide open. There stood two top foreign affairs advisers with several secret cables—and a clear view of the woman in bed. Never bothering to close the door, Kennedy cooled down, read the dispatches and made his decisions before returning to his friend.

It was not uncommon for some of Kennedy's closest male friends to send willing young women to the White House. One newspaper columnist was once overheard telling an attractive brunette how to get into the mansion with a note that he wanted delivered to Kennedy.

The President later called the columnist back to confirm: "I got your message—both of them." Secret Service agents would pass such casual women under presidential instructions, although they worried about it. More frequent visitors, including a number of airline stewardesses, underwent full Secret Service investigations.

Years after the event, *Time Magazine* reported that, "Recent reporting has put one celebrated Kennedy anecdote into a different perspective. Newsmen watching Kennedy's movements on the night before he was nominated as the 1960 Democratic presidential candidate caught him climbing over a backyard fence near his suburban Los Angeles hideaway. Kennedy shouted that he was going off 'to meet my father.' Reporters have since learned that the stealthy visit was more likely to the nearby home of a former diplomat's wife he had known for some time."

One book which describes both the sexual adventures occurring within the White House and the manner in which they were carefully concealed from the public was *Dog Days at the White House,* by Traphes Bryant. Bryant was an electrician and kennel-keeper at the White House from the days of Harry Truman to those of Richard Nixon.

According to Bryant, the housekeeping staff engaged in a "conspiracy of silence" to keep Jack's romantic activities a closely guarded secret.

Sometimes, he reported, Jack would lounge naked around the White House swimming pool when Jackie was away, and women would arrive, undress and join him.

Bryant also tells of once taking the elevator past the family quarters in the course of his duties after the First Lady left the White House:

"Just as the elevator door opened, a naked blonde office girl ran through the hall between the second-floor kitchen and the door leading to the West Hall. There was nothing to do but to get out of the vicinity fast and push the basement button."

The staff, according to Bryant, always scurried around after a woman had visited Kennedy, to retrieve such telltale signs as hairpins. Once Jackie allegedly found a woman's undergarment tucked into a pillow slip. She is supposed to have said calmly to Jack: "Would you please shop around and see whose these belong to. They're not my size."

Jack Kennedy's friends in the press kept what was well known to almost everyone in official Washington a carefully guarded secret from the American people. They were, indeed, the last to know. Not until 1975 and the public declarations by Judith Campbell Exner did the truth start to come out.

"Mrs. Exner's story," Newsweek declared, "broke a kind of gentlemen's code of silence that has long sheltered Kennedy's private diversions from public view. She was the first of the supposed Other Women in his life to come forward out of the shadowland of gossip with documentation for her claim to his interest. Old Kennedy associates angrily denied her story. But some privately found it at least imaginable in the context of all the other backstairs whispers of supposed Kennedy amours—with stenographers and stewardesses, an off-Broadway star and a Hollywood star-in-the-making, a syndicated reporter and an ambassador's wife. Comedian Mort Sahl once praised Kennedy as 'Our first sexually viable President.' An old New Frontiersman, less impressed, said sourly: 'It was a revolving door over there. A woman had to fight to get in that line.'"

During the years of Jack Kennedy's presidency, and in the years which followed, all of these things were never much discussed. The press created an image of a loyal and faithful family man—the kind of a man the vast majority of the American people want as their President.

It is time the full story is known.

7

Placing Style Before Substance

THE DAY BEFORE John F. Kennedy was to take office was cold and bleak. A blizzard threatened to bury the Capitol and ruin the gala atmosphere of the Inauguration. The snow came suddenly when everything had been arranged with stop watch precision and continued to build up inch by inch. By dusk on the eve of the Inauguration, ten thousand cars were stalled in Washington. The control tower at the National Airport ordered planes elsewhere. In fact, it seemed in these dark hours that the Inaugural itself would be buried beneath a white carpet.

However, the following morning dawned clear and cold and three thousand men, using 700 plows and trucks, were able to remove more than 8 inches of snow from Pennsylvania Avenue and other major thoroughfares. The National Park Service, trying to guarantee that if winter came spring could not be far behind, had sprayed fresh green dye on the lawns surrounding the Lincoln Memorial. Trees along the parade route were splashed with bird-discouraging Roost-No-More so that no pesky starling would perch in branches above the two hour and forty six minute procession. The White House and the Capitol glistened under new coats of sparkling white paint.

Early on the morning of January 20th, Mr. and Mrs. Kennedy

attended Mass at Holy Trinity Church. Afterwards they drove to the White House for coffee with the Eisenhowers, the Lyndon Johnsons and the Richard Nixons. Then Kennedy and Eisenhower stepped into the Presidential limousine for the drive down Pennsylvania Avenue toward Capitol Hill.

The imposing facade of formal morning dress and politicians' public smiles, successfully concealed the true feelings of the outgoing and incoming Presidents, intent on their responsibility to make a smooth governmental transition. Only a few months before, President Eisenhower had vowed he would never let the young Senator sit in his chair in the White House. He believed Kennedy was ill prepared for the responsibilities of his high office and lacked the experience to be the Chief Executive of a great nation. Perhaps, on that cold Inauguration day, he felt partially responsible for the failure of his Party's candidate. Certainly he had not campaigned very strenuously for Richard Nixon. Few Americans realized that Eisenhower had been seriously ill during much of the 1960 campaign and was thereby rendered unable to support his Vice President as vigorously as he had planned to do.

And now the young President-elect mounted the temporary platform in front of the Capitol. His father, speaking more to himself, said, "This is what I've been looking forward to for a long time. It's a great day." All around were the human symbols of this most moving of American ceremonies. Boston's Richard Cardinal Cushing, the ecclesiastic closest to the Kennedy family, united to them in profound friendship over many years, was there to bless the young man he loved. Robert Frost, the salty octogenarian New Englander, America's true poet laureate, spoke his simple moving words of "miles to go and promises to keep."

The majesty and might of the Government of the United States sat in official silence in the clear bitter cold. The real strength of the United States—its people, old, young, middle-aged—was massed in expectant rows before the flag-draped platform; and wherever there was a television set in the nation it was tuned to hear John Fitzgerald Kennedy take the oath of office as President of the United States and give his thoughts and views to the country.

There was an expectant hush. Finally the young President's breath frosted the air as he spoke.

He spoke brave words, full of promise. His theme was clear. The country was stuck on dead center. He called on everyone to help him get it moving again.

"Let the word go forth from this time and place, to friend and foe alike, that the torch has been passed to a new generation of Americans, born in this century, tempered by war, disciplined by a cold and bitter peace, proud of our ancient heritage, and unwilling to witness or permit the slow undoing of those human rights to which this nation has always been committed, and to which we are committed today.

"Let every nation know, whether it wishes us well or ill, that we shall pay any price, bear any burden, meet any hardship, support any friend, or oppose any foe, to assure the survival and success of liberty."

His words formed a magnificent Inaugural address.

". . . Let us never negotiate out of fear. But let us never fear to negotiate . . .

". . . All this will not be finished in the first 100 days. Nor will it be finished in the first 1000 days, nor in the life of this administration, nor even perhaps in our lifetime on this planet. But let us begin . . ."

The words thrilled the nation. Many of the words were written by Ted Sorenson. Others had been written many years before. The most memorable phrase of all had been taken from an article written by the Lebanese philosopher Kahlil Gibran, author of the international best-seller, *The Prophet,* which has sold more than a million and a half copies and has been translated into more than twenty languages.

The title of the article Gibran had written was titled, "The New Frontier," the very title of the entire Kennedy program. And in the article appeared the source of Kennedy's phrase, "Ask not what your country can do for you, but ask what you can do for your country." Gibran had written, "Are you a politician asking what your country can do for you or a zealous one asking what you can do for your country."

Following the Inauguration, the fulfillment of the promises he had made—promises of action, motion, great deeds—became an obligation. In the White House, and in many Washington bureaus, scores of assistants were soon preparing hundreds of bills for the legislative hopper.

Many of these bills were prepared by the gung-ho academic types who were as impatient as Kennedy himself to "get the country moving again." It was an early version of the Jimmy Carter White House operation to come years later. The Kennedy White House staff operated largely cut off from the Cabinet officers. Decisions were made in a hurry.

It would be impossible in a single chapter to describe the scope of all the legislation hurriedly prepared by the Kennedy Administration. It embraced the whole gamut of economic and social philosophy of the young intellectuals the new President brought to Washington. In one year there were 405 distinct and separate proposals for Congressional enactment.

Apparently Kennedy had little doubt that this flood of legislation would be approved by Congress, otherwise he would have felt the need for restraint in proposing it. Because the new President had a definite philosophy on this. "Every President, moreover, has to husband his bargaining power for its more effective use," he once said. "There is no sense in putting the office of the President on the line on an issue, and then being defeated."

However, there didn't seem to be much cause for worry. The Democrats controlled Congress by a heavy majority. In the Senate they outnumbered Republicans almost two to one, and in the House by four to three. In the even more Democrat-weighted House Rules Committee, Kennedy's advantage was great. Under the House Rules Committee's peculiar powers, this group could make it impossible for the Representatives to pass any legislation of which they did not approve. Similarly, no bill passed by both Houses in differing forms could pass to a Senate-House conference unless the House Rules Committee granted a rule. And here Kennedy had the leverage of 8 Democrats to 4 Republicans.

Despite this favorable majority, the President did not get instant compliance. Congress did a double-take at the torrent of proposed legislation pouring from the White House. Many of the bills were invested with an Alice-in-Wonderland quality. There was an impractical, unsound quality about many of them which surprised and shocked the seasoned legislators in the House and Senate.

One of the most able and skilled legislators ever to work in Washington, Sam Rayburn, spoke of the men who prepared the bills. Rayburn said to Kennedy's Vice President Johnson, "They may be every bit as intelligent as you say, but I wish just one of them had run for sheriff once."

One of the bills Kennedy proposed was the "Quality Stabilization Act." Now while the Federal Government had dabbled in price ceilings for a good many years, this was the first time anyone had sought to fix levels below which merchants would not be permitted to sell their merchandise. Opponents quickly attacked the bill on the ground that it would raise the cost of living by $100 to$250 annually for the average American family and add $5,000,000,000 to $15,000,000,000 to our total inflation. The Congress turned the bill down.

Another hastily contrived bill which the White House recommended was a cotton bill designed to "encourage increased consumption of cotton and maintain the income of cotton producers." The Administration hoped that the bill would also benefit the public by lowering cotton textile costs. However, there was something very wrong with the arithmetic. Fourteen Republican members of the House Committee on Agriculture pointed out that if the bill became law, a taxpayer buying a five dollar shirt made from a little more than a pound of cotton, would receive a six per cent price break. Yet he and other taxpayers would have to provide an extra $221,000,000 in taxes each year to finance the bounty—about two dollars from every taxpayer.

The massive Housing bill, which Kennedy finally pushed through the Congress, provided another example of faulty calculation. Before amending, the proposal called for forty-year, no down-payment loans. The bill would have created a situation in which every home-buyer with a forty-year mortgage on his house would not own any part of it until the twenty-sixth year. The first twenty five years would have been devoted to paying interest alone!

Another example of impractical legislation was the "Double Overtime Bill." The purpose of this proposal was to create new jobs by discouraging overtime. It did not limit the amount of overtime the government could force companies to pay. It merely set a floor limit of two times regular pay. Once again the bill touched off sharp objections. Seasoned legislators pointed out that small businesses which could not afford to pay this heavy overtime, or hire more workers, would be unreasonably and unfairly handicapped.

Such impractical and hazily conceived proposed legislation was commonplace in the days of the New Frontier. Some critics pointed out that the new President's lack of business experience and his protective upbringing in one of America's richest families were responsible for his impractical proposals. Furthermore, many of the new men he had brought to Washington were similarly lacking in the common sense approach to money and economics. They were steeped in theories which sounded great in the give-and-take of professor and student in the classroom without the need of being tested.

The first Federal Education bill which the President sent to the Congress in 1961 was so drawn that the House refused even to consider it. One Democratic Congressman remarked that, "This Federal Education Bill got exactly what it deserved. We do not have money in Washington to give anyone. It is the taxpayers money and this was a victory for the taxpayers and for local and state control of education." In 1962 and 1963 the Congress again turned down the President's education bills.

In his January 31, 1962 message to Congress, President Kennedy called for farm legislation which he described as "a comprehensive long range program to replace the present patchwork of short run emergency measures." In general, he proposed that producers of wheat and feed grains, the major surplus crops, accept strict limits on acreage and sales, or lose government price supports. Wheat acreage was to be cut ten per cent to 49,500,000 acres. The bill would, for the first time, require dairy farmers to accept controls on the marketing of milk.

The wary Congress passed the legislation but not before adding the stipulation that two-thirds of the farmers approve it in a referendum. In a move to assure satisfaction of that proviso, the Administration sought the backing of the National Grange, the National Farmers Association, the National Association of Wheat Growers and the Missouri Farmers Association. The pressure that was applied in various ways was one of the first indications the Administration was determined now to use old and new techniques to get its way in achieving legislative success.

In spite of everything the Administration could do, however, the American Farm Bureau Federation came out against the program, charging the Administration with, "misuse of Federal power" and "scare tactics and threats of retaliation." The President not only failed to get a two-thirds vote of the farmers but a majority of them actually voted down the bill.

The President was determined to override the farmers and he sent his aides back to Congress the next year and this time the bill was passed. Kennedy worked on friendly Senators who pressured their fellow Senators to approve the wheat section, which had never been approved by the House, then add it to a cotton bill. When this bill came to the House, the Administration tried to get that body to approve it without hearings, committee reports or floor debate. There were strong objections from House members. The Administration then agreed to let the House Agricultural Committee judge the bill. However, in the Committee meeting the wheat section was approved before minority members were even allowed to have copies of the bill.

It was not often, however, that the President was able to get pet legislation passed by such ingenious methods or by applying White House pressure.

When the President had been Senator he had not extended himself to be a real hard-working member of that body—the most exclusive club in the world, as it is called. Nor had he gone out of his way to endear himself personally to older members. He had been absent a great deal; and while much of this was due to his serious back injury he had the habit of "no-show" from his days as a young Representative from Massachusetts.

Those who knew President Kennedy well have said that although he enjoyed being President and liked the prestige and power of the position, he often expressed annoyance at the need to attend to all the deadly minutiae and boring routine that, of necessity, is part of the job of Chief Executive. This could, perhaps, explain the many mistakes he made in what he regarded as the least glamorous aspect of a President's job—domestic legislation.

One bill which he rushed through the Congress without adequate thought or attention to detail had almost ludicrous consequences. In the summer of 1963 the gold outflow from this country was rapidly reaching a dangerous level. On July 18, 1963, the President requested Congress to put a special tax on Canadian securities. Following the President's request, and without sufficient study on its own, the Congress passed the bill. Almost immediately our nearest neighbor to the north was drained of $190,000,000 in gold and

United States dollars. This seemed to be good for the United States and, indeed, it was. But the President had not foreseen other repercussions which were so great that within two days after the bill had gone into effect the Congress had to rescind the special tax.

Not every piece of legislation which Kennedy submitted to the Congress was poor or faultily conceived. Much has been written about the successful aspects of President Kennedy's tenure in the White House. And, unquestionably, his youth, and wit, and the special style which he brought to the office, were appreciated at home and abroad. However, these graceful attributes of a cultivated young man are not adequate subsitutes for experience and practical common sense.

Much of the legislation which the Kennedy Administration succeeded in getting through the Congress may be criticized on these grounds. For instance, there was the so-called Project 60, another case in point. This bill allowed fifteen politically appointed procurement officers to use national defense dollars to pour economic help into certain areas. The officers simply rushed orders for weapons, missiles and other defense items to the specified sections.

"The Pentagon can control material sources, manpower, tools and entire segments of the economy with its $53,000,000,000 baseball bat," one Congressman commented. Worst of all, Project 60 violated Public Law 601 passed by the Eighty-sixth Congress which prohibited the Defense Department from using its funds to direct contracts into areas with economic problems.

"So far as practicable," the law stated, "all contracts shall be awarded on a competitive basis to the lowest possible bidder."

It is interesting to note that in 1962 the Space Administration let contracts for $28,000,000,000. Of that huge sum, contracts amounting to $18,000,000,000, or sixty-five per cent, were granted without formal or competitive bidding of any sort.

As Congress began to balk more frequently at bills submitted by the President, the Administration sought ways to bypass the Congress. There was the time, for example, when the President created a domestic Peace Corps by executive decree, and then asked for the "modest sum" of $5,000,000 to $6,000,000 to get the project off the ground.

Some Congressmen attacked the proposal because there were millions of teachers, social workers, law enforcement officers and clergymen already performing the functions of a Peace Corps. But objections did not prevent the Administration from going ahead with the project and spending on it tax money appropriated for other purposes. One Congressman pointed out at the time that this was actually illegal.

These are but a few examples of President Kennedy's mistakes on the home front. His program of domestic legislation seemed to be designed to give an appearance of tremendous drive and purpose. But the Congress, faced with the obligation of enacting legislation which would work, opposed the President over and over again, even though the majority of the men in both House and Senate were of his own party. They opposed his legislation not from political caprice or dislike of the young President but because, as hard-headed realists, they knew what would work and what wouldn't. The Congress received the bills, studied them, and of the 405 received in one year, voted only 37 into law. The other 368 bills were either rejected or died in Committee.

The President tried to blame the Republican Party for his defeats. At least that was the impression he gave the American people in statements to the press. But, as many in Washington knew, although the chairmen of the sixteen standing committees in the Senate were Democrats, these experienced men voted against the President no fewer than 596 times.

Finally President Kennedy decided that the House Rules Committee was where the bottleneck was. The Committee was composed of eight Democrats and four Republicans but Howard Smith, Virginia Democrat, and William Colmer, Mississippi Democrat, frequently voted with the Republican minority.

Kennedy now seized enthusiastically on the obvious solution which was to reform the House Rules Committee. At first he demanded that Smith and Colmer be purged, but wiser heads persuaded him that this would be politically unwise. In the end, House Speaker Sam Rayburn came to Kennedy's rescue with a compromise; two Democrats and one Republican should be added to the Committee, bringing its strength to fifteen. As soon as Rayburn stated the proposition the battle was on and the infighting grew vicious. Every tactic was used—patronage, sentiment, campaign commitments. Drawn into the thick of the fight were the Chamber of Commerce, the National Association of Manufacturers, the American

Management Association and the American Farm Bureau Federation.

When the noise and the furor subsided, the proposal to increase the size of the Committee had carried 217 to 212, but the casualties were heavy. Kennedy had opened old wounds and made life-long enemies. He surveyed the damage and with his gift for self-criticism noted, albeit a bit grimly, that, "With all that going for us, with Rayburn's own reputation at stake, with all the pressures and appeals a new President could make, we won by five votes."

While 64 Democrats voted against the President, 22 Republicans voted with him, 17 of them from states he had carried. Without the votes of one-third of the Southern Democrats and one-eighth of the Republicans, he would not have won at all.

From that moment the handwriting was visible on the wall. No bill could pass the House without picking up 40 to 60 Southerners and Republicans of the 70 or so who, while outside the confines of The New Frontier, were still not entirely alien to the President.

Scarcely was the victory won than Kennedy tested the new enlarged Committee with his proposal for a Department of Urban Affairs. This was not the first mention of the proposal. Kennedy's earliest endorsement of such a plan had been in October, 1960, when, as a candidate, he had addressed a Pittsburgh Urban Affairs Conference which he had called to give himself a forum.

In that campaign speech he complained about the "shameful record of neglect" of the cities. Republicans in Congress, he charged, had kept the nation from getting larger grants of federal tax funds for urban renewal, public housing, private housing, public schools, hospitals, mass transportation, water and air pollution and relief from juvenile delinquency.

The solution, Kennedy now told the revised House Rules Committee members was a Deptmartment of Urban Affairs. Members listened to the President but were not impressed. In spite of the new members just added, the Committee again felt it necessary to give the Chief Executive a strong rebuke. It turned down the suggestion of a Department of Urban Affairs.

That was an insult which the President felt he could not let pass. He announced that he would create a Department of Urban Affairs by executive order and that he would name as director Robert C. Weaver, who would become the first Negro in the Cabinet.

Victor Lasky wrote of this in his book *J.F.K.: the Man and the Myth,* that "the idea was to twist things around so that a vote against Urban Affairs could be construed as a vote against having a Negro in the Cabinet . . . The strategy was so raw that Kennedy found himself speedily accused of racism. People remembered that while during the 1960 campaign Henry Cabot Lodge, the Republican Vice Presidential candidate, had predicted a Negro in the Cabinet in the event of a GOP victory, candidate Kennedy had stated:

"I am not going to promise a Cabinet post or any other post to any race or ethnic group. This is racism at its worst."

Congress had sixty days in which to ratify the reorganization plan. Kennedy chose to make his first fight in the Senate. Although he had a two to one majority there, it wasn't enough to put through the reorganization. For the first time since 1936 every Senator showed up to vote. Senator Edmund Muskie, Maine Democrat, who had been hurt in a motor accident, came into the chamber in a wheelchair. The final vote was fifty-eight to forty-two against the motion.

In the wake of this new confrontation Congress grew to resent President Kennedy. Then, in the spring, there occurred between Kennedy and business leaders, a dramatic battle with Congressional overtones.

At three o'clock on an April morning a ringing telephone bell wakened an Associated Press reporter. The man on the other end of the line introduced himself as an agent of the Federal Bureau of Investigation and told the A.P. man to expect an early visit from the FBI. One hour later FBI agents rang his doorbell.

Two hours after that, a reporter for the *Wall Street Journal* was rooted out of bed by other FBI agents. At 6:30 a.m. a newsman working for the Wilmington, Delaware *Evening Journal* found FBI men waiting at his office door.

The reporters were not involved in any crime. They had merely written that the steel industry was raising prices and it had become important to President Kennedy to know the source of the story.

The special early morning attentions of the FBI were given as well to major executives of large steel corporations which had announced price increases. These invasions of privacy were at the order of the President's brother, Robert Kennedy. As Attorney General he misused his authority.

Later in the day the pattern and purpose became evident. A grand jury was impanelled to investigate possible criminal collusion in connection with the increased price of steel. An Administrative Committee in Congress undertook a probe. Orders went out from the Pentagon to withhold government business from any steel company which had increased its prices. United States Steel, which held a patent to make a super-steel for nuclear submarine hulls, lost its contract and was told to turn over the secrets of its process to a competing corporation.

In one of the most threatening misuses of authority of all, Attorney General Robert Kennedy let it be known that he was having the Internal Revenue Service start work on the tax returns of steel company officers.

U.S. Steel Chairman Roger M. Blough and the President had a dramatic confrontation in the newspapers and on television. Afterwards Kennedy made his famous statement that his father had told him "all businessmen" were of doubtful parentage. He used the plain language expressed in the vernacular phrase "S.O.B." The Stock Market collapsed. Prices plunged.

President Kennedy, in trouble with Congress, and completely inexperienced in handling business, was genuinely frightened by this turn of events. He and his advisers searched feverishly for a way to check the sliding economy. The President decided a quick tax cut was the prop to put under a tottering financial structure, and Congress and the nation were led to believe the Administration would make this proposal. But when Kennedy went on television in mid-August, he failed to come out for a tax-cut proposal. Instead, he said that emergency tax legislation "could not now be either justified or enacted." Washington insiders and Congress-watchers everywhere knew that the key word was "enacted." The President would not be able to put his bill through Congress.

By this time jokes about the Kennedy predicament were circulating widely. To Kennedy, this was no laughing matter. Sensitive to jokes and preoccupied with appearances, Kennedy made an effort to minimize his problems in the eyes of the nation. He set out to control the way news stories were written.

8

How Kennedy Managed
The News

IN 1957 WHEN Joseph P. Kennedy was formulating his plans to get his son Jack elected President, he told his old friend Arthur Krock, the *New York Times* columnist, "We're going to sell Jack like soapflakes."

Joseph P. Kennedy, Sr. had a consuming ambition: the advancement of the Kennedy name and fortune. His lifelong drive had been for money; and for power for his children. He wanted one of his sons to be president—any one of the four. When the leading candidate, Lt. Comm. Joseph P. Kennedy, Jr., groomed for politics and naturally attracted to it, was killed in a bomber crash in World War II, it became a matter of tapping the next in line, John F.—for Fitzgerald—his maternal grandfather's name.

Joseph P. Kennedy, Sr. well understood that the way to accomplish his goal was through the power of money—and the proper exploitation of newspapers, magazines and, above all, television.

With his good looks, John F. Kennedy was the ideal television candidate. Author David Halberstam described him as "the first of a new kind of media candidate flashed daily into our consciousness by television during the campaign, and as such he had managed to stir the aspirations and excited millions of people. It had all been deliberately done; he had understood television and used it well, knowing that it was his medium."

He put an equal effort into cultivating news reporters and making certain that he was well reported in the nation's newspapers and magazines. From the beginning of his campaign for the nomination Kennedy's charm and wit won over the nation's news people. And his liberal views on domestic issues had a natural appeal to them.

Few realized how these views had been shaped and planned by Joseph P. Kennedy, Sr. Prior to the start of the campaign, at a dinner for two in the New York apartment of Henry Luce, the publisher of *Time* and *Life*, Joe Kennedy made his preparations to get his son elected president.

Luce and his magazines had long taken a conservative view on both foreign and domestic questions. Warm with wine and over dessert, the elder Kennedy gave his word that his son, even though a Democratic presidential nominee, was still a man to be relied upon.

Joe Kennedy and Henry Luce were old friends. Luce had written an introduction to the first book by Kennedy's son Jack, entitled *Why England Slept*, while Joe Kennedy had arranged to get Luce's son Hank his first job after college, as special assistant to the chairman of the Securities and Exchange Commission—who happened to be Joseph P. Kennedy.

At their private dinner, the two elder statesmen, Luce and Kennedy,· discussed, in effect, what it would take to neutralize *Time* and *Life* during the coming presidential campaign. Together, they created the ideal candidate.

Luce tried to divide the issues between the foreign and the domestic, implying that Jack Kennedy should run on a campaign of liberalism on domestic issues. Joe Kennedy reacted strongly. "No son of mine is going to be a goddam liberal," he is reported to have said.

But Luce had the game plan mapped out. He replied that, of course, Jack had to run as a liberal. He had to turn left to get the votes he needed in the large Northern cities, Luce said, adding that *Time* and *Life* would not hold that against him. But on foreign policy, Luce insisted, if the younger Kennedy showed any signs of weakness toward the anti-Communist cause, or if he was not firm in defending the cause of the free world, then *Time* and *Life* would have to turn on him. Joe Kennedy assured his friend that there was no chance of that. "No son of mine is going to be soft on Communism," he confided. Well, Luce replied, if he is, we'll tear him apart.

The Kennedy cultivation of the press started at that early meeting. And from then on John F. Kennedy devoted a tremendous amount of his personal time and energy in winning the nation's news reporters to his side. His handling of the press was repeatedly hailed as "brilliant." Favored correspondents . . . and they were numerous . . . were provided briefings and frequent access to the Kennedy inner circle. Rarely had newsmen been so close to their subject. The result: almost totally favorable copy. "But the very fact that his publicity has generally been uncritical has done him anything but a service with other Democratic politicians," wrote columnist William S. White as early as May, 1958. "They suspect him, soundly or not, of running a vast public relations stable."

By the time his campaign for the White House was officially announced, Jack Kennedy understood the importance of the new brand of political public relations necessary to win elections. He also initiated what was to be the hallmark of his brief presidency, a relationship with the press more intimate and involved than that of any President who had preceded him. From the start, reported Paul Martin of Gannett Newspapers, "What seems to be developing here is an after-hours elite press corps, a sort of unofficial oligarchy of wealth and wit and intellect."

That the image and the Kennedy reality were radically different was understood only by a handful. Professor James MacGregor Burns was one. He commented that, "The bright charm is only skin deep; underneath there is a core of steel—metallic, sometimes cold, sometimes unbending, unusually durable—Actually, he is a serious, driven man—about as casual as a cash register."

The other side of John F. Kennedy . . . the side that was virtually never revealed to the public . . . was seen in the early primaries. The Kennedy strategy in the primaries was simple: stress Kennedy's position as an underdog. *The Baltimore Sun*'s Thomas O'Neill, for example, devoted entire columns to the problems Kennedy faced. "Wisconsin is a tough one for Senator Kennedy," O'Neill wrote.

Yet, this was contrary to what Kennedy's own full time pollster Lou Harris was finding. Robert Kennedy, learning of these polls, gleefully said, "Wisconsin is in the bag." He was overheard by a C.B.S. correspondent who reported the statement and suggested that the Kennedy campaign was taking the Catholic vote for granted. Bobby went into a rage, calling the reporter, "a Stevenson Jew." After berating the reporter, Bobby called Sig Mickelson, the head of C.B.S. News, in New York and, as *Hollywood Daily Variety* put it, engaged "in a heated conversation with him."

John Kennedy finally got Bobby to apologize to the reporter. A newsman who had witnessed Bobby's bitter attack, William Lawrence of the *New York Times*, a good friend of the Kennedys, failed to report the incident. Through the years, many such incidents . . . and many more newsworthy . . . remained unreported by Kennedy friends in the media.

Kennedy, it became clear from the start, could be a nitpicking critic of the media. During the Wisconsin primary, according to David Wise's book, *The Politics of Lying*, Kennedy called C.B.S.' Frank Stanton. "Jack called from the airport in Fort Wayne," Stanton said. "His voice was very strident. He objected to the C.B.S. analysis of the primary vote in Wisconsin and said that we had raised the religious issue." Stanton agreed, but he noted that it wasn't "something we invented. The papers are commenting on the religious issue, too." "But," Kennedy said, "This is different. You're licensed."

Stanton was further outraged, he told Wise, when he learned that Kennedy had told a C.B.S. correspondent, "Wait till I'm President—I'll cut Stanton's balls off."

These revealing slips by Kennedy, however, were few and far between. His charm and wit impressed almost all the reporters who covered him. His views agreed to a great extent with theirs. In addition, Kennedy knew how to appeal to the vanity of the news people. "Jack called me the other day," a noted correspondent announced shortly before the Democratic nominating convention in Los Angeles, "and asked me who I thought should be his floor manager. I told him Ribicoff."

By the time Jack Kennedy assumed office as President, his romance with the press was at full bloom. Even such otherwise Olympian commentators as Walter Lippmann were enthralled. So much so, in fact, that the nation's other venerable columnist of the era, Arthur Krock, once stormed out of his office, smoke streaming from his cigar, saying: "Well, I may be getting old, and I may be getting senile, but at least I don't fall in love with young boys like Walter Lippmann."

From the day after the election, Kennedy became the most accessible President in U.S. history. *The Economist* of London reported: "It is a long time since a President has enjoyed such a mixture of liking and respect from the majority of American reporters; Mr. Kennedy's recent activities—from playing golf with Mr. W.H. Lawrence of *The New York Times* to banging on Mr. Joe Alsop's door in the small hours—seem designed to enhance this feeling."

Publishers were invited to lunch at the White House. Reporters were given exclusive interviews. Photographers and television cameramen were invited to tour the White House and meet with the First Family.

Book after book was published about Kennedy, almost all adoring. This was often carried to such extremes that even journalistic friends of the President, such as *The New York Times'* Tom Wicker, thought it was somewhat excessive. In his review of William Manchester's biography, *Portrait of a President: J.F.K. in Profile,* Wicker compared Manchester to "the dazzled artist who has gazed upon his subject with loving eyes and found redeeming beauty in his every flaw."

Adulation carried too far, Wicker warned, might be damaging. He wrote: "The question is whether any President is well-served by the sort of adulation that Mr. Manchester allows himself and Mr. Kennedy has too often been accorded in the press. May it not tend to give both him and the public a sense of euphoria? And when trouble comes, as it always will, the fall from glory will be just that much harder. President Kennedy deserves better of his chroniclers . . ."

Jack Kennedy, however, was not embarrassed by the mythology being woven around him by his supporters in the press. His good friend Ben Bradlee declared that, "Kennedys by definition want 110 per cent from their friends, especially their friends in the press, and feel cheated by anything less."

When Kennedy attempted to place an old family friend, Francis Xavier Morrissey, a Boston municipal court judge whose legal abilities, according to Bradlee, "were taxed by parking ticket cases," on the federal bench, even some friends were mildly critical. In response, Kennedy shouted at Bradlee and several others, "Jesus Christ, you guys are something else. When I was elected, you all said my old man would run the country in consultation with the Pope. Now here's the only thing he ever asked me to do for him, and you guys piss all over me."

Kennedy was furious with Bradlee about the Morrissey story. "Jesus," he said, "there you are really plugged in, better than any other reporter except Charlie (Bartlett), getting one exclusive after another out of this place, and what do you do but dump all over us."

From regular contact with Kennedy—dinner at the White House once or twice a week, frequent phone conversations—Bradlee was isolated from the President, like a small boy being punished for misbehaving. It was three months before he saw the President again. If there was anything Kennedy could not tolerate, Bradlee and other friends quickly learned, it was a journalist who gave anything less than "110 per cent."

Bradlee recalls the incident: "It seems strange now, so many years later, that a friendship like ours could not survive such a minor irritant. Some of the reasons have their roots in that wonderful law of the Boston Irish political judge, 'Don't get mad, get even.' He never got mad, but he plainly got even, cutting me out of a mainstream of information that had been enormously valuable to me and to *Newsweek*. At issue, then and later, was the question that plagued us both. What, in fact, was I? A friend or a journalist? I wanted to be both. And whereas I think Kennedy valued my friendship . . . he valued my journalism most when it carried his water."

Bradlee and the others quickly learned that to receive White House exclusives, one had to pay with complete loyalty. Writing in *The New Republic*, James MacGregor Burns reported: "The adjectives tumble over one another. He is not only the handsomest, the best-dressed, the most articulate, and graceful as a gazelle. He is omniscient; he swallows and digests whole books in minutes; he confounds experts with his superior knowledge of their field. He is omnipotent . . . The buildup is too indiscriminate. The build-up will not last. The public can be cruel and so can the press. Americans build their triumphal arches out of brick, Mr. Dooley said, so as to have missiles handy when their heroes have fallen."

In his lifetime, Kennedy never fell. But some reporters did persist in doing their jobs, attempting to find out the truth about what was happening in government and sharing this information with their readers. Those who told too much of the truth were victimized by an Administration which could tolerate no criticism and which was determined to "get even" with anyone viewed in any way as "an enemy."

The Billie Sol Estes scandal was an early case in point. The Estes case related to the misuse of Agriculture Department funds and the suspected murder of investigators as well as an attempted cover-up. Writing in *The New York Herald Tribune,* reporter Earl Mazo told readers that the Justice Department had done nothing to stop Estes' activities until they had reached the front pages of the nation's newspapers.

Bobby Kennedy, then Attorney General, was furious. He summoned Mazo to his office to, he said, reason with him. In fact, Mazo was subjected to a heated verbal assault. "Bobby's so-called 'lecture' as it has been described, was in reality a childish outburst," Mazo recalled. "He was so enraged over our coverage of the Billie Sol Estes scandal that I expected at any moment he would throw himself to the floor, screaming and bawling for his way. Instead, he paced back and forth, storming and arguing. It was something to see."

Columns on the Estes case by the Allen-Scott team also inspired bitter phone calls to Robert S. Allen questioning both his facts and his motives. Even the soft-spoken Roscoe Drummond, a widely respected *New York Herald Tribune* columnist, was berated for his comments on the Estes case.

In the end, the charges made about Estes turned out to be true. Still, as a result of its exposes on the subject, *The New York Tribune* was exiled from the White House—all subscriptions to the paper were immediately cancelled. President Kennedy, enraged that any journal would dare to look into wrong-doing in his Administration, sought to teach the *Herald Tribune* and other potential critics a lesson.

Ben Bradlee recalls that Jack Kennedy "relished whatever displeasure he was causing the *Tribune* and was oblivious to the criticism of his act as demeaning and petty."

"Why," Kennedy asked Bradlee, "don't you get Phil Graham (of *The Washington Post)* to buy the *Tribune* syndicate? That's all they've got." Kennedy said of the *Herald Tribune:* "We read enough shit. We just don't have to read that particular brand."

During this same period, the President did his best to further the political career of his brother Ted. Ted was then engaged in a bitter battle with Edward McCormack, nephew of Rep. John McCormack, for the Democratic nomination to the Senate in Massachusetts. The President asked Ben Bradlee, "When are you going to send one of your ace reporters to look into Eddie's record?"

Asked what he meant, Kennedy responded that McCormack had resigned his commission in the Navy on the day he graduated from Annapolis, on a medical disability. "Half of it was nerves and half of it was a bad back," Kennedy continued, "and he's been drawing a 60 per cent disability ever since up until six months ago. David Powers (receptionist at the White House and one of the President's closest friends and admirers) has all the information and he'll give it to you."

Even from the White House itself, Jack Kennedy sought to manipulate the press in the interest of his family's political ambition. But Bradlee would not participate in this questionable enterprise. "I never did talk to Powers about McCormack," he recalled, "but reflected once more on that 'don't get mad, get even' maxim."

Then, the press was subjected to the kind of high-handed governmental treatment usually associated with totalitarian and authoritarian states when the Kennedy Administration sought to show its outrage at the decision by U.S. steel companies to raise their prices.

Rather than expressing its views to steel company executives themselves, the Kennedys engaged in what has been referred to as "midnight raids" on reporters' homes and offices.

Even the accounts of this incident most favorable to the Kennedys tell a chilling story. Ray Hoopes, in a sympathetic account appearing in his book, *The Steel Crisis*, reported: "At about 3 a.m. the telephone rang in the two-story duplex in Philadelphia's Burnholme Park section. It was the home of Lee Linder, a business reporter for the Associated Press. Linder had covered the Bethlehem Steel stockholders meeting in Wilmington for the A.P. on Tuesday, and it was in his story that Bethlehem's President Martin had been quoted as saying that he was opposed to a rise in the price of steel. It had been an ambiguous statement, made all the more confusing by the fact that on Wednesday a Bethlehem official had said that Martin had been misquoted. When Linder answered the phone, a voice on the other end said: 'This is the F.B.I., and we're coming right out.

Attorney General Kennedy says we're to see you immediately.' 'Who is it?' demanded Linder's sleepy wife. 'The F.B.I.,' replied Linder. 'They've got a nerve,' his wife shot back. 'Hang up on them.'"

Hoopes' report continues: "Two F.B.I. agents arrived about an hour later. They showed the I.D. cards and Linder let them in. They settled down in the living room and proceeded to question Linder . . . about President Martin's statement . . . About 4 a.m., John Lawrence, Philadelphia editor for *The Wall Street Journal*, was called by the same F.B.I. agents. They wanted to come out to talk to him about Martin's statement, but he refused to let them come. 'I told them I had nothing to say,' says Lawrence, 'so they gave up.'"

When James T. Parks, Jr., a business writer for *The Wilmington Journal*, arrived at his office at about 6:30 a.m., F.B.I. agents were waiting. *The New York Times* called the Kennedy Administration's anti-steel campaign "a personal vendetta." Max Lerner wrote in *The New York Post:* "There was one thing I found distasteful about the Administration's behavior. It was the use of F.B.I. agents to track down aspects of the steel story by dawn interviews of reporters. This may make sense if you want to catch a spy before he vanished, but these were reporters, not spies, and the invasion of their privacy suggested a police operation."

President Kennedy himself, Ralph De Toledano reported, "tried to laugh off the whole episode by telling his press conference that newspapermen were always waking up people, so that the F.B.I.'s midnight ride was simply poetic justice. And Bobby grinned and said the questioning 'could have waited until morning.'"

Vendettas against newsmen who challenged any of the Administration's policies or practices continued. The tactics varied. Some were denied access to information as punishment for expressing contrary views. Others, however, were given the full treatment, including audits by the Internal Revenue Service and other forms of official harassment.

Columnist Walter Winchell, who had been sharply critical of both Jack Kennedy and his brother Bobby, suddenly found his income taxes being carefully audited. He told columnist Victor Lasky: "The Kennedys are out to get me." Lasky reported that, "Winchell told me he had never before had that much trouble with the I.R.S., even when Truman, whom he had attacked just as vigorously, had been President."

Another prominent journalist, Jim Bishop, found himself in the same boat. "They started about the time Bobby Kennedy became Attorney General," he said. "I wrote a story and said he acted as though the rest of us were working on his old man's plantation. After that, audits."

Victor Lasky aroused Bobby Kennedy's fury for having written a highly critical book about his brother, *JFK: the Man and the Myth*. After the book moved to number one on the bestseller lists, it was disclosed that federal officials had launched an investigation of Lasky.

At first, in a letter to Senator Kenneth Keating of New York, Bobby denied that he had ever authorized an investigation of Lasky. Only later, after evidence was produced, did he concede that "overzealous" officials had undertaken the probe.

As it turned out, these "overzealous" officials had served under Bobby as Senate investigators. Both were known to have engaged in wiretapping and, following the 1960 election, had been placed on the payroll of the Immigration and Naturalization Service. Senator Keating discovered that the F.B.I. had originally been asked to conduct the investigation of Lasky but that J. Edgar Hoover refused to involve the Bureau in what he called "a political vendetta."

The Kennedy operatives sought to link the conservative Lasky to "subversive" activities. Suddenly, several Democratic Party chairmen in Western states publicly accused Lasky of being an ex-Communist while Democratic National Chairman John Bailey described him as "a Birchite."

In his later book, *It Didn't Start with Watergate*, Lasky recalls: "Thus, the executive wing of government, under the Kennedys, used its enormous power in an attempt to defame one of its critics. In retrospect what made the entire episode even more significant was the total lack of interest shown by the same liberal press which was to become outraged—and quite properly so—by the Nixon Administration's misuse of the F.B.I. in conducting a field investigation of Daniel Schorr. Such newspapers as *The Washington Post* and *The New York Times* couldn't have cared less about the violations of the civil liberties of an anti-Kennedy author. If anything, liberal publicists like James Wechsler treated the episode as a joke."

Finally, when the facts were too well known to any longer deny, Bobby Kennedy, not known for his penchant for apology, was forced to get in touch with Lasky and beg his pardon. Bobby asked Lasky's publishers if the author would cease his criticism of the incident. Lasky said he would if he received an official letter of apology. A few days later, John F. Kennedy was assassinated, bringing the issue to an end. Later, on June 12, 1971, J. Edgar Hoover told Lasky that Bobby Kennedy had wiretapped his telephone for several weeks in the summer of 1963.

Mazo, Lasky, Winchell, Bishop—the list goes on and on. The attempt to intimidate and silence press critics became a basic feature of the White House strategy. Rep. Bob Wilson (R-California) recalls one instance "where a publisher was invited to the White House where he was wined and dined . . . and then was asked to go down the street to the Department of Justice, where he had a conference with the President's brother. The conference had to do with a possible anti-trust violation. So, the orders soon went out—and we have this on good authority—that the critical columnists and newspapermen on this particular paper were to let up on their criticism of the New Frontier."

Rep. Wilson also reported that other critical newsmen were offered "very cozy and very attractive jobs. One columnist told me that he was offered a very exciting job at the State Department. He turned it down. Shortly thereafter his income tax returns were being checked."

If a reporter could not be successfully harassed and intimidated into ceasing any criticism of the Kennedy Administration, the President had yet another ace up his sleeve. He could attempt to have the offending reporter removed from his job, or at least silenced, by putting pressure directly upon the publisher.

One of these troublesome reporters targeted for removal from his job by President Kennedy was David Halberstam. Later the author of an in-depth study of the Kennedy years, *The Best and the Brightest,* Halberstam was then a *New York Times* correspondent in Vietnam. His reports from the battlefield and from Saigon infuriated the President. Jack Kennedy called Arthur Hays Sulzberger, the *Times* publisher, and attempted to have Halberstam fired. *The Times* refused.

On another occasion, the President was outraged over an article appearing in *Fortune Magazine* by Charles J.V. Murphy about Cuba. He not only telephoned publisher Henry Luce in an effort to have Murphy rebuked but sent a personal envoy—General Maxwell

Taylor—to New York to argue with Luce executives about alleged errors in the article. Discussing this effort at intimidation and manipulation of the press, columnist James Reston said of the Kennedys that, "They are almost psychopathically concerned about that dreadful modern conception of their image."

When the President's effort at having Charles Murphy either rebuked or removed failed, the White House did not give up. The next move was vengeance. This involved a variety of other methods at harassing this independent-minded reporter. After his article on the Bay of Pigs, Murphy found most doors closed to him in official Washington. For years, Murphy, a Colonel in the Air Force Reserve, had a mobilization assignment in the office of the Air Force Chief of Staff. Suddenly, he found that, as a result of White House pressure, the Air Force had been forced to shift him to a minor post elsewhere.

There was another side to the Kennedy effort to manipulate the way news stories appeared. Friendly reporters often printed material provided to them by the White House which was of a questionable nature, in order to help Jack Kennedy salvage his image. One case which reflects this widespread approach was that of E.M. "Ted" Dealey, the publisher of the *Dallas Morning News*, who attended a White House luncheon and told Jack Kennedy to his face that he and his administration appeared to be "weak sisters."

"The general opinion of the grass-roots thinking in this country," Dealey declared, "is that you and your administration are weak sisters." The President was livid.

One of the President's best friends in the press corps, Charles Bartlett was called in. It was Bartlett, then serving as Washington correspondent for the *Chattanooga Times*, who had introduced Kennedy to Jacqueline Bouvier. Bartlett received from the President an "exclusive" report on what Kennedy had said in response when he was challenged by Dealey. Bartlett, who was not present at the luncheon, used exact quotations, even though no one was supposed to quote the President at such luncheons.

The President was quoted as saying to Dealey that everyone is, of course, entitled to his opinion. "But the difference between you and me, Mr. Dealey, is that I was elected President of this country and you were not and I have the responsibility for the lives of 180 million Americans, which you do not have." Further, the President is quoted as saying: "Wars are easier to talk about than they are to fight. I'm just as tough as you are, Mr. Dealey, and I didn't get elected by arriving at soft judgments."

These remarks were obviously eloquent, designed to make the President appear to be a strong and wise leader. They obtained much coverage in the press, far more than Mr. Dealey's original statement which had prompted them.

The question remains, however, whether the President ever made such an eloquent response. In fact, none of the 18 other Texas journalists who were present at the luncheon remembered the President's remarks. Dealey himself said: "I think the whole story was cooked up by the Administration and Bartlett stating what Kennedy wanted to say to me in rebuttal to my statement. Only the President didn't say it at the time."

Dealey said that the episode demonstrated "pretty sorry newspapering." It demonstrated, in addition, the extraordinary lengths to which President Kennedy was prepared to go to maintain what he considered to be a proper image.

The manipulation of the press by the Kennedy Administration, however, reached even more damaging proportions when it came to such crises as the Bay of Pigs invasion and the removal of Soviet missiles from Cuba.

Discussing the falsification of facts engaged in by the White House, James Reston described the Administration's handling of the Bay of Pigs invasion this way: "When the landings started, American reporters in Miami were told that this was an 'invasion' of around 5,000 men—this for the purpose of creating the impression among the Cuban people that they should rise up to support a sizable invasion force. When the landing, not of 5,000 but of around 1,000 men, began to get in trouble . . . officials here in Washington put out the story—this time to minimize the defeat in the minds of the American people—that there was no 'invasion' at all, but merely a landing of some 200-400 men to deliver supplies to anti-Castro guerrillas already in Cuba. Both times the press was debased for the Government's purpose. Both times the Castro Government and its Soviet advisers knew from their own agents in the anti-Castro refugee camps and from their own observation on the beaches that these pronouncements were false and silly. And both times the American people were the only ones to be fooled."

President Kennedy's real attitude about the whole idea of a free press became evident as the Bay of Pigs crisis unfolded. Later on, Richard Nixon would meet a torrent of criticism, much of it wholly justified, when he sought to conceal certain information in the name of "national security." Jack Kennedy, however, was able to call for what was, in effect, a managed press without receiving the overwhelming hostility of the nation's media leaders.

In a speech before the American Newspaper Publishers Association in New York, shortly after the Bay of Pigs fiasco, Kennedy declared that, "Every newspaper now asks itself, with respect to every story: 'Is it news?' All I suggest is that you add the question, 'Is it in the national interest?' . . . And should the press of America consider and recommend the voluntary assumption of specific steps or machinery. I can assure you that we will cooperate wholeheartedly with those recommendations."

Fortunately, some in the nation's press corps understood the real meaning of the President's word and reacted to them. *The St. Louis Post Dispatch* declared: "He suggested that the press submit itself to a system of voluntary censorship under government direction, as has been customary during shooting wars. Such a system would make the press an official arm of government, somewhat as it is in an official arm in totalitarian countries."

The Indianapolis Star was even more shocked. It stated editorially: "It was obvious that the President was trying to intimidate the press into going easy on criticism of his policies and actions. At the same time he was trying to make the American people believe that if it had not been for the press the Cuban affair might have succeeded. This is nonsense. Until the President finds a clear case of injury to national security as a result of newspaper publication, he should stop trying to accuse the press of errors that are his alone."

British commentator Malcolm Muggeridge lamented that, "These are ominous words. Some variant of them has been the prelude to every assault on freedom of the press."

The manipulation of the press in matters of important public policy became even more clear at the time of the Cuban missile crisis. Following this confrontation, the Pentagon's Arthur Sylvester acknowledged that news was being deliberately manipulated by the Kennedy Administration. This, he said, was "part of the arsenal of weaponry." On December 6, 1962, Sylvester said: "The inherent right of the Government to lie—to lie to save itself when faced with nuclear disaster—is basic."

What Sylvester was referring to, of course, was not nuclear disaster but the manner in which Jack Kennedy had denied the Soviet buildup in Cuba prior to the confrontation. Sylvester said that when the Administration was on the defensive, "I would always be suspicious of what it said, or any other administration—and I do not expect virtue to come out of men, complete virtue, or even 75 per cent virtue. If any of us are virtuous 51 per cent of the time in life, that, I say, is a good record, and in politics, an amazing record."

While virtue may be difficult to define, truthfulness is less problematic. The question involved in the Cuban missile crisis was whether or not the Soviet Union had placed large numbers of offensive missiles in Cuba.

On September 4, 1962, Senator Kenneth Keating of New York was interviewed by Martin Agronsky on NBC-TV's *Today Show*. Keating said that he had been "reliably informed" that some 1,200 men in Soviet army uniforms had landed in Cuba in August and he suggested that the American people had not been sufficiently alerted to the dangerous situation.

Even before Keating left the studio, presidential press secretary Pierre Salinger was on the phone with the network, sharply criticizing Agronsky. Salinger said that the White House was not happy with the manner in which the questioning was conducted, that it showed Agronsky knew little about Cuba. The White House, Salinger said, resented Keating's "erroneous" estimates of the Cuban threat.

"By dusk it was clear to N.B.C. that the White House would not be happy," wrote Ted Lewis in *The New York News*, "unless an Administration Democrat had a chance to rebut Keating on the same show. Senator Claire Engel was picked quickly by the White House, for he had just received a complete fill-in on the Administration's Cuban line."

As expressed by Engle, that line was: "My good friend from New York, Ken Keating, was just as wrong as he could be . . . He didn't get his facts right."

The truth was the precise opposite. Keating's facts were quite correct and, if anything, were under-stated. And at the very time

Engle was misinforming the television audience at the request of
Jack Kennedy, calling Kenneth Keating wrong, Pierre Salinger, in an
off the record briefing, was telling reporters that, "the general
information that he (Keating) made public has been made public by
the government before."

Jack Kennedy himself admitted that the White House was guilty of
managing the news in the Cuban affair, but he denied that this was a
regular policy of his Administration. Speaking privately to Ben
Bradlee he said of the press, "You bastards are getting more
information out of the White House—the kind of information you
want when you want it—than ever before. Except for the Cuba
thing, I challenge you to give me an example of our managing the
news."

Bradlee did not rise to the challenge at that time but later recalled:
"I felt I was a potential example, but it seemed almost impolite to
bring it up . . . The President says the people who are charging him
with managing the news are the people who aren't getting as much
news as some others . . . I feel very comfortable right now in that
second category, and will not look this gift horse in the mouth."

One of the most extensive descriptions of how the Kennedy
Administration was managing the news appeared in the April, 1963
issue of the *Atlantic Monthly* in an article written by the dis-
tinguished *New York Times* correspondent Hanson Baldwin. Baldwin contended that "the blatant methods used by the administration
and its tampering with the news deserve considerably more criticism
and discussion than they have received."

One form of news control, he wrote, was "the tremendous
strengthening in government of the federal police power (the F.B.I.
and especially the C.I.A.) and of the 'intelligence mentality' which
tends to enshrine secrecy as an abstract good. The free-wheeling use
of federal cops to investigate leaks has grown to menacing proportions. Some of the most respected reporters in Washington have
experienced 'the treatment,' which included visits by the F.B.I. to
their homes, tapping of telephone lines, shadowing of reporters,
investigations of their friendships and other forms of intimidation."

Another method was blocking the press from access to the news.
Arthur Sylvester, for example, issued an order requiring the
presence of a third person during any interview, or alternatively, the

filing of a report by the person interviewed. This rule, said Baldwin, "has gone a long way toward restricting news to the 'Poppa knows best' kind, to stories and data which the government *wants* to release."

Another tactic used by President Kennedy, wrote Baldwin, was the calculated leak, "the carefully disseminated canard or half truth from someone close to the throne." One example was the account in *The Saturday Evening Post* by Stewart Alsop and Charles Bartlett which purported to depict the "softness" of Adlai Stevenson during the 1962 Cuban crisis and which also added "hawks" and "doves" to the political vocabulary.

"There was a time when the word of the government was its bond," wrote Baldwin. "The people could have faith in what Washington told them. Public confidence has been shaken severely many times since World War II: the U-2 case exposed the dangers of government falsehood for all to see. But the Kennedy Administration does not appear to have learned from these horrible examples . . ."

The Kennedy effort at manipulating the press was eagerly joined by some journalists. Others, however, understood precisely what was happening and attempted to warn the public. One of these was *New York Times* columnist Arthur Krock who, incidentally, was an old friend of the Kennedy family.

"A news management policy not only exists," wrote Krock during the third year of the Kennedy Administration, "but in the form of *direct and deliberate* actions has been enforced more cynically and more boldly than by any other previous Administration."

This policy took many forms. "One principal form that it takes," reported Krock, "is social flattery of Washington reporters and commentators—many more than ever got this treatment in the past—by the President and his high-level supporters."

Bobby Kennedy was also deeply involved in the manipulation of the press. He was guilty of attempting to use the press for his own personal vendettas, particularly when it came to Teamsters Union leader Jimmy Hoffa. On the first day of Hoffa's trial in Nashville, Tennessee, for example, a person representing himself as a reporter for *The Nashville Banner* telephoned some of the jurors.

Acting to protect the good name of his staff, James G. Stahlman, publisher of the *Banner*, announced a $5,000 reward for the arrest and conviction of the imposter. Bobby Kennedy quickly got on the phone to Stahlman and urged that news of the incident be suppressed. Stahlman disclosed that Bobby felt that "if a detailed story in connection with this matter were made, it might very well lead to a mistrial."

"What has happened," Stahlman answered, "has made it necessary for me to defend the reputation of my newspaper, which has existed for 86 years, and I don't intend to have it sacrificed to Jimmy Hoffa, the federal government, or anyone else."

In another instance, Bobby Kennedy was instrumental in placing a derogatory story in *Life Magazine* entitled: "Roy Cohn: Is He A Liar Under Oath?" Senator Edward V. Long (D-Missouri), who held hearings on the episode, said: "This smells to high heaven." *The Chicago Tribune* declared that the practice of an Attorney General in promoting prejudicial magazine pieces about individuals under federal indictment called for "the fullest kind of investigation by the responsible committees in Congress. It is one of the most serious charges ever made against a high officer of Government."

From the beginning of his administration until his tragic death, Jack Kennedy never learned how to take criticism. Whenever and wherever a critic reared his head, even in the most unlikely and obscure place, the Kennedys did their best to silence him. "How can they spot an obscure paragraph in a paper of 3,000 circulation, 2,000 miles away is beyond me," said senior White House correspondent Merriman Smith of United Press International. "They must have a thousand little gnomes reading the papers for them."

The Kennedys used the press. They assaulted those who dared to disagree. "Never," wrote Fletcher Knebel in *Look Magazine* in August, 1962: "have so few bawled out so many so often for so little as the Kennedys battle reporters."

Yet in the end, they created for themselves the illusory media image of Camelot which has still not faded from public view. The assassination ended for good any disillusionment which many in the media had come to feel. Author Richard Whelan summed it up this way: "The news media, and the liberal intellectuals, whose jurisdiction overlapped in the American communications system, enthroned and mythologized John F. Kennedy and then, quite predictably, became displeased with him for behaving as the cautious politician he had always been. His martyrdom, however, transformed him into a figure of instant legend, and the liberals were again greatly pleased with Jack Kennedy. For now they could devote themselves to making the Kennedy myth permanent and to protecting their heavy investment in the illusory liberalism recast in his image."

9

Betraying Black Voters' Trust

JOHN F. KENNEDY'S speech writers put the problem of the American Negro in forceful language when they had the 1960 Presidential candidate say, "The Negro baby born in America today, regardless of the section of the nation in which he is born, has about one-half as much chance of completing high school as a white baby in the same place on the same day, one-third as much chance of completing college, one-third as much chance of becoming a professional man, twice as much chance of becoming unemployed, about one-seventh as much chance of earning $10,000 a year, a life expectancy which is seven years shorter, and the prospects of earning half as much."

The candidate's statistics were accurate. To all who listened, they made clear the inequities faced by Negroes in America.

To overcome these inequities millions of Negroes had already left the South and moved to the North and West. It is hard to gauge this resettlement, which has been called the "greatest geographic migration in American life since the settlers took their covered wagons west."

The Negro migration from the South has been said to be as low as 100,000 a year and as high as 200,000 a year. In 1910 ninety per cent of all American Negroes lived in the states of the Old South. But, by the time of the presidential campaign of 1960 the percentage had shrunk to fifty-two. Almost half of the Negro population—a total of about nine million—then lived in the North and West. Most of these were crowded into the great metropolitan centers of the North and they were an important voting bloc.

In 1960, Washington, the nation's capital, became the first major city of the world to count a Negro majority—fifty-four per cent of the population. New York City had seen its Negro population grow from 775,000 or 9.8 per cent in 1950, to 1,087,000, or 14 per cent, in 1960. Philadelphia was 26 per cent Negro, and Detroit 29 per cent in 1960. Newark had almost doubled its Negro population in a decade, from 17 per cent to 35 per cent. Abraham Lincoln's home state of Illinois had increased its Negro count from 646,000 to 1,037,000; and most of them were in and around Chicago.

This Negro voting strength, especially in the industrial cities of the North, was to prove a vital factor in 1960. In Theodore H. White's 1961 book, *Making of the President 1960,* he said that: "Even more than in the election of 1948, the outcome of 1960 was to be dependent on Negro votes. And the leadership of the Negroes, like the leadership of so many minorities in the great cities of the United States, was to exert its electoral strength. For the Northern cities of the United States, commanding the electoral votes necessary to make an American President, have for generations provided a leverage on American power to shape and alter the world itself. During the years of World War I, the Irish of the great Northern cities had provided the leverage to free Ireland from Britain; the Czechs of Pennsylvania had actually written the first Constitution of the Free Czechoslovak Republic in Pittsburgh in 1919. During and after World War II, the Jews of the great Northern cities had exercised their political leverage to win and guarantee the independence of Israel.

"And so, in 1960, the Negroes of the Northern cities meant to exercise their leverage on the Presidential election, to compel equality for their kinfolk in the South. Deeply motivated, Negro leaders watched the electoral campaign begin the summer of 1960 . . ."

They were to see John F. Kennedy make a vivid appeal for the Negro vote.

Before 1960 Kennedy had a weak civil rights record. Negroes tended to view him with misgiving. They had reason to do so for in the 1957 showdown on civil rights Senator Kennedy clearly identified himself among the party unity compromisers. A Southern newswriter noted that Kennedy, "voted with Lyndon Johnson, and against the Northern liberal bloc, for the crucial compromise that made that year's civil rights bill so eminently acceptable to the South that half a dozen Southern Senators actually voted for it."

He was careful to tread a path midway between those who advocated strong civil rights legislation and those who opposed it. *The New York Post* noted that, "While he dare not desert the antifilibuster cause lest he be totally repudiated in the North, the other side of his mouth is addressed to the South. The total result, as in his evasion of the McCarthy issue, is a portrait of irresolution."

His position was so ambivalent that Roy Wilkins, executive secretary of the National Association for the Advancement of Colored People, attacked him as a "compromiser with evil." Kennedy wrote to Wilkins explaining his position. Wilkins refused to answer Kennedy's letters.

Thirteen months before the 1960 Convention, in June, 1959, Alabama Governor John Patterson had Kennedy to breakfast in the Georgetown home of Sam Englehardt, a leader of the White Citizens Councils. Patterson was a bitter foe of integration and once, during a governor's race, he waved a blown up photograph of a Negro being pushed in Little Rock, declaring, "This is how I will treat them if you make me your Governor."

Soon after the meeting, Patterson endorsed Kennedy for President, saying, "I think he's a friend of the South. I will use all the influence I have to see that he gets the nomination."

Negro leaders reacted violently to the Patterson endorsement. Harlem's Adam Clayton Powell called on delegates to the 1960 Convention to repudiate Kennedy because he had accepted support from "Negro-hating Alabama officials."

NAACP executive director Roy Wilkins said: "It is very difficult for thoughtful Negro leaders to feel at ease over the endorsement."

Jackie Robinson, the Negro baseball star, described Kennedy as "the fair-haired boy of the Southern segregationists."

Kennedy then became concerned about going so far to please the South that he would lose black support. He responded to Robinson:

"Although it is true that I once had breakfast with them (Patterson and Englehardt) it is equally true that a few days later I had lunch with Mr. Thurgood Marshall. No implications can be drawn from either of these meetings other than my own public statements."

Robinson responded: "If Kennedy thinks he can use a luncheon with the NAACP's Thurgood Marshall to counterbalance his endorsement by Governor Patterson, then his view of the intelligence of Negro Americans must be very low indeed."

Black journalist Chuck Stone, then editor of the *New York Citizen Call,* wrote of Kennedy's ability "to talk out of both sides of the face simultaneously . . . There's one thing money can't buy. And that's a liberal and forthright attitude toward Negroes and their fight for equality. Senator Kennedy just does not have this attitude . . . Senator Kennedy has been equivocating on civil rights so long, he wouldn't know a forthright statement on racial equality if it were dragged across his breakfast table. Search his Senate speeches. Has he ever condemned the South's barbaric attitude? Has he ever spoken out against the inequities of housing discrimination or job discrimination? Has he ever shown deep concern about the second-class citizenship of Negroes?"

Mr. Stone continued: "Kennedy is the same man who sat down to breakfast with Governor Patterson, one of the staunchest Negro-haters in America . . . He has never urged the South to hurry and shake off its Neanderthal racial blinders. He has never once urged speedy compliance with the Supreme Court school desegregation decision of 1954. Where in Senator Kennedy's career can one point to a single aggressively definite stand on racial integration . . . In the present spectrum of Democratic and Republican candidates, Senator Kennedy is unquestionably the worst of the lot for the American Negro, and this includes Lyndon Johnson."

Thereafter, up to the time of the Convention, Kennedy made every effort to avoid committing himself on civil rights. He was so careful that, although he was Chairman of a Senate Subcommittee on African Rights, he never called a meeting of the group. And he was one of a few Senators who did not respond to the American Veterans Committee's questionnaire on civil rights. The NAACP criticized him for not voting on two key amendments to the 1957 Civil Rights Act—one to establish a permanent Commission on Equal Job Opportunity Under Government Contracts—the other to provide technical assistance to areas desegregating their schools. Both were defeated.

Within the Labor Committee, Kennedy voted against a motion to create a special subcommittee to study the need for legislation to ban racial discrimination. Then, when President Eisenhower asked passage of a bill to establish a Commission on Equal Job Opportunity Under Government Contracts, Kennedy's own subcommittee—of which he was chairman—never brought the bill to a vote.

The press did not fail to notice and comment on Kennedy's not-so-artful dodging. One of the most astute, Victor Lasky, in a subsequent book, *J.F.K., the Man and the Myth*, wrote that, "During the 1960 Southern filibuster, when most civil rights advocates were stumbling groggily through the pre-dawn hours to answer quorum calls in order to keep the Senate in session, John F. Kennedy was conspicuously absent from the scene.

"On March 10, 1960, *The New York Times* reported that Kennedy had failed to appear for a single post-midnight call. By contrast, Senator Lyndon Johnson, whose newly found devotion to the cause was even more suspect, turned out for every call during the graveyard hours of early morning when the going was roughest."

The filibuster went on through March and April. Kennedy came into Washington only occasionally in these months. He was campaigning in Wisconsin and West Virginia, ahead of the primaries in those states.

When Kennedy's politically wise campaign managers realized Negro and liberal anger could wreck his drive for the presidential nomination, they had Kennedy take several steps to strengthen his position on civil rights. One move they made was more important than any of the others: they asked for help from Harris Wofford of the Notre Dame Law School.

Wofford had come to Washington two years before, in 1958, to be counsel to the Civil Rights Commission and chief of the Commission's inquiry into discrimination in housing. He stayed to join the Kennedy team as an expert on Asian matters. As the Negro matter grew into a problem and then a crisis, Kennedy shifted him over to civil rights, in which he was informed and experienced. Under Wofford's tutelage, Kennedy took stands on civil rights which promised a good political harvest.

The turning point came on the eve of the Convention. Michigan

Governor G. Mennen "Soapy" Williams invited ten Negro delegates to meet Senator Kennedy. Negro and white waiters served guests on the patio. One of the guests remarked that "they served a subtle punch before lunch. I thought there was gin in it, but I heard it was cognac. There was chicken and some fancy kind of eggs. That man must have given away $100 worth of cigars from some foreign country. Mrs. Kennedy was present, too, and later they had the press conference for television and everything. We were all impressed."

Soon Kennedy and Negro leaders exchanged views in a series of meetings arranged by Wofford who told the candidate what to say. The meetings showed results. At the Convention, Kennedy insisted on a strong civil rights plank. It pledged full use of federal powers and leadership "to assure equal access for all Americans to all areas of community life, including voting booths, schoolrooms, jobs, housing and public facilities."

In addition, the platform promised "to support whatever action is necessary to eliminate literacy tests and the payment of poll taxes as requirements for voting." It stated that "every school district affected by the Supreme Court's school desegregation decision should submit a plan providing for at least first-step compliance by 1963."

Further, the platform held that "peaceful demonstrations for first-class citizenship which have recently taken place in many parts of this country are a signal to all of us to make good at long last the guarantees of our Constitution." And it called for the establishment of a fair employment practices commission to assure equal opportunity for jobs.

The press hailed the platform which, in its sweeping promises of government-enforced equality for Negroes, reached far beyond any previous party platform, Democratic or Republican.

To reinforce his position even further, after a special session of Congress in August, Kennedy joined twenty-three other Democratic Senators in a statement condemning the Republican civil rights record. The Eisenhower Administration, the Senators declared, had failed to end discrimination in federal housing programs which "the President could do by a stroke of the pen." The Senators, including Kennedy, pledged "action to obtain consideration of a civil rights bill by the Senate early next session that will implement the pledges of the Democratic platform."

Kennedy, who prior to his campaign for the nomination had done nothing and said nothing to advance the Negroes' cause, now was on the record in favor of a powerful civil rights bill.

Then followed the election campaign of 1960. With his eye on the millions of Negro voters, Kennedy quickly declared himself in favor of introducing a civil rights bill. In opening his formal campaign with the Labor Day speech in Detroit, he said, ". . . this bill (civil rights) will be among the first orders of business."

To be sure, the old ambivalence was still there. In the same talk he insisted that the civil rights fight fell more on the Presidency than it did on Congress. "The next President," said Kennedy, "must exert the great moral and educational force of his office to help bring equal access to public facilities, from churches to lunch counters; and to support the right of every American to stand up for his rights, even if on occasion he must sit down for them. For only the President, not the Senate and not the House and not the Supreme Court, can create the understanding and tolerance necessary as the spokesman for all the American people."

The Vice Presidential nominee, Lyndon B. Johnson, echoed Kennedy in his campaign tour through Dixie in October. He promised that, "Under Jack Kennedy, the Democratic Party will guarantee the Constitutional rights of every American, no matter what his race, religion—or what section of the country he comes from."

And so it went all through the campaign. Although as a Senator he had repeatedly avoided any confrontation which would put him on record in favor of civil rights, now in speech after speech Kennedy reiterated his promises to the Negro people.

The Negroes liked Kennedy's assurances of a raise in minimum wages. They liked his civil rights pledges. But it might not have been enough to convince the nation's Negroes that Kennedy had really had a change of heart if Wofford had not had a stroke of inspiration.

On Wednesday, October 19, Richard M. Nixon and Kennedy were addressing the American Legion in Miami on national defense. At about the same time Martin Luther King, Jr. and fifty-two other Negroes were arrested in Rich's Department Store in Atlanta for refusing to leave its Magnolia Room restaurant.

The following Monday all the other sit-ins were released but King was held, sentenced to four months' hard labor on a technicality, and whisked away to the Reidsville State Prison. Mrs. King, six months pregnant, expressed her fear he would die on a Georgia chain gang.

The American Negro communities armed for battle, and so did Southern whites. Tension mounted as the crisis grew.

Kennedy's strategists met on the night of October 25, just two weeks before the election—to find some way to exploit the situation to political advantage. Wofford suggested that Kennedy place a phone call to Mrs. King, and express his concern to her.

The next few hours were desperately critical as aides tried to find Kennedy. Wofford, after considerable difficulty, reached his immediate superior, Sargent Shriver, head of the Civil Rights Section of the campaign—and Kennedy's brother-in-law. When he finally located Shriver early Wednesday morning, Shriver was able to grab Kennedy at O'Hare Inn at Chicago's International Airport just as he was about to take off on a day of barnstorming in Michigan.

Kennedy reacted instantly to the suggestion by picking up the phone and placing a long-distance call to Mrs. King. He told her of his interest and concern in her suffering and assured her that, if necessary, he would intervene on behalf of her husband.

Whether the act was simple and humane, as some have claimed, or merely cold, calculating and designed to get Negro votes, as others have contended, it was a stroke of genius from the standpoint of the practical politician. Says White in *Making of the President 1960*, "Mrs. King, elated yet still upset, informed a few of her closest friends. Through channels of Negro leadership, the word swiftly sped northward from Atlanta, and thus to the press, that Kennedy had intervened to protect the imprisoned Negro leader. And Bobby Kennedy, informed in the course of the day of the command decision, proceeded even further and the next morning telephoned a plea for King's release from New York to the Georgian judge who had set the sentence; on Thursday King was released from Reidsville Prison on bail, pending appeal—safe and sound."

White adds that in the Negro community the Kennedy intervention rang like a carillon. It convinced Negroes that Kennedy was sincere in his promises that civil rights legislation would be the first order of business if he was elected. Confident and reassured, the Negroes went to the polls and their vote gave Kennedy the election.

A total of 68,832,818 Americans voted and the finish was close. Neither candidate won a majority. John F. Kennedy received

34,221,463 votes or 49.7 per cent; Richard M. Nixon, 34,108,582, or 49.6 per cent of the vote.

Thus Kennedy was elected by one-tenth of one per cent of the whole.

Nixon carried more states, 26 to 23, but Kennedy took those with the highest electoral votes. His total of electoral votes was 303 to 219.

The importance of the Negro vote can be readily seen. Kennedy carried Illinois by only 9,000 votes. It was estimated that 250,000 Negroes voted for him in that state. Similarly, Kennedy carried Michigan by 67,000 votes. Again it was estimated that 250,000 Negroes voted for him in that state. He carried South Carolina by 10,000 votes, and an estimated 40,000 Negroes voted for him there.

Loss of Illinois and Michigan alone would have beaten Kennedy.

The Gallup and Harris polls said from 68 to 78 per cent of all Negroes voted for Kennedy across the country. Had only whites gone to the polls, Nixon would have taken 52 per cent of the vote.

Dwight Eisenhower recognized the importance of the Negro vote. When asked to discuss the King episode, the President said that a couple of telephone calls "had swung the Negro vote to him (Kennedy) and gave him the election." Nixon echoed his sentiments, declaring in an interview, "I just didn't realize such a call would swing an election."

But swing the election it did, and it placed John F. Kennedy in the position to deliver on his repeated promises to the Negro voters.

After the election King lost no time reminding the new President of his promises. In an article in the *Nation*, he demanded that Kennedy act in two areas as he had promised. In the legislative area, said King, Kennedy should fight for a civil rights program with emphasis on the right to vote. In the executive area, by a stroke of the pen, the President should stop the use of federal funds to support housing, hospital and airport construction in which discrimination was open and notorious.

Although he was under a campaign pledge to do both, as King well knew, Kennedy was now set to make another great mistake. He was about to fail, for two long years, to deliver on his promises to millions of American Negroes and, in so doing, stir their wrath to spill over in marches, demonstrations and violence from one end of the country to the other.

The American people had returned to Congress a Senate of sixty-

four Democrats and thirty-six Republicans; and a House of Representatives of 262 Democrats and 175 Republicans, a gain for the
Republicans of two Senate seats and 21 House seats.

At first glance, the arithmetic appeared to be on Kennedy's side,
but uncertain of the Southern Democrats, Kennedy felt it was risky
to introduce a civil rights bill. He decided to renege on his campaign
promises for, in spite of all the pledges to the Negroes when he was
running for office, he did not want to alienate Southern Congressmen. He was afraid of a debate and a filibuster over a civil rights bill.

So he began his Administration with a series of executive actions
which got him considerable publicity and which he hoped would
hold the confidence of the Negro community.

After his Inaugural he pointed out that he had seen only white
faces among the Coast Guard who paraded past him. When Robert
Kennedy resigned from the Metropolitan Club, charging it discrimi-
nated against Negroes, John Kennedy said, "I personally approved of
my brother's action." He urged appointment of more Negroes to
government jobs. As early as February he made Clifford R. Wharton
Ambassador to Norway. And in October Thurgood Marshall was
nominated to the Second Circuit Court, the first of five Negroes
made lifetime judges.

But Kennedy declined to issue the order on housing, and he
refused to introduce a civil rights bill. His failure to fulfill his solemn
promises in these two areas infuriated civil rights leaders. Martin
Luther King, Jr., the man he had saved from a Georgia prison and
the author of the *Nation* article putting him on the spot, said, "The
President did more to undermine confidence in his intentions than
could be offset by a series of smaller accomplishments."

While conceding that "the vigorous young men" of the Administration had "reached out more creatively" than their predecessors and
had "conceived and launched some imaginative and bold forays,"
King pronounced the broad record "essentially cautious and defensive," directed toward "the limited goal of token integration."

Roy Wilkins praised Kennedy for "his personal role in civil rights
and very plain indications of his concern that conditions be im-
proved," but expressed his "disappointment with Mr. Kennedy's
first year" as a result of his failure to issue the housing order; and
even more of the "basic error" of the strategy of "no legislative action

on civil rights." Frustrated and angry, Negroes began to stir restlessly across the country.

The press reported the appearance of "freedom riders." The first band was led by James Farmer of the Congress of Racial Equality (CORE), and rolled through the Carolinas and Georgia with only a few fights and arrests. There was no real trouble until the "freedom riders" got to Alabama, where John Kennedy's old friend Patterson was Governor. One of the buses was burned at Anniston. A white mob attacked and beat the riders at Birmingham. Armed with clubs and pipes, a throng set upon the riders and assaulted many of them. This forced Attorney General Bobby Kennedy to send 600 deputy federal marshals into the state to protect the Negroes.

About the same time, a young Negro named James Meredith sought admission to the University of Mississippi. When the school rejected Meredith's application, he carried the case all the way to the United States Supreme Court which found that Meredith had been refused admission solely because he was a Negro. Governor Ross Barnett heard the decision and responded by saying, "We will not surrender to the evil and illegal forces of tyranny."

On September 20 James Meredith presented himself for registration at Oxford, Mississippi. Students marched around the campus singing, "Glory, Glory, Segregation," while Governor Barnett stood at the door and read a long proclamation rejecting Meredith's application.

Later, when Meredith was refused admission a second time, the whole state caught fire. County folks for miles around gathered in Oxford, many of them with guns. As Meredith, flanked by marshals, approached to be registered, Barnett decided the situation was too dangerous. The mob might break out of control. He backed off.

Because he had refused to register Meredith, the Governor was found guilty of civil contempt and ordered to purge himself by the next Tuesday or face arrest and a fine of $10,000 a day.

Now a series of negotiations took place over the long-distance phone between the nation's capital and Montgomery, the capital of Alabama. By this time the university town of Oxford was an armed camp. An angry mob of some 2,500 pelted the federal marshals with bottles and bricks. After taking the bombardment for an hour the marshals fired tear gas into the crowd, and a call for troops was made.

Before they arrived and restored order, two men were killed and scores of persons wounded.

The next morning, with the bayonets of the soldiers enforcing a truce, James Meredith appeared at the Lyceum, which was administrative headquarters for the university. The crisis was past. He was enrolled as a student.

The whole terrible affair caught the headlines and flavored television news, but it did little to advance the cause of civil rights for the Negro. None recognized this fact more readily than the Negro leaders themselves. They pressed harder for legislation and for the executive order on housing which the President had promised.

People who recalled the Kennedy campaign assurances about "a stroke of the pen" in regard to the housing order, inspired a sarcastic campaign to goad the President into signing such an order by flooding the White House with cheap pens.

Once again the President felt he had reason not to act. He had intended to put out the order when Congress adjourned in the fall of 1961, according to his biographer, Arthur M. Schlesinger. He decided to put it off, however, because he needed Congressional support for a Department of Urban Affairs, which Robert Weaver would head as Secretary. He also wanted Democratic votes from the South for the trade expansion bill in 1962. And there is some indication he feared such an executive act might interfere with the start of new buildings and thus slow up business recovery.

In his State of the Union message in 1962 the President had recognized there was more to be done "by the Executive, by the courts, and by the Congress." However, the only solid achievement for the entire year was the action of Congress in August when it passed a Constitutional Amendment declaring that a poll tax must not be a bar to voting in federal elections. The Amendment was later ratified by the States.

But now even more than before, the Negro leadership felt that Kennedy had failed them. Martin Luther King, Jr., said sorrowfully that 1962 was "the year that civil rights was displaced as the dominant issue in domestic policies . . . The issue no longer commanded the conscience of the nation."

A young freedom rider named Jerome Smith revealed the intense resentment of Negroes. Smith said he felt like vomiting when he had to be in the same room with Robert Kennedy. Far from criticizing

Smith, the other Negroes defended him. The younger Kennedy resented the remark, and more so because of the way the other Negro leaders rallied behind Smith.

Novelist James Baldwin was acidly critical of the Administration. He said the only reason the government had sent federal troops into Alabama was because a white man was stabbed.

Negro resentment spread and grew through the winter and by the spring of 1963, Negro leader A. Philip Randolph could say, without fear of contradiction, "The Negroes are already in the streets. It is very likely impossible to get them off. If they are bound to be in the streets in any case, is it not better that they be led by organizations dedicated to civil rights and disciplined by struggle rather than to leave them to other leaders who care neither about civil rights nor about non-violence? If the civil rights leadership were to call the Negroes off the streets, it is problematic whether they would come."

Randolph was correct. Tired of waiting for the President to act, the nation's Negroes felt they had to move to force his hand.

On April 2, Dr. King himself opened a major campaign against segregation in Birmingham. Within three weeks more than 400 Negroes had been arrested for loitering, for trespassing, for parading without a permit. Dr. King was among the leaders arrested. Like the others, he was fined $50, and freed on bail pending appeal.

By early May civil disobedience was a running flame across the nation. More than 75,000 Negroes rioted in cities from coast to coast. In Birmingham, police used dogs, and firemen high pressure hoses, to disperse the demonstrators. There were 2,500 persons arrested, including many children.

Then, briefly, there was a break in the violence while Dr. King and other Negro leaders worked out a limited desegregation agreement with white businessmen. The truce was ruptured on May 9, when the home of a Negro leader and a desegregated motel were bombed. The explosions triggered new rioting in which fifty persons were hurt.

President Kennedy attempted to stem the wildfire spread of the rioting by going on a tour of the South toward the middle of May. He spoke at Vanderbilt University about racial violence across the country, "The nation—indeed the whole world—has watched recent events in the United States with alarm and dismay," he said. "No one can deny the complexity of the problems involved in assuring to all of our citizens their full rights as Americans. But no one can gainsay the fact that the determination to secure these rights is in the highest traditions of American freedom."

It was a strange statement, for he seemed to be criticizing himself for his own failure in trying "to secure these rights."

In June Negro rioting increased, sweeping Washington, New York and Philadelphia, and cities in Maryland, North Carolina, Tennessee, Georgia, Alabama, Mississippi, Virginia, Florida, California, Missouri, Ohio, Nebraska, Rhode Island, Massachusetts and New Jersey. And this nationwide "attack" finally persuaded Kennedy he must act to carry out his campaign promises to American Negroes.

The President on June 19 finally asked Congress to enact an Omnibus Civil Rights Act which, he said, "will go far toward providing reasonable men with the reasonable means of meeting these problems," and "will thus help end the kind of racial strife which this nation can hardly afford."

This time the Kennedy rhetoric was not enough. The Negroes had been disappointed and misled too often. The speech failed to end the violence. In New York City there were demonstrations against discrimination in employment and more than 700 were arrested. And in Cambridge, Maryland, whites and Negroes clashed until National Guard units had to restore peace and order.

Three years had now elapsed since the President had first started to talk about civil rights legislation. The Negroes' patience was exhausted. They wanted immediate action. Congress was under such strong pressure to push the long awaited Civil Rights bill through it could not give it the scrupulous care its importance demanded. To meet the necessity, the bill would have to be hurriedly and imperfectly drawn. For one example, the Public Accommodations Section of the new bill would embrace any establishment in which a lodging or eating place was located. A physician whose offices were in a hotel or similar building covered by the law also found himself bound by its provisions.

Any owner-occupied hotel, motel, lodging-house with "five or less" rooms was exempt from the bill, since this was interpreted as a "social" rather than a "business" situation. But a man with six rooms to rent could be fined or jailed if he chose to deny accommodations on grounds of race, religion or other factors.

Clearly, this kind of anti-discrimination legislation—which made it illegal for one man to discriminate but legal for his competitor to do so—was in itself discriminatory. But such jarring discrepancies were typical of the Omnibus Civil Rights Act hurriedly proposed to stem the rioting.

As Congress debated the new bill, Negroes were still unsure of what to expect from the Administration. Seething unrest still troubled the nation.

Negro leaders needed a channel into which to drain off the violence. One way to harness the steam of the rioting was a march on Washington. For several weeks Negro leaders had thought of a march on the Capitol similar to the one Randolph had proposed to Franklin D. Roosevelt twenty years before. Now they saw it as a means of forcing enactment of the Civil Rights Act.

President Kennedy was not too happy about the idea. He saw it as a pistol pointed at the collective head of Congress. But there was not much he could do about it.

On August 28th, 200,000 persons—mostly Negro but including thousands of whites—marched on Washington. They came from every section of the United States and they demanded full civil rights immediately.

On that lovely summer day this formidable crowd gathered at the Washington Monument, signed a pledge of dedication to the civil rights struggle, and marched down Constitution Avenue and Independence Avenue to the Lincoln Memorial.

The marchers sang hymns and spirituals and the now well known song, "We Shall Overcome." They carried thousands of banners emblazoned with such lettered challenges as, "Effective Civil Rights Laws—Now!" "Integrated Schools—Now!" and "Decent Housing—Now!"

The operating word was NOW. They knew their power. Thoughtful persons realized this and knew the Negroes would never again underestimate their power. Their actions since have proved this for in subsequent years, Negro riots rose to an even higher pitch.

So much for President Kennedy and civil rights. He had entered the 1960 campaign with a poor record from the standpoint of the Negro. During the campaign, in order to win the Negro vote, he made wholesale promises—promises to introduce a civil rights bill, promises to help the Negro's cause with executive action.

Only when the President they trusted did not fulfill his promises did the Negroes come out into the streets and riot in almost every major city of the country. Only then did the President move to introduce a civil rights bill.

This was one of Kennedy's saddest mistakes. It was also his most ignoble one. By exploiting a heart-rending problem for his political gain, and by failing then to honor the promise, the President betrayed the Negroes.

In recent years, John F. Kennedy has been remembered as a friend of civil rights and of black Americans. The activities of his Administration would lead to a more ambivalent conclusion. Consider, for example, the treatment of the Rev. Martin Luther King, Jr.

At the direction of Attorney General Robert Kennedy, wherever Martin Luther King went, he was the object of electronic surveillance. Room bugs were installed in his hotel rooms. According to Arthur Murtagh, a retired agent attached to the F.B.I.'s office in Atlanta, the action against King was second in size "only to the way they went after Jimmy Hoffa."

A study of King's personal life, with emphasis upon his relations with women, was circulated among government officials. *The New York Times* reported that when the President himself became aware of what was going on, he ordered F.B.I. Director Hoover to call back every copy. But the President did not order an end to the surveillance of Dr. King.

Kennedy friend Charles Bartlett reported that the surveillance of King was done "in a spirit of anxiety" over King's associations. Bartlett wrote that, "The Kennedy brothers were initially puzzled over King's intentions. He appeared to have links that reached into both the Rockefeller and Communist camps. Uncertain whether he was conspiring to overthrow the country or the Kennedy Administration, they readily assented to Hoover's plans for close scrutiny."

Later on, the Justice Department admitted that the purpose of the surveillance was "investigating the love life of a group leader for dissemination in the press." The group leader was later identified as King. Professor Alan Dershowitz of the Harvard Law School, writing in *The New Republic*, estimated that 5,000 separate conversations went on tape, violating "the privacy of hundreds, perhaps thousands, of King callers and visitors."

One of the secret recordings was of a party held by King and other black leaders at the Willard Hotel in Washington, D.C. in the summer of 1962 at the time he was to deliver his *"I have a dream"* speech. A copy of the recording was sent directly to Dr. King's wife, Coretta, by William Sullivan, then in charge of the F.B.I.'s counter-intelligence operations, on orders from Hoover.

While John F. Kennedy and Martin Luther King have been linked as allies in death, while both men were alive their relationship was clearly more one of adversary than friend.

10

The Cuban Missile Crisis

SEPTEMBER 3, 1962, was Labor Day. The sun shone, the air was warm, and millions of Americans went to the beaches, mountains and highways for their last long summer weekend. Few people anywhere took time to read the newspapers.

It was a pity, for the front page headlines confirmed what a great many had feared:

MOSCOW AGREES
TO ARM AND TRAIN
MILITARY IN CUBA
Soviet Will Also Provide
Economic and Industrial
Aid under New
Pact
GUEVARA WINS ACCORD
Actions Termed Response
To Threats by Imperialists
Against Castro Regime

In a sense, the story was misleading. From the day Fidel Castro had seized power there had always been a trickle of Russian arms and men into Cuba. Months after the Bay of Pigs, on December 2, 1961,

Castro had made a grandstand announcement to the world. "I am a Marxist Leninist," he said, and added he was taking Cuba into the Communist bloc.

Washington made no response to this threat. The Kennedy Administration was still unsure of itself after the "colossal mistake" of the Bay of Pigs. Above all else, the President wanted to avoid another involvement, and in Moscow his silence must have spoken louder than words. The Russians decided that they could do pretty much as they pleased in Cuba without worrying about the United States. The trickle of Soviet aid became a stream of arms, ammunition, equipment and Russian men as Russian ships moved toward Cuba in ever increasing numbers during the winter and spring of 1962.

These developments were a direct challenge to the Monroe Doctrine, a United States policy which previous Administrations had upheld for 139 years. During the Russian build-up of arms in Cuba in the fall of 1962, few remembered that Russian activities on our West Coast had led to the promulgation of the Doctrine by President Monroe in his annual message to Congress on December 2, 1823.

The major assertion of the Monroe Doctrine was that the United States would consider as dangerous to its peace and safety any attempt of the European powers to extend their political system to any portion of the Western hemisphere.

There were actually two threats to the Western hemisphere that year.

The first arose when Czar Alexander of Russia issued an imperial order in which he claimed the entire Pacific Coast of North America and the surrounding seas down to the 51st parallel, which is the northern tip of Vancouver Island.

President James Monroe reacted to the Czar's ukase by directing John Quincy Adams, his Secretary of State, to draft a protest and Adams informed the Russian minister in Washington, "that we should contest the right of Russia to any territorial establishment on this continent, and that we should assume distinctly the principle that the American continents are no longer subjects for any new European colonial establishments."

In frank language Adams told the Russian minister, "There can, perhaps, be no better time for saying, frankly and explicitly, to the Russian government, that the future peace of the world, and the

interest of Russia herself, cannot be promoted by Russian settle-
ments upon any part of the American continent."

A dispute between France and Spain kindled a second threat of
foreign encroachment on Latin-American States, the independence
of which had been recognized by the United States.

While Monroe was debating this new danger, Britain's Foreign
Minister, George Canning, proposed a joint declaration by England
and the United States. Monroe was agreeable but laid down the
condition that Britain would first have to recognize the independence of the former Spanish colonies.

When Canning balked, Monroe determined to go it on his own. In
his State of the Union Message to Congress he inserted two
paragraphs which are the bones and flesh of the Monroe Doctrine.

"The occasion has been judged proper for asserting," he said, "as a
principle in which the rights and interests of the United States are
involved, that the American continents, by the free and independent
condition which they have assumed and maintain, are henceforth not
to be considered as subjects for future colonization by any European
powers."

In his second paragraph, Monroe pointed out that the "political
system of the allied powers" is "essentially different" from that of
America, and then went on to promulgate his doctrine:

"We owe it, therefore, to a candor and to the amicable relations
existing between the United States and those powers to declare that
we should consider any attempt on their part to extend their system
to any portion of this hemisphere as dangerous to our peace and
safety. . . . It is impossible that the allied powers should extend their
political system to any portion of either continent without endanger-
ing our peace and happiness; nor can anyone believe that our
southern brethren, if left to themselves, would adopt it of their own
accord. It is equally impossible, therefore, that we should behold
such interposition in any form with indifference."

Since President Monroe's declaration, in only two instances did
New World nations fall under European domination. Both occurred
while the United States was preoccupied with the Civil War. In
1861, on invitation of the Dominican president, Spain reassumed its
rule over Santo Domingo; and four years later France set up
Maximilian as Emperor of Mexico.

As soon as the Civil War came to a close, Secretary of State

William H. Seward turned his attention to these violations of the Monroe Doctrine. With 1,000,000 men under arms in the United States, Spain lost no time getting out of Santo Domingo; and Napoleon thought better of his bargain in Mexico and started withdrawing his legions in 1866. A year later, Maximilian died before a firing squad.

Time after time in the latter half of the nineteenth century the Monroe Doctrine was invoked, once against Great Britain in South America and several times against Germany when her admirals urged the seizure of islands for naval bases in the Caribbean. On each occasion cooler heads insisted the inevitable clash with the United States was too high a price to pay.

Early in this century, President Theodore Roosevelt extended the doctrine to include the acts of European countries which seek to redress wrongs or collect debts. In 1902 when Germany undertook a blockade of Venezuelan ports to force the government to pay claims, public opinion in the United States became so aroused that the Germans called off the blockade.

Until 1962, the Monroe Doctrine was virtually the keystone of American foreign policy. President Kennedy had ample precedent for using the highly successful policy to thwart Russia's second attempt to establish herself in the Western hemisphere. The danger was even greater in 1962 than in 1823, for we had seen many examples of Soviet tyranny and treachery in Europe's satellite states as well as inside the seventeen so-called Republics of the Soviet Union itself.

The threat to our welfare and safety was real in Cuba. Kennedy's failure to invoke the Monroe Doctrine to protect the nation was a tragic and nearly fatal mistake.

Khrushchev, who had boasted that the Monroe Doctrine was dead and that its remains had "best be buried, as every dead body is, so that it does not poison the air by its decay," now was sending vast amounts of munitions and even Russian troops into this hemisphere.

At first, he anticipated a challenge to the 1962 inflow of arms and men into Cuba and shouted a bombastic warning that, "America cannot now attack Cuba and expect that that aggressor will be free from punishment for this attack. If such an attack is made, this will be the beginning of unleashing war."

Similar threats had been made during the long history of the

Monroe Doctrine, but this time the response from Washington was far different from the strong words of the past.

The President followed the same line he had used when Russia constructed the Berlin Wall. Kennedy announced that, "Castro is in trouble. Along with his pledges for political freedom, his industries are stagnating, his harvests are declining, his own followers are beginning to see that their revolution has been betrayed."

"Russian shipments into Cuba," he said, "Do not constitute a serious threat to any other part of this hemisphere." Because that was so, "universal military intervention on the part of the United States cannot currently be either required or justified."

Kennedy's mistake of misjudging the reports coming out of Cuba even alarmed apologists for his Administration. Max Lerner of *The New York Post* grew worried when Khrushchev threatened nuclear war if we attacked Cuba.

"The importance of the recent Soviet statement," said Lerner, "is that the Russians have now made a daring move to appropriate Cuba as one of their own don't-touch-me areas. That is why it is, to put it mildly, astonishing for President Kennedy to say that nothing has happened in the recent Soviet moves to threaten American vital interests. Nothing has happened except Khrushchev's attempt to steal the Monroe Doctrine so far as Cuba is concerned, and turn it upside down and inside out, so that Russia assumes the role of protector of the outraged integrity of a Latin American country and the United States is put into the role of the big bad foreign power."

Lerner echoed the sentiments of *The New York Times*, which said editorially, "The increasing close relationship between the Soviet Union and Premier Fidel Castro's regime poses the most serious challenge to the (Monroe) doctrine since Emperor Napoleon III took advantage of the Civil War in the United States to set up a puppet monarchy in Mexico."

Through it all, the President belittled the threat. Berlin was a continuing crisis. The Negro student, James H. Meredith, was being denied admittance by the University of Mississippi and this required delicate handling.

The President turned his attention elsewhere. It wasn't until October 15, when the consequences of his inaction were inescapable, that he was forced to move.

Even on the subject of Cuba considerable attention was paid to aspects other than the shipment of Russian arms and technicians into the country. For instance, there was the much publicized ambassadorship of New York attorney, James Britt Donovan, to Havana to obtain the release of some twelve hundred Cuban prisoners.

Directly after the Bay of Pigs fiasco Kennedy had promised Cuban leaders he would do everything in his power to save the Freedom Fighters captured on the Cuban beaches. First a high level attempt had been made to meet Castro's offer of a swap of the prisoners for tractors. Walter Reuther, the United Auto Workers labor leader, Mrs. Eleanor Roosevelt and Dr. Milton Eisenhower, brother of the former President, were named to serve on the Committee. The President tried to keep his name out of the questionable plan. However, Dr. Eisenhower left no doubts about the President's direct involvement. In his book, *The Wine Is Bitter,* he states flatly he was solicited by President Kennedy himself and began what he described as "the most exasperating, frustrating and enervating six weeks of my life."

The intermediary between the committee and President Kennedy was Richard Goodwin, 29-year-old protege of the Administration. The negotiations ran into obstacles almost from the start. It was soon obvious that Castro did not want ordinary farm tractors but heavy D-8 type bulldozers which were suitable as war materiel. He also refused to talk about a swap for prisoners and insisted instead that any payment made be considered indemnification for invasion damage.

A wave of opposition to the deal arose in Washington. Homer Capehart, as well as other Senators, called it "Castro blackmail." Senator Everett Dirksen joined the critics saying, "Now President Kennedy has added to that loss (the Bay of Pigs) by announcing his official sponsorship of a so-called citizen movement that proposes to make the American people pay blackmail to Fidel Castro."

As events proceeded, the problem not only demanded more and more of the President's precious time, it also upset him. There was reason for this. The attempt to fool the world as to who was behind the plan began to fail. It was remarkably similar to the previous attempt on the part of the President to hide the United States' participation in the invasion of Cuba. The President sensed another debacle and sought to absolve himself from responsibility for the committee's work. He said officially, "The Government of the United

States is not, and cannot be, a party to these negotiations." That brought a response from Dr. Eisenhower, who wrote later, "I now realized, in chilling clarity, that the President intended to maintain the fiction that all aspects of the case, from negotiations to critical decision, from raising funds to actually freeing prisoners, were private."

When it became clear that Castro was going to hold out for 500 heavy bulldozers costing about $28 million, the negotiations fell through. This further upset the President. One observer said, "President Kennedy not only lost interest but became irritable whenever the subject was brought up, and he issued an order to his top aides that Cuba wasn't to be mentioned publicly."

Castro was furious when the deal fell through. He staged a communist-type trial of 1,179 prisoners which was widely televised. Said the *Chicago Tribune*, "While we continually hear paeans to the quality of leadership we are getting these days from Washington, let no American forget that the conscience of the United States is also, in some measure, on trial. For the men in the dock were equipped, trained and transported by the United States to the invasion beach, and it was a failure of will in the Kennedy inner circle which deprived them of the air cover which alone could have made the landing successful."

The collapse of the first transaction had been almost a relief to many Americans who found the deal repugnant. But President Kennedy was openly disappointed at the denouement and embarrassed by the hippodrome trial that followed in its wake. The fate of the prisoners weighed on his conscience and he undertook a second ransom effort through the Cuban Families Committee. The White House secretly dubbed this new try, "Project X."

James Donovan, who was the President's agent in this effort, had first become a public figure in 1957 when the United States District Court in Brooklyn appointed him to defend Rudolf Abel, the chief Russian spy. Later, in 1962, the government chose him to negotiate the exchange of U-2 pilot Francis Gary Powers, who had been shot down over Soviet territory. Robert Kennedy, the Attorney General, assured Donovan the new negotiations for the release of the Cuban prisoners would not be a violation of the Logan Act which prohibits private citizens from negotiating public matters. This opinion Kennedy gave despite the fact that the Act was designed to prevent a civilian from actions apparently in the exclusive purview of the Departments of State and Defense.

On August 30, Donovan held a press conference before leaving for Havana. At his first brief meeting with Dr. Santiago Cubas, Castro's Attorney General, it was immediately obvious that Castro would insist on his principal point—any sum paid would not be a swap for prisoners but an indemnification to the Cuban government for damages, something that previous American negotiators had refused to admit.

Castro met with Donovan then and stated his price: $62 million in cash. Negotiations produced an agreement that the sum would be paid in food products and medical supplies to be bought at wholesale rates.

Soon there were complications, however. The Cuban Families Committee obviously could supply only a fraction of the money. The unavoidable conclusion was reached that much of the sum was to come from American taxpayers by way of the President's contingency fund or through some other channel. When the terms were conveyed to Washington, cries of anger and protest again erupted from Capitol Hill. Senators John Stennis of Mississippi and John J. Williams of Delaware spoke out against the use of federal funds to meet Castro's demands.

Nor was that all. The shipment of food alone would require 30 to 68 ships, and longshoremen threatened to picket the loading of them. Moreover, Donovan came under attack for agreeing to run on the Democratic ticket against Senator Jacob K. Javits. The *Washington Post* raised a question about this unforeseen development: "Suppose the Cubans are freed before election. The suspicion will exist, fairly or not, that the United States had paid a bribe to the Castro regime at least in part to help publicize a candidate for office."

Donovan was still deep in negotiations for what would eventually be a successful settlement of the deal when on Monday, October 22, 1962, national attention was focused again on the alarming Russian build-up of arms and men in Cuba, which had apparently been almost completely overlooked by the President.

Cuba was something John F. Kennedy wanted to forget. He had admitted that he had mishandled the Bay of Pigs. Thereafter he talked about it as little as possible. In his 1962 State of the Union message he had made no mention of it at all. On February 3, he did order an embargo on American trade with Cuba, but that was as far as he had gone.

Six weeks afterwards, on March 21, he informed a press conference there was no evidence of a build-up in military strength around our big naval base at Guantanamo. Then, in vague language, he volunteered, "We are always concerned about the defense of American territory wherever it may be, and we take whatever steps are necessary."

All through the summer of 1962, the President appeared to ignore the question of Cuba as much as he could.

Yet during those months, 61 vessels from Russia and Iron Curtain countries had delivered arms, supplies and men at Cuban ports. The cargoes included MIG-19 jet fighters, tanks, battlefield artillery, rockets, trucks and small weapons.

The Administration paid little heed to this but on August 22, in response to a direct query from a newsman, the President confirmed that Russia had been shipping substantial quantities of modern war equipment and military technicians during August and July. "What we are talking about are supplies and technicians of rather intensive quantity in recent weeks," he said.

Just two days later, government intelligence sources reported that Russian-made transportation, communications and electronic equipment and, most important of all, guided missiles similar to our Nike anti-aircraft missiles, were now in Cuba.

When questioned about this at a news conference six days later, the President said to the correspondents, "I don't know who told you at the State Department that they are going to operate Nike missiles, because that information we don't have at this time."

Roger Hilsman, Director of the State Department's Intelligence and Research Office, in a briefing on August 24, had explained that the Soviet block ships steaming into Cuba were merely carrying electronic gear and construction equipment for coastal and air defenses. He conceded that government intelligence sources had reported that the Russians in Cuba included 3,000 to 5,000 specialists, two-thirds of them military technicians. He added, however, that these men were not organized in combat units nor had hey ever been seen in uniforms.

John McCone, Director of the Central Intelligence Agency (CIA) had different ideas. He believed the military build-up was to introduce offensive weapons. Reporters James Daniel and John Hubbell tell us in their book, *Strike in the West:* "In early August (1962), it is now known, the C.I.A.'s John McCone began warning responsible officials that the temptation to Khrushchev to plant attack missiles in Cuba would be almost irresistible."

He was virtually alone among the Administration group in this interpretation until evidence obtained on October 24 proved him correct.

In the meantime, on September 5, Senator Keating said that Russian ships had landed in Cuba at least 1,200 troops wearing "Soviet fatigue uniforms." Kennedy then admitted that Russia had brought in missiles "with a slant range of 25 miles similar to early models of our Nike, and motor-torpedo boats bearing shipto-ship guided missiles having a range of fifteen miles."

The President "insisted," according to news magazines, that there was no evidence "of any significant offensive capability either in Cuban hands or under Soviet direction or guidance."

The Russian arms, he said, were defensive in nature.

Time Magazine replied to this, "The distinction between offensive and defensive weapons is a dangerous one; it all depends on how the weapons are used, whom they are pointed at, and how mobile they are. It is a bitter fact that many tyrants—including Hitler—have built aggressive war machines while claiming to arm only for defense."

The President also said there was no evidence of "any organized combat force in Cuba from any Soviet-bloc country." He emphasized that the Russians in Cuba were technicians. This was another fine distinction, because technicians could be working on missiles.

The New York Times raised an editorial eyebrow in its September 3 issue by commenting that "United States specialists disagree as to whether missiles have already been delivered."

New York's Senator Kenneth B. Keating had no doubts, however. On August 31, he told his fellow Senators that: "Ominous reports suggest that the Soviets are constructing missile bases and sending over technicians and experts to man them."

Again, on September 2, over a nationwide radio and television hookup, he said: "The very least the United States can do is call upon the Organization of American States to send a mission to Cuba to investigate reports of Cuban missile bases."

And a week and a day later he stood up again in the Senate to warn solemnly that, "Construction has begun on at least a half dozen launching sites for intermediate-range tactical missiles. My own sources in the Cuban situation . . . have substantiated this report completely."

The Administration was silent. But now other voices in Congress from both parties took up the alarm. Connecticut's Democratic Senator, Thomas Dodd, told a television audience, "I don't call it Castro's Cuba. I call it Khrushchev's Cuba. I suggest we start with a partial blockade. If it isn't adequate, we move to a total one. How much of a threat does it have to become? How many lives will we have to pay to stop it? It would have taken very few in the beginning, some more later on, many more now. I think it will be a catastrophe if it goes any further."

On the same television program Florida's Senator George Smathers said a blockade was not enough. He proposed a kind of Western Hemisphere NATO—"an admittedly military group of nations that feel about communism just the way we do; that are prepared to fight and will fight."

Senator Jacob K. Javits believed a blockade or intervention might be necessary eventually.

The New York Senator said: "I call upon him (the President) to be blunt not only with us but with his Administration. I call upon him to recognize the urgency plainly required by the situation. The American people are disturbed about the Cuban situation, disturbed as they have not been since the Korean war."

Senator Alexander Wiley of Wisconsin urged the creation of a peace fleet to rescue Cuba from the Soviets. Senator Homer Capehart of Indiana said we had a right to land troops on the soil we had wrested from Spain in 1898. Senator John Towers of Texas clamored for an invasion. The entire Congress, alarmed about the Soviet military presence in Cuba, demanded action from the Administration.

The 87th Congress had been critical of the President in other ways. Despite the fact that the Democrats controlled the House by a three-to-two margin, and the Senate by a two-to-one margin, Congress had consistently defeated the Administration's programs. It was now nearing election time and all 435 members of the House and one-third of the Senate were up for re-election. If the Republicans gained control of the House and reduced the Democratic majority in the Senate, an already bad situation for President Kennedy would become intolerable.

And that could well have happened, because the election campaign was not going well for the Democrats. Despite the Administration's various diversionary moves, Cuba had become the foremost issue. People were worried about the communist dictatorship only 90 miles off our shores and talk of Russian missiles and men on the island underscored it in the minds of voters.

Demands to do something about Cuba grew so vehement they threatened to overwhelm the Democrats at the polls. Everywhere the President went he heard gibes about his do-nothing policy. On October 13, in a campaign speech for Birch Bayh, Democratic opponent of Senator Capehart in Indiana, Kennedy struck out harshly at "self-appointed generals and admirals who want to send someone else's sons to war."

But it was plain that the President was not turning the election tide that was running against him, and he was forced finally into taking some effective action before the people went to the polls. A tragic and foreboding development demanded that he recognize that Cuba was the issue and act decisively.

On October 14, a U-2 plane flying over western Cuba, photographed a launching pad, a series of buildings for ballistic missiles and, on the ground in San Cristobal, one missile. This information was to prove crucial.

U-2 planes had made previous flights over Cuba—on September 5, 17, 26 and 29, and October 5 and 7, when they were suddenly halted. The Administration explained that Hurricane Ella had grounded them. But the Weather Bureau said the storm did not make flying impossible until the 16th and the flight of October 14 seemed to confirm this.

Up to this time the CIA had controlled the independent U-2 squadron but now Secretary of Defense McNamara moved into the picture and insisted that U-2 flights be placed under the jurisdiction of the Air Force. The CIA had trained the U-2 pilots and was experienced in this branch of intelligence gathering. Reluctant to complicate and delay matters at this crucial time, it appealed to the White House. However, McGeorge Bundy, Presidential Assistant for National Security Affairs, supported McNamara.

At this point, two regular Air Force majors, Rudolf Anderson, Jr.

of Spartanburg, South Carolina, and Richard S. Heyser of Battle Creek, Michigan, were ordered to take a U-2 on a reconnaissance sweep over Western Cuba. They took off on October 14.

Their flight was uneventful. They encountered no ground fire. When they landed, their film magazines were transferred to a waiting jet and flown to Washington.

The films they brought back from their photographic target—an installation near the town of San Cristobal—showed a clearing in the woods. In it were missile erectors, launchers and transporters, all inside a quadrilateral pattern of two parallel and two non-parallel sides. A surface-to-air missile (SAM) had been installed at each corner. The photo analyst recognized that the pattern was a duplicate of the medium-range missile sites that intelligence had seen before only in the Soviet Union.

A tragic footnote to the discovery on October 14 by the Anderson-Heyser team of the first missiles deployed by the Soviet Union in the Western hemisphere records the death of the valiant Major Anderson only two weeks later. He was shot down by a "defensive" weapon on October 27.

The October 14 evidence was irrefutable, especially since other planes had joined the reconnaissance. Some Navy planes flew only 200 feet above the ground, cameras whirring, gathering sensational confirmation of earlier reports. In all there were some forty slim, 52-foot medium-range missiles, many already on their mobile launching pads pointed toward the United States.

These missiles, with an established range of 1,200 miles and armed with one-megaton warheads, could hit cities as far away as Houston, St. Louis and Washington.

The photos spotted the missiles at about ten locations. Besides San Cristobal they were at Guanajay, Remedios and Sagua la Grande.

Under construction at the same time were a half dozen bases for 2,500-mile missiles with five-megaton warheads which could blast American cities from coast to coast with a nuclear holocaust.

The photos showed too, that the Russians had moved in at least 25 twin-jet Ilyushin-28 bombers which could carry nuclear bombs thousands of miles.

It was clear that so much offensive power had not just suddenly sprung up where only defensive weapons had existed before. However, a story to this effect was given out to the American news media and distributed by them to the American people by newspapers, magazines, radio and television.

Actually, the inaction and failure to appraise the evidence properly had now permitted the situation to develop into a serious threat to the country.

The President returned to Washington at 2 a.m. Monday, October 15, after campaign appearances.

Throughout Monday experts pored over the photos. What they saw were Soviet-made medium-range ballistic missiles—the MRBM's which had been brought to Cuba in the Soviet ships *Omsk* and *Poltava* on September 8 and 15, respectively.

Bundy was among the first to learn of the discovery of Soviet missiles in Cuba. When he saw the photographs and the intelligence reports and resolved all his doubts, he went to the President, early Tuesday morning, with the photos and the bad news.

The President called a meeting for 11:45 a.m. of a special security committee. In that executive committee session were Vice President Johnson, Secretary of State Rusk, Secretary of Defense McNamara, Attorney General Robert Kennedy, General Maxwell Taylor, CIA Director McCone, General Carter of the CIA, Douglas Dillon; the President's chief assistants, McGeorge Bundy, Theodore Sorensen and Kenneth O'Donnell; George Ball, Edwin Martin, Llewellyn Thompson, Roswell Gilpatric.

This group became known as the Executive Committee of the National Security Council. For a week they debated how the President should proceed. On Monday, October 22, one week after the photographing of the missile bases, Kennedy went on television to give the American people a message of the "highest national urgency." It was a grim speech. The President said the United States had two objectives: "To prevent the use of these missiles against this or any other country, and to secure their withdrawal or elimination from the Western Hemisphere."

The President had decided on a naval blockade. Estimates showed there were, at that time, 25 Soviet or satellite cargo ships headed for Cuba probably carrying more missiles and bombers. Kennedy assigned Navy P2V, P5M, and P3V patrol planes, flying out of East Coast and Florida bases, and from carriers encircling Cuba to put the communist ships under constant surveillance 800 miles off Cuba.

The 80 ships of Task Force 136, under command of Vice Admiral

Alfred G. Ward, were to move to intercept the Russian ships.

A striking force was quickly mobilized near Cuba for use if the need should arise. Forty thousand marines were sent to the area. The Army's 82nd and 101st Airborne Divisions went on alert. One hundred thousand soldiers were gathered in Florida. Strategic Air Command bombers left Florida airfields to make room for tactical fighters flown in from bases all over the country. Fourteen thousand reservists were recalled to be ready to fly transport planes.

Thus, having made the great mistake of permitting the installation of the missiles, the President was compelled to save the United States from disaster by bold and decisive acts. He issued an ultimatum to Khrushchev to remove his missiles from Cuba. And then, after thirteen black days in as golden an October as Washington could remember, Premier Khrushchev yielded to the President's demands.

It has been widely accepted that this was the young President's finest hour in office. Indeed, faced with as terrible a crisis as any ever before thrust upon a President, Kennedy did not waver in his "eyeball to eyeball" confrontation with Khrushchev. He met the crisis and forced the Russian leader to back down.

His firmness in this action saved America not only from possible nuclear attack but from Russian nuclear blackmail which would have been made possible if Russia had been able to complete its installation of missiles inside America's missile warning system.

There was another result—a political one. Kennedy's courageous confrontation with Khrushchev turned the tide of the November election. Joseph Alsop wrote, "As to why it (the election) is in the President's favor, the answer is equally clear. Until a fortnight ago, the atmosphere of the Democratic campaign was downright dank, to put it mildly. The President's barnstorming on domestic issues had lighted no bonfires among voters. There was no enthusiasm, no spark to ignite the faithful with excitement."

"Then came the Cuban crisis . . . The President took the kind of action most Americans wanted to see taken. . . . Cuba was the spark that had been lacking before. In some states the way the resulting fire singed the Republicans was easy to see."

A Republican Congressman, however, had a more critical view. Representative Bob Wilson of California said Kennedy had not been wholly candid in stating to the nation that he had learned of the

Soviet missiles only the week before his television presentation on October 22. He said the government had photographs of Russian missiles which were as clear and convincing as the photos released by the Administration with great fanfare just two weeks before election. According to the California Congressman, this worked to the political advantage of the Democrats and cost the Republicans 20 House seats.

One Congressman with access to CIA information said that Congress was told about Russian offensive weapons in Cuba "weeks in advance of President Kennedy's announcement of October 22."

Even that "friend of the Administration," columnist Walter Lippmann, talked of a "crisis of confidence." He pointed out that the President had asserted on September 13 that Soviet shipments to Cuba "do not constitute a serious threat to any other part of the hemisphere." And, two weeks later, Undersecretary of State George Ball had told a Congressional Committee there were no offensive weapons in Cuba. In commenting on these two statements of Kennedy and Ball, Lipmann noted, "But in fact there were. On October 10, Senator Keating insisted there were intermediate-range missiles in Cuba, and five days later the President received the photographs that confirmed the charge."

Other repercussions unfavorable to the Administration followed. It became known that a worried Kennedy had won Khrushchev's promise to take the long-range missiles out of Cuba by pledging the United States would not invade Cuba and overthrow Castro by force.

That alone was a considerable concession on our part, but to those who looked deeper it soon developed that we had made further concessions. Although the Administration denied it, Castro first revealed, and Khrushchev later confirmed, that we had agreed to take our medium-range missiles out of Turkey where they were aimed at vital Russian oil fields; and out of Italy and England as well.

Here is the series of events that led up to this trade with Khrushchev.

In one of the executive sessions during the crisis, W. Averall Harriman told members of the President's committee that before they could expect Khrushchev to order the dismantling of the Cuban bases, they must give the Soviet Premier an "out." Someone suggested the Turkish bases as a bargaining point.

The information was tipped to columnist Walter Lippmann, who on October 25 wrote in *The New York Herald Tribune,* "The only place that is truly comparable with Cuba is Turkey. This is the only place where there are strategic weapons right on the frontier of the Soviet Union. The Soviet missile base in Cuba, like the U.S.-NATO base in Turkey, is of little military value. The two bases could be dismantled without altering the world basis of power."

On October 27, just two days after Lippmann's suggestion of dismantling the Turkish bases was published, Premier Khrushchev wrote to President Kennedy that, "We agree to withdraw those means from Cuba which you report as offensive . . . Your representative made a statement that the United States . . . would withdraw similar means from Turkey."

The very same day our Administration responded that "if your letter signified that you are prepared to discuss a detente affecting NATO and the Warsaw Pact, we are quite prepared to consider with our allies any useful proposal."

Khrushchev then announced the withdrawal of missiles from Cuba, commenting that "we are prepared to continue to exchange views of this question."

He referred to a detente, which in diplomatic language means the relaxation of strained relations between two nations.

And shortly after the election the Administration did, in fact, take the missiles out of Turkey.

When Americans began to feel that perhaps we had surrendered under Khrushchev's pressure, the Administration said the removal of these missiles was merely because they were no longer needed. Actually, Washington said, we were giving up nothing. We were doing only what we intended to do anyway.

What most Americans did not know was that in October of that very year the Department of Defense had published a background paper stating that the Turkish missile bases were then vital to the Free World's defenses.

What we still do not know today is whether Russia really did remove all of its missiles from Cuba, for after winning Khrushchev's promise to remove all of them, Kennedy backed down on his original demand that the United States inspect Cuba to make certain of Russia's compliance. Reports continued to come in of intermediate-range nuclear missiles hidden in Cuban caves.

Kennedy's indecisiveness and lack of experience were never more clearly evident than they were during the Cuban missile crisis. The origin of the crisis can be traced back to the Kennedy-Khrushchev meeting in Vienna.

George F. Kennan, former U.S. Ambassador to the Soviet Union, said of that meeting that Kennedy was a "tongue-tied young man, not forceful, with no ideas of his own." It was Kennan's belief that the impression Kennedy made on Khrushchev probably led the Kremlin to send the missiles to Cuba.

Kennedy's inexperience, and the almost fateful consequences of it, was commented on indirectly when The Senate Preparedness Investigating Subcommittee subsequently reported that the almost fatal delay in believing the evidence that nuclear missiles were in Cuba was due to "the predisposition . . . that it would be incompatible with Soviet policy to introduce strategic missiles into Cuba."

In 1965, *Foreign Affairs,* the journal of the Council on Foreign Relations, also commented on this "frame of mind" that offensive missiles in Cuba were unthinkable.

Dean Acheson, the highly respected Secretary of State during President Harry S. Truman's Presidency, accused President Kennedy and his brother Robert of "high school thought" during the Cuban missile crisis. He was present as an adviser to Kennedy at the time.

Acheson's observations are repeated here because they serve to confirm the thrust of this book: that America cannot afford to elect as President men who are not thoroughly qualified to handle the problems of that high office.

Acheson's view was that President Kennedy "did not have incisiveness and he was out of his depth where he was. I hate to say this because I know it's going to be misunderstood, but his reputation is greater because of the tragedy of his death than it would have been if he had lived out two terms . . . he did not seem to me to be in any sense a great man. I did not think he knew a great deal about any of the matters which it's desirable that a Chief of State or a President of the United States should know about. He was not decisive."

During the meetings about what to do about the Russian missiles in Cuba, Robert Kennedy described the situation as "a Pearl Harbor in reverse."

Acheson told the President that "this was a silly way to analyze a problem . . . What we were now faced with was the introduction of nuclear weapons into Cuba and what we were going to do about it. To talk about that as a Pearl Harbor in reverse seemed to me high school thought that was unworthy of people charged with the government of a great country."

11

Words vs. Deeds
South Of The Border

WHEN JOHN F. Kennedy took office at noon on January 20, 1961, the position of the United States in the cold war, then sixteen years old, was good. Despite the scare stories of an alleged missile gap which Kennedy had falsely used to help bring about his election, stories later admitted to be untrue, the nation was militarily strong and held the respect of the entire world.

A system of alliances bound together the free, anti-communist nations of the world. In Europe NATO, eleven years old, stood from Iceland to Turkey as a massive breakwater against the Red tide.

In the Middle East, with age-old tensions that made the area a tempting target for Communist exploitation and subversion, the Baghdad Pact, later called the Central Treaty Organization, or CENTRO, kept out Red influence. That the treaty worked was demonstrated when President Eisenhower sent troops to Lebanon to stamp out a communist brushfire.

In Asia the Red Chinese continued to threaten Formosa with extinction but the United States stood behind Nationalist China with the might of the Seventh Fleet. In Southeast Asia the Southeast Treaty Organization, or SEATO, gave hope of a firm and united defense against communist encroachment.

195

In Africa former colonies, now beginning to breathe the air of independence, showed signs of impending troubles and careful measures would have to be employed to prevent the communists from exploiting the confusion attending the birth of new and inexperienced governments.

In Cuba the bearded director Castro still held sway but our Good Neighbor Policy was working among the Latin American republics and a carefully thought-out plan was going into operation for the overthrow of the Castro regime.

At noon on January 20, 1961, we were a stronger military nation than any in all history. Anticipating with optimism the opportunity to use our position of strength to help correct many of the world's problems, the new President brought to the White House a complex plan for the continued economic and military stability of the Atlantic Community. The vast blueprint came to be known as *The Grand Design* after the title of a book which Joseph Kraft published in 1962 setting forth the new Administration's vision of a Western Europe and America joined by common bonds and pursuing prosperity in a peaceful world.

In its narrowest sense The Grand Design applied only to the North Atlantic community. Stewart Alsop gave one of the best descriptions of it in *The Saturday Evening Post:*

"The Grand Design," he said, was in two parts.

"The political-economic part was largely inspired by France's Jean Monnet. Its chief American sponsors were Undersecretary of State George Ball and White House security advisor McGeorge Bundy, both personal friends and passionate admirers of the brilliant Monnet. This portion of The Grand Design can be summarized in three sentences. First, the British would join the Common Market. This would lead to a "United Europe," including Britain, united politically as well as economically. The United States would in turn form with United Europe what the President in more hopeful days called a 'concrete Atlantic partnership.'"

". . . The military-strategic portion of The Grand Design was the brainchild of Secretary of Defense Robert McNamara and his 'whiz kids' in the Pentagon. It can also be summarized in three sentences. The United States would contribute to the Atlantic partnership a 'centrally controlled' atomic deterrent—meaning controlled by the United States. Meanwhile the Europeans would bring NATO's strength up to thirty divisions, to provide the 'conventional option.' Thus the West could resist a limited Soviet attack without resorting to the weapons which might destroy the United States as well as the Soviet Union."

This explained the limited view of The Grand Design. Actually, however, the Kennedy Administration faced the future with grand ideas for the whole world so that the concept of its Grand Design could be enlarged to take in all its foreign policy.

The implementation of this Grand Design began when, in Latin America, on March 31, 1961, the Administration announced the formation of the Alliance for Progress. This was a John F. Kennedy idea, and, as such, received a highly publicized send-off in speeches and TV statements.

The Alliance for Progress was established formally at the Uruguayan resort of Punta del Este. The charter read, "We, the American republics, hereby proclaim our decision to unite in a common effort to bring our people accelerated economic progress and broader social justice within a framework of personal dignity and political liberty."

"Common effort" would be behind the backing and leadership of the United States, pledged by the President. The new regime in Washington would, he said, initiate and guide many of the steps to be taken and, of course, provide a great deal of the money. The cooperation of our neighbors to the South would be required but, with their help, a new and better way of life would be achieved for all the peoples of the hemisphere. The goals were noble and the hopes of their achievement were high.

From the start, however, the Alliance for Progress was a disappointment. One project after another failed to work out. The people of South American countries were not being helped to achieve the goals they had been promised. By 1963, in fact, many people felt the Alliance was doing more harm than good.

It was helping overthrow one government after another. At the time Oregon's Senator Wayne Morse said, "We are reaching one of the most serious crises in U.S.-Latin American relations in a quarter of a century. We are either going to support constitutional government, or we are going to lose any following that we can hope to obtain by throwing billions of dollars into Latin America." And Alaskan Democrat Ernest Gruening was suggesting $700,000,000 in military aid be cancelled to prevent its use as "an instrument for the overthrow of established democracies."

What had happened? The fact of the matter was that the Alliance for Progress was failing because of lack of resolve in Washington. It had been launched with a flurry of promises, but too little top level attention was paid to fulfill those promises. Latin-Americans themselves said that in every area of economic, educational, social, political and industrial progress, the Administration had failed to fulfill the invested responsibilities of its own brainchild.

For instance, Brazil and Argentina represent more than half the total population of Latin America. During the three years the Kennedy Grand Design was in operation both countries suffered enormously. From 1959 to 1964 the cost of living soared 600 per cent in Brazil and 400 per cent in Argentina. Gold reserves of both nations were dissipated. Totaling two billion dollars after World War II, they shrank to $670,000,000 in 1964. In 1963 Brazil's internal budget deficit was a whopping sixty nine per cent of its total revenue. Argentina's was forty eight per cent. On our scale this would amount to a $50 billion to $70 billion deficit—a figure which would be catastrophic.

The hoped for success of The Grand Design in South America was based on the Kennedy belief that if we sent enough of our taxpayers' dollars into Latin America our neighbors there would become better clothed and, consequently, friendlier to us and less susceptible to communist influence.

However, this simplistic view did not look very deeply into the problems. Argentina was a case in point. In 1962 alone we poured $110,000,000 into that country. What did it accomplish? Did Argentina become friendlier to us or less inclined toward communist ideology? Argentina showed its gratitude for American aid by annulling all American oil contracts in Argentina and refusing to indemnify the American companies for their lost investment.

This seizure of American property in many South American countries led to the undermining of the Alliance for Progress—an eventuality the Kennedy Administration should have foreseen. When he proposed the Alliance the President carelessly guaranteed that the United States would supply $300,000,000 a year in private investments by American companies in Latin America. In 1963 private investment not only fell short of the $300,000,000 mark but there was a net withdrawal of $38,000,000 in investments. At the rate of 3.6 per cent return on investments American companies could not afford to do business, not when they ran the risk of confiscation without indemnification.

Between July, 1961, and March, 1964, as a result of the Kennedy plan, our government advanced Brazil $625,000,000. Were there worthwhile benefits from these loans? Did they further solidify the Alliance? Brazil reacted to our financial support by resuming relations with Russia, by defending Castro's claims before the Organization of American States, by adopting a law severely limiting profits of foreign countries, by confiscating the assets of American businesses and by naming known communists to top government posts. Knowing full well that we expected our foreign aid to be used as much as possible for the purchase of American goods and services, Brazil used its newly acquired American credit to make a trade agreement with the Russians. The USSR would get coffee and cocoa. Brazil would get Russian oil, wheat and machinery.

Just how absurd this Latin American deal was can be seen when we remember that at the time Russian grain was in short supply. Russia was buying wheat from Canada and Australia and Brazil could have obtained all she needed from our billion-bushel surplus.

Much of the failure of the Alliance must be attributed to the pressures on the President who, as we have seen, was overwhelmed by the problems of his office. Often this pressure and the failure to prepare himself in advance for important decisions, or for important statements, had most unfortunate results. When President Kennedy greeted President Victor Paz Estenssoro of Bolivia as a guest to the White House, he hailed Bolivia as the precursor of the Alliance for Progress and as a model for other American republics seeking economic and social development.

When these comments were printed in the press accounts of the day the *New York Herald Tribune* corrected the President editorially, "Bolivia's eleven year revolution, under the leadership of Paz Estenssoro and his colleagues, is a model of disaster. Instead of improving an admittedly bad situation in the mines, whose private owners had exploited the ignorant and illiterate Indian labor force, he and his revolution made it worse. They virtually killed Bolivia's basic industry—the mining of tin.

"Instead of improving an equally bad situation in agriculture, his ostensibly laudable land reform measures took the land away from the handful of greedy oligarchs, parcelled it among ignorant peasants, who did nothing but sit on it and let it go to seed, and resulted in the ruin of Bolivian agriculture."

"The outcome of Paz Estenssoro's revolution is that Bolivia has become indigent—a pathetic dependent on handouts from the United States for its day-to-day survival."

"Is that the model Mr. Kennedy had in mind for the Alliance for Progress? We prefer to believe that he simply pulled the wrong speech out of his pocket—or some of his State Department advisers played a bad joke on him when they briefed him on Paz Estenssoro and the Bolivian revolution."

It was bad enough for the President to urge the disastrous Bolivian land reform measures as a model of good government. Unfortunately he also often idealistically, but impractically, criticized other governments and their policies. This was spread throughout South America, working more mischief than the administration ever dreamed of, for communists used this "propaganda from the North" to help them overthrow governments.

For example, the publishers of a Santiago, Chile, paper charged that the Kennedy slogans and criticisms, which local Alliance for Progress administrators echoed, were responsible for a communist takeover.

"Our friends of the United States are killing democracy in Latin America," one paper said. "If the President or one of his advisers says the land should be subdivided, and if we are told by the Alliance for Progress that we don't know how to handle the government in our countries, and that we must raise our taxes, that has more impact in favor of the communists than if the Reds say these things."

Some of Washington's actions were harmful to the United States in other ways. It was in Chile that the government expropriated American-owned copper mines, agreeing to pay only about $209,000,000 for them over a twenty-year period. Instead of protesting the seizure and the settlement, which would cover only a small fraction of the true worth of the mines, Kennedy sent Chile another loan of $200,000,000 over the next two years. This meant the American taxpayers made good for the payment to cover the theft.

Still another South American country, Ecuador, was in desperate need of reform. The unemployment rate was twenty five per cent.

Half of the people of the larger port cities lived in waterless, lightless, evil-smelling shanties. Illiteracy was widespread. There was a threat of a communist takeover once the majority of the Indian population realized they existed as serfs under a feudal government.

Only a revolution would help Ecuador and one came in the nick of time. The military junta that overthrew alcoholic Carlos Julio Arosemena first outlawed the communist party, then it taxed the feudal oligarchs who had previously refused to pay any taxes whatsoever. The junta consolidated some eight hundred tax agencies which had drained away receipts for personal pleasure, returned "government-owned estates" to individual farmers and planned a breakthrough in the war against illiteracy.

How did the United States react to this improvement? The Washington Administration thwarted the new regime at every turn. It seemed almost as if we felt communism, illiteracy, corruption, disorder, graft and unemployment preferable to reform, anti-Communism, planned education and general welfare.

The Kennedy reaction to another revolution in the Dominican Republic echoed the reaction in Ecuador. When leaders of the Dominican government ousted communist sympathizers, the unprepared Administration went into a state of shock. To help Kennedy decide what to do, twenty-two "liberal" Senators drew up a petition demanding that the President withdraw our diplomats, military people and AID personnel, and asking him not to recognize the new anti-Red government.

President Kennedy was at a loss on whether to follow the advice. In frantic sessions, Alliance for Progress chief Theodore Moscoso, Assistant Secretary of State of Inter-American Affairs Edwin M. Martin and White House Aide Arthur Schlesinger, Jr., could reach no agreement. The AID branch in the State Department clearly wanted a hard policy against the new anti-communist government. The Pentagon advised a soft policy. The State Department couldn't decide which line to take. And Kennedy did not make the Presidential choice.

Eventually Secretary Dean Rusk took a tough policy stand and withdrew all AID personnel from the Dominican Republic. Afterwards, in a statement revealing the Administration's amateurish thinking, Edwin Martin announced, "We all have respect for motherhood and abhor sin," but we cannot "as a practical matter, create effective democracy by keeping a man in office through the use of economic pressure."

The following facts show how mistaken the White House could be. In the twenty-one months just prior to the Dominican coup we had poured $80,000,000 into pro-communist Santo Domingo. After the anti-communist government took power we gave them surplus rice but not one dime in AID money. We withdrew our ambassador and our Foreign Aid Mission.

The shape and color of the Dominican Republic's changing government was discernible to the most shortsighted. The pattern, too, was plain. First, the Trujillo dictatorship was overthrown by the Dominican people in favor of a presumably democratic form of government led by Juan Bosch. But the Bosch government was indulgent of communism, and it was turned out in favor of a triumvirate which started functioning under a democratic constitution in September, 1962. Despite this obvious design, the Kennedy Administration turned its back on the anti-communist government and gave its support to a member of the former leftist regime, Dr. Juan Casasnovas. This mistake went a long way towards explaining why the communists and communist sympathizers in the Dominican Republic were encouraged to strike again in 1965, and made it necessary for President Johnson to dispatch United States Marines to Santo Domingo on April 28 of that year.

Kennedy tripped over the same kind of political trick when Dr. Cheddi Jagan was elected Prime Minister of British Guiana. The President hailed Jagan as a confirmed neutralist. He was wrong. The Administration's office of Intelligence and Research, in Report 4489-R 12, entitled "World Strength of the Communist Party Organizations," stated that the victory of the Jaganite group was a victory for a faction that is openly pro-communist. The report added that Cheddi and Janet Jagan "are recognized as the representatives in British Guiana of the International Communist Movement and have contacts with Communists in the United Kingdom and the United States." FBI files showed that Janet Jagan had studied in Soviet training schools, signed contributions to the London Daily Worker and was a member of the Young Communist League. Yet, no sooner was her husband, Dr. Jagan, elected than he met with Everett Melby, American Consul at Georgetown, requested American aid, and the aid was granted.

Kennedy's mistakes were criticized by many, but nobody made as serious a charge as former President Miguel Ydigoras Fuentes of Guatamala when, in April of 1974, he accused President Kennedy of ordering the coup that overthrew him in March, 1963, eight months before Kennedy was assassinated.

It had been in Guatamala that part of the invasion force which landed at the Bay of Pigs had been trained. Ydigoras Fuentes said the attempt on Fidel Castro's regime had failed because of "the great indecision of President Kennedy . . . As always, he had to find a scapegoat, and that scapegoat was Ydigoras Fuentes. It was through Kennedy's orders that my government was destroyed."

Through an extraordinary series of mistakes President Kennedy's handling of relations in Central and South America doomed the Alliance for Progress to failure. It had been launched with the highest of goals. But as in so many of President Kennedy's projects, the rhetoric and promises so glibly made were unmatched by the performance that followed. And in April, 1967, at the very site of the birth of the Kennedy program, Punta del Este, Uruguay, a new summit conference was held to rescue the Alliance and launch in its place a Latin American Common Market designed to weld the nations of this hemisphere into a giant trading bloc by 1985.

12

The Failure in Europe

ONE OF JOHN F. Kennedy's most serious mistakes in foreign policy took place in Europe where our government had previously built up NATO to resist communist aggression against the Western Powers.

At the beginning, NATO was a simple military alliance. It was put together in April of 1949 when twelve Atlantic countries joined in an integrated defense against a threatened attack by Russia.

The original countries were the United States, Canada, Britain, France, Holland, Belgium, Luxembourg, Iceland, Norway, Denmark, Portugal and Italy. Later, Greece, Turkey and West Germany came into the alliance, forming a crescent-shaped shield extending from the Arctic, across Western Europe all the way to the Middle East.

Neither President Kennedy nor General Charles de Gaulle stood at the helm of state at the time NATO was conceived. But both subscribed to its principles as soon as they took office. General de Gaulle was at that time a supporter of the United States. Eisenhower had, in 1958, refused de Gaulle's proposal of an executive committee for NATO, charged with formulating a common policy all over the world. But de Gaulle had not yet been entirely alienated from us. De

Gaulle expressed himself in detail on April 11, 1961, just before the General and President Kennedy talked in Paris.

"No one is more convinced than I that it is necessary for the free peoples to be allied in case of a conflict between East and West. Of course, this applies particularly to those who are on one or the other side of the Atlantic. What I question, therefore, is not the Atlantic Alliance, but the present organization of the Atlantic Alliance," said de Gaulle.

"Everyone feels that a change is necessary, and with regard to this change I can say, that, in my view, it must take into account three essential points.

"First, the right and the duty of the European continental powers to have their own national defense. It is intolerable for a great state to leave its destiny up to the decisions and action of another state, however friendly it may be. In addition, it happens that, in integration—for it is integration that I mean—the integrated country loses interest in its national defense, since it is not responsible for it. The whole structure of the alliance then loses its resilience and its strength. And what would it be like in time of war?

"Another point: it is necessary to clarify thoroughly the question of the use of nuclear weapons by the two Western powers which possess them, and also the question of the use of their own arms. For the European states of the continent, which are by far the most exposed, must know exactly with which weapons and under what conditions their overseas allies would join them in battle.

"Finally, the third point: since the Atlantic Alliance was created, the threats of war are no longer limited to Europe. They extend over the entire world, Africa and Asia in particular. Under these conditions the Atlantic Alliance, in order to endure, must be extended to all these new fields. If it does not do so, it would lose the basic, the close solidarity between its members, which is indispensable to it. If it does so, then it must revise its organization which does not encompass these extra-European questions."

The French President did not say much more except that, "We shall soon have, I repeat, the great honor and the great pleasure of seeing President Kennedy. I suppose that this is one of the subjects which we will discuss as good friends and good allies."

Kennedy and de Gaulle met, and talked together politely, but it soon became obvious that each was failing to win over the other to his point of view. Kennedy, like Eisenhower, wanted The Grand Design with himself as its boss, while de Gaulle favored sharing responsibility among all the countries in NATO. When the two men concluded their Paris talks they were miles apart. In their inability to agree on basic questions they inevitably moved toward an impasse.

Soon the U.S. press found the Kennedy Administration in trouble in Europe.

The basic United States policy was to create a Europe integrated politically as well as economically, but our allies became bewildered by the erratic shifts in policy line on vital matters. British officials said openly that President Kennedy and his advisers stumbled from one blunder to another in a frenzied attempt to salvage their position in Europe.

One such blunder was the Kennedy decision to scrap the Skybolt program. That story began in 1960 when the British government decided to write off its own program of missile development—for technical and economic reasons—and concluded an agreement with the United States for the purchase of one hundred Skybolt missiles.

Britain felt it had to have the missiles by 1965. Its independent nuclear force was built around Vulcan jet bombers, and survival of the system depended on getting the missiles. In Britain the question of an independent nuclear deterrent long had been politically explosive. It was the last remaining symbol of vanished empire. The British government was counting on the United States to deliver the Skybolt missiles as agreed.

Then, in December of 1962, without warning—indeed, without consulting or even notifying the British government officially—the Administration in Washington "leaked" the news that we had decided to scrap the Skybolt project.

Harold Macmillan, the British Prime Minister, was in Brussels, where negotiations for Britain's entry into the Common Market were entering a critical stage, when the news hit London like a bombshell. Already in serious trouble at home, Macmillan faced the threat of a revolt among his Conservatives in the House of Commons. With matters in such an uproar he could not possibly offer the concessions that would win British admission into the Common Market.

The Kennedy Administration appeared ignorant of the storm it had raised. When Defense Secretary McNamara flew to London on December 11 he was startled to learn of the tempest that raged. By the time McNamara left, two days later, Macmillan was deep in a political crisis. Many of his own supporters felt Washington had deliberately killed the Skybolt project to strangle Britain's independent nuclear deterrent.

Said Alastair Buchan, director of Britain's Institute of Strategic Studies and a close friend of many top officials in Washington, "The Kennedy Administration made a profound and unnecessary mistake of timing in cancelling Skybolt at the very crisis of Britain's negotiations with the European Economic Community (the Common Market)."

The mischief had to be repaired, and repaired quickly, if Macmillan was to save face in Europe as well as Britain. A thirty-six hour conference was arranged at Nassau in the Bahamas. There the young President and the older British Prime Minister put their heads together to find a solution. The deal they came up with caused even greater damage than the mistake it was intended to correct.

At Nassau the President agreed to sell Polaris missiles to the Macmillan government and to help the British build nuclear submarines to launch these missiles. The agreement underwrote continuation of a nuclear deterrent for Britain over a fifteen to twenty year period. This was Kennedy's way of making up for cancelling the Skybolt program. The armed nuclear underwater craft were to be the substitute.

However, it soon became apparent the President had not done his homework. Apparently he did not know that for the past 18 months Secretary of State Rusk (who was not included in the Nassau party) had insisted we take no step to form a nuclear force for NATO until Great Britain had entered the Common Market. Not only that, but less than a week before the Nassau agreement, an American official had told a group of NATO foreign ministers in Paris that "we cannot move very far on a NATO deterrent until the Common Market negotiations with Britain are resolved. We will not know what Europe really is until that happens. And many of these questions will depend upon the shape of Europe."

In Paris, too, after he'd been to London and just before Nassau, Defense Secretary McNamara had insisted that the United States would do nothing to prolong the life of small, national nuclear deterrents which he considered unnecessary and dangerous.

Yet, when Kennedy and Macmillan met in Nassau to offer and

accept the face-saving deal, after the Skybolt fiasco, they acknowledged that it sought to create a "multi-lateral nuclear force" within NATO.

The Nassau agreement marked an abrupt reversal of basic American nuclear policy, which was to keep full control of our atom bombs. It also flaunted French objectives which aimed at keeping NATO conventional and uncomplicated.

Inexperience and lack of caution, plus a few strokes of the pen at Nassau, threw all that into the diplomatic ashcan. Nassau's worst result was on our relations with France in general, and on President de Gaulle in particular.

"Over a period of months," according to *U.S. News and World Report,* "President Kennedy had tried hard to overcome the suspicion of the French and other Europeans that the United States accorded Great Britain a special and privileged role among her allies. Administration officials were under particular orders to eliminate the idea that Britain, inside the Common Market, would act as a stalking horse for the United States.

"President Kennedy himself tried to overcome these European suspicions. Then, in the agreement made at Nassau, he seemed to reaffirm the 'special Anglo-American relationship' by providing Britain with an entirely new nuclear-weapon system at a time when the United States was refusing to consider any nuclear cooperation with the French and opposing small national nuclear forces of any kind."

"Ever since Britain applied to join the Common Market in July, 1961, it had been taken for granted that success or failure of the negotiations would depend upon French President Charles de Gaulle. Yet, in Nassau, the American President and British Prime Minister signed an agreement in which President de Gaulle was neither informed nor consulted."

De Gaulle looked upon the Nassau deal as a personal affront. He saw it as conclusive proof that Britain and the United States were bent on dictating Western policy without consulting France. At his first press conference in 1963, de Gaulle duly announced his intention to veto Great Britain's entry into the Common Market.

The French President said the six members of the World Market were, economically speaking "of the same nature," and moving forward "at more or less the same pace," and were free of "rivalry for domination or power." Then he added, in an implied rebuke to Britain and the United States, "Finally, they have a feeling of solidarity because not one of them is linked on the outside by any special political or military agreement."

In explaining further why he rejected Britain's entry, de Gaulle said, "Britain, in effect, is insular, maritime and linked by her trade, her market and her suppliers to a great variety of countries, many of which are distant ones . . . the nature, the structure, the combination of circumstances proper to Britain differ profoundly from those of the Continentals."

He predicted a possible increase to eighteen members and continued:

"It is foreseeable that the cohesion of all its members who would be very numerous and very diverse, would not hold for long and that in the end there would appear a colossal Atlantic Community under American dependence and leadership which would soon completely swallow up the European Community.

"In the Bahamas, America and Britain concluded an agreement and we were asked to subscribe to it ourselves," the French President said, pointing out that the British "receive privileged assistance from the Americans."

"You know—and I say this in passing—that this assistance was never offered to us and you should know, despite what some report, that we have never asked for it. France has taken note of the Anglo-American Nassau agreement. As it was conceived, undoubtedly, no one will be surprised that we cannot subscribe to it."

Alastair Buchan shrewdly summarized the consequences of the Nassau pact. It was, he said, "a public reaffirmation of the special Anglo-American military relationship and, consequently, it has strengthened President de Gaulle's resistance to British entry (into the Common Market), and we may now face a period of considerable uncertainty in Britain's political as well as in her economic relationship with Europe."

Said Theodore Sorensen in *Kennedy*, his biography of the President, "The Nassau Pact itself showed signs of hasty improvisation and high-level imprecision, of decisions taken by the President in Nassau before he was ready to take them in Washington, of excellent motivation and poor preparation. The pact was accompanied by an offer to the French 'similar' to Kennedy's offer to the British, but the French promptly rejected it." It came much too late.

In a cryptic remark at a press conference, President Kennedy summed up the situation in the winter of 1962 as well as anybody. "If you ask me whether this was the winter of our discontent I would say no. If you ask me whether we were doing quite as well this winter as we perhaps were doing in the fall, I might say no."

Throughout the rest of the winter the United States made desperate efforts to salvage something from the wreckage. Former Ambassador Livingston Merchant was called out of retirement. His new assignment called for selling a new hastily-devised Kennedy plan which was also doomed to failure: a "multilateral nuclear force," namely a fleet of twenty-five surface ships disguised as freighters and armed with nuclear missiles. The nuclear freighters were to have crews of several nationalities and would be owned jointly by the sponsoring NATO powers.

The object of the new proposal was to isolate France and dissuade West Germany from going along with the de Gaulle plan for a European Third Force built around French nuclear power. Washington estimated the cost at five to six billion over a ten-year period. The United States would pay one-third and supply nuclear warheads.

The allied reaction to the U.S. Merchant plan was cool. Britain made no financial commitment. Norway and Denmark expressed themselves as unwilling to take part in the multi-national nuclear force. Italy put off a decision because of an election. Greece, Turkey and Portugal were too poor to contribute much. And France, of course, was disdainful of the whole business, calling the proposed fleet "the multilateral nuclear farce." It realized the transparency of the Kennedy scheme which provided for multi-national forces to "operate" the ships, but reserved to the United States alone the decision to "operate" the missiles they carried.

These were not the only weaknesses of NATO in 1963. Across the waist of Europe Soviet forces were prepared for a forty-kiloton war; NATO forces for a two-kiloton conflict. The Russians were supported by twice as many aircraft as there were to defend NATO countries. The NATO units lacked a sound logistical set-up. The Russians had more armor and artillery. And the terrain features of Central Europe gave the Russians an edge in launching big forces across the North German plains.

However, so long as there was any threat of massive nuclear retaliation by the United States this made no real difference and, under Eisenhower, the NATO ground forces remained relatively limited. But when Kennedy came into office and McNamara installed his cost-accounting methods and philosophy in the Defense Department, we changed our strategy to one of "graduated deterrent." (This was the so-called "Taylor Doctrine" which General Maxwell Taylor had enunciated.) What the West Europeans feared was that a big Russian army could occupy a large section of their territory while Washington "negotiated" with Moscow.

Other NATO allies, too, were cooling perceptibly towards the United States. President Kennedy's instinctive desire to be on the side of the underdog led him into many emotional errors of judgment. He had repeatedly encouraged insurrections in Europe's African colonies, especially in Portuguese Angola. The intrusion into the affairs of Portugal dismayed an ally which was being forced to spend about 45% of its budget for military expenses to patrol a 1,000-mile long area on Africa's west coast where communist forces, directed from the Congo, operated among Angola's eleven tribal groups, much as in Vietnam.

Kennedy's stubborn belief he could work with the Russians, despite his discouraging experience with Khrushchev in Vienna, was responsible for many of these mistakes. Our European allies had as evidence his public speeches, as well as his actions, to bolster their growing dismay and distrust. For one thing, he repeatedly applied pressure to keep West Germany away from a closer union with the rest of NATO. This, in itself, convinced de Gaulle he could not count on United States nuclear support when and if he needed it. Realistically, then, de Gaulle being de Gaulle, he decided to go it alone and also negotiate with the Russians.

This was the background of the Franco-German pact signed in the last months of Chancellor Adenauer's term as head of the West German Government.

Adenauer had worked closely with Frenchman Robert Schuman and Italian DeGaspari in creating the European Coal and Steel Community and the Common Market. He was not at odds with France. But he knew his country's safety depended primarily on the

United States and he trusted Eisenhower and Dulles implicitly. Kennedy's policies convinced him he could no longer do so, and he sought a second support in the alliance with France.

It had not always been so with the resolute German leader who had been responsible for the reconstruction of Germany after the war, and whose death brought the world's leaders to his funeral where they uniformly praised him as one of the great leaders of modern history. Adenauer had had great faith in John Foster Dulles who, as Secretary of State, had repeatedly helped him during the trying reconstruction. However, his misgivings over Kennedy were known throughout Europe.

These misgivings had started when he visited Washington three months after Kennedy's inauguration. What he found there not only surprised but shocked him. He described the people around the new President as "flippant whippersnappers." As time went on he more and more began to talk of Kennedy and his advisers as "unserious." Some of his criticism was no doubt the result of a rather human reaction to such comments as the one made by Jacqueline Kennedy at an official dinner in Europe during the famous Paris-Vienna trip. She confided to a dinner companion that she considered the German Chancellor "ga-ga." Germans interpreted Mrs. Kennedy's unfortunate word as an accusation of senility and the remark soon reached Adenauer. He was as shocked at this tactless expression of rudeness on the part of the President's wife as he was when Pierre Salinger, the President's Press Secretary, during a press conference, had used an unprintable word to describe Germany's ambassador to Washington.

These were but two of many incidents which impressed Adenauer as a flippant approach to diplomacy, to resolution of world problems and, more important, to a proper concern for the welfare of Europe. There were, however, more serious reasons for his doubts and fears.

There was the building of the Berlin Wall which Kennedy permitted with virtually no objections of any import whatsoever. There was the by-passing of Western Europe with the "Hot Line" which ran directly from Washington to Moscow without any connections to Berlin, France or London, so that in time of emergency our European allies would be consulted only "subsequently" as second class nations, their security and very survival to be decided for them by Kennedy.

And there were the withdrawing of our missiles from Greece and Turkey after the Cuban missile crisis, and, as noted above, the Kennedy decision to change from "massive retaliation" to "flexible response" in the defense of NATO in case of attack from the East.

Finally, there was the Kennedy decision to withdraw some United States troops from Germany which was not even announced and was changed only after alarmed cries appeared in the German press.

Adenauer was convinced that Kennedy was more concerned with the appearance of things than with their soundness. The performance of the Kennedy administration dissuaded him from placing his country's security too firmly in the hands of Washington. Whereas he had admired and respected the United States he now turned towards his southern neighbor. He regarded Charles de Gaulle as a wise and experienced statesman.

It was poetic justice, in a way, this movement of Germany's elder statesman toward true rapprochement with France. Directly after World War I, Adenauer had been a Rhineland separatist with France's support. The wheel had come full circle.

No one should really have been surprised by de Gaulle's subsequent actions with respect to NATO. Nevertheless, it was a bitter dose for Americans to swallow when in 1966, President de Gaulle himself announced his intention of getting France out of NATO and ordered NATO to get its troops out of France. In one year of costly change, thirty thousand American troops, fourteen United States air bases, two Canadian air bases and many supply depots were moved and relocated among the member nations in NATO, which established new headquarters in Brussels.

There is an inclination on this side of the Atlantic to lay the entire blame for the collapse of NATO on France's President. This is due in some measure to efforts of members of the Kennedy Administration to avoid being blamed for its errors. In *A Thousand Days*, Schlesinger says he endeavored to persuade the President that the roots of de Gaulle's actions "lay deep in the view of Europe and the world de Gaulle had stated and restated throughout his career."

This is true. From the time of his years of wartime exile in England, de Gaulle had been convinced that the United States and Great Britain were ganging up to deny France her rightful position as a great power—or as a power at least equal to Britain. Repeatedly he referred in bitterness to bilateral agreements between the United

States and Britain without including or even consulting France. Instead of allaying de Gaulle's suspicions, Kennedy confirmed them.

An astute political observer in Britain said, "The Skybolt affair revealed how insensitive the Kennedy Administration was to the realities of British politics. The Nassau affair revealed how insensitive it was to the realities of French politics." Further than that, in signing the Test Ban Treaty, the Kennedy Administration again insulted France by dealing directly with Moscow.

By June of 1964 the world situation had deteriorated to such a point that even former Democratic President Truman felt impelled to comment, "It is all too obvious that the position of the United States in the affairs of the world is not what it should be. Our leadership has been steadily losing effectiveness. Our hopes for a world committed to peace, freedom and security seem to have faded in the resumed struggle for power and trade. It serves no useful purpose to protest or to ignore this unpleasant state. We had better face up to it."

Much of that 'unpleasant state' could be blamed on the mistakes and errors in judgement made by a youthful, inexperienced President who was, as Dean Acheson said, "out of his depth" and really not able to hold his own with the wise elder statesmen of the world such as de Gaulle and Adenauer. In NATO, too, he made misjudgements and hasty, ill advised decisions without sufficient preparation or knowledge of all the background problems and future implications of his actions.

13

The Greatest Mistake
In U.S. History?

ON MAY 5TH, 1961, Commander Alan B. Shepard soared into space in the world's first sub-orbital manned space flight. It was a great success for the United States, one very much needed to counteract the nation's feeling of failure which had followed the defeat at the Bay of Pigs in April.

Twenty days later, on May 25th, President Kennedy appeared before Congress in what he termed his second State of the Union message. The speech contained a dramatic announcement.

"I believe that this nation should commit itself to achieving the goal, before this decade is out, of landing a man on the moon and returning him safely to earth," the President said.

The announcement surprised Congress as much as it did the American people. There had been no previous mention of it. There had been no hearings before Congress; no meetings of experts to determine the feasibility of such a massive undertaking which would certainly cost tens of billions of dollars. Apparently the idea had been conceived suddenly by the President himself.

A few unkind critics immediately suggested that the announcement, coming so soon after the President's Bay of Pigs mistake, was more than a coincidence. Word went around Washington that it could be an adroit bit of political misdirection designed primarily to raise the stature of the President himself. The Administration denied this. The reason for the announcement was the urgency of beating the Russians to the moon—a dramatic new national goal—which the President said would cost the nation twenty billion dollars.

It was clear that a race was on, one which appealed to the sporting blood of Americans and captured the imagination of people all over the world.

But was there really a race? The Russians denied it. Nikita Khrushchev blandly told reporters, "We are not at present planning flights by cosmonauts to the moon. . . . I have a report to the effect that the Americans want to land a man on the moon by 1970-1980. Well, let's wish them success . . . We shall take their experience into account. We do not want to compete with the sending of people to the moon without careful preparation."

The Khrushchev statement drew many comments. One which appeared later in *Newsweek* noted that "Khrushchev may have been out to trick the Americans, but it is more likely the statement was true. In fact, Khrushchev's frankness may have contributed to his downfall."

At any rate, Khrushchev did not accept Kennedy's challenge. Suddenly the main reason given by the President for the United States spending twenty billion dollars disappeared. Americans waited to see what he would do. By early fall they had the answer.

To a surprised country, and to the world, the President now proposed that instead of racing Russia to the moon we should pool our resources in a joint endeavor and reach the moon together. He spoke before the United Nations and said, "Surely we should explore whether the scientists and astronauts of our two countries—indeed of all the world—cannot work together in the conquest of space, sending some day in this decade to the moon not the representatives of a single nation but the representatives of all of our countries."

It was an idealistic suggestion but many Congressmen felt the President had not thought through all the implications of sharing with Russia some of our most closely guarded secrets of rocketry and missiles. Many in Congress were appalled at the idea. Some called it Kennedy's "lunacy." Warnings were sounded; and later, in approving a National Aeronautics and Space Administration appropriation, the Congress actually took the unusual action of prohibiting the use of any of this twenty billion to finance a joint flight to the moon with Russia.

President Kennedy, however, believed we should stay with the program, and in response to many queries the Administration now gave a new reason for the moon flight. In statements and speeches the country was told we should go to the moon "because it is there." Kennedy also felt the project would build up our national prestige. Had not man always sought out the unknown?

As time went on and work progressed it became evident that the President's cost figure had been very wrong, probably because he had arrived at his decision without asking a single scientific group to study the project or a single Congressional Committee to review it. Experts were soon estimating the actual cost of sending a man to the moon and return would cost in excess of forty billion dollar.

By the year 1966, after President Kennedy had been dead two years, criticism of the moon project became general in the country. A United States nuclear physicist, Dr. Vance L. Sailor, said on his return from a tour of Russia's scientific institutions, "Our Man-on-the-Moon program is just a sensational stunt of little scientific value. There is too much manpower and research going into space when they could be used to energize our society through peaceful applications." It was Dr. Sailor's view that United States nuclear technology might be employed to greater advantage to improve man's life on earth in the areas of medicine, agriculture, oceanography and in many other ways. It was clear that the United States simply did not have enough money to work thoroughly in these areas in addition to spending forty billion dollars on the moon project. Aviation Week magazine's editor Donald C. Winston wrote on his return from Russia, that the two Soviet leaders, Leonid Brezhnev and Premier Alexei Kosygin, had changed the direction of Russia's space program. The emphasis was now on the military, he wrote, because propaganda-oriented manned spectaculars were draining resources from "more important activities."

Then, in January, 1967, America's most famous astronaut also commented on the moon race. John Glenn, who had raced around the world at 17,500 miles per hour, said that he'd "never been in favor of the space-race concept. A hundred years from now nobody will remember who got to the moon first. The importat thing then, as it should be now, is all the wonderful boons that will have come from the technological strides both countries are taking today."

In the spring, Dr. Arthur F. Burns, who had been Chairman of the President's Council of Economic Advisers under Eisenhower, added his name to the growing number of people criticizing President Kennedy's decision. Dr. Burns, a leading economist, spoke out forcefully. The Government could not continue spending huge sums on projects "of marginal or even doubtful value," he said, adding that President Kennedy's moon program is "draining the universities and business firms of needed scientists for the sake of an athletic race to beat Russia to the moon."

By the end of March, 1967, *The New York Times* had joined the objectors 'We fail to see that it makes any great difference who reaches the moon first or whether the landing takes place in the 1960's or the mid-1970's," said an editorial on March 27th. "Moreover, we see large unsatisfied needs here on earth—in this country and elsewhere—that could very usefully employ some of the vast resources now being devoted to the Apollo program and its Soviet analogue. A cutback in those resources and their diversion to more pressing needs would make more sense. The moon is not going away, and it can wait a little longer for visitors."

It is the opinion of thoughtful and competent minds in high military and technical circles that there are still more important reasons why the decision to land a man on the moon by 1970 was a great mistake. By committing unprecedented resources of money, materials, manpower and brainpower to the race-that-wasn't-a-race, chiefly for national prestige, the United States created a true technological gap in weaponry directly related to the future military capacity upon which our very survival may depend.

Contributing to this gap was another of President Kennedy's momentous decisions to implement the famous Test Ban Treaty with Russia. The decision to negotiate this treaty, which committed both Russia and the United States to cease testing nuclear explosions in the atmosphere, was also made without prior submission to the Congress. It was brought to the Congress only after negotiations were complete, under circumstances which made it difficult for any Congressman to vote against it.

The Test Ban Treaty had as its background a three-year voluntary moratorium on atomic testing agreed to between the United States and Russia during the Eisenhower administration. The Russians violated the moratorium. In 1961, the year in which President Kennedy announced his moon race proposal, Colonel Oleg V. Penkovsky, a high-ranking Russian intelligence officer, passed on top secret military information to American and British agents about secret Soviet tests.

Among the statements Penkosky made was this . . ."testing of various new types of nuclear weapons is conducted daily. Nuclear test explosions take place more often than reported by TASS or the Soviet press. All this talk about the Soviet Union advocating the prohibition of nuclear tests is nothing but lies. He (Khrushchev) is not ready for it. He will sign an agreement prohibiting nuclear tests only after he becomes convinced that the U.S.S.R. is ahead of the United States in the use of nuclear energy for military purposes."

As Russia continued testing atomic devices, fall-out became a subject of wide concern. All through 1961, 1962 and 1963 air contamination made major headlines especially when the United States finally followed Russia's lead and again began testing. Yet, the most significant tests were those conducted by Russia in which, for the first time in history, massive explosions of 25 and 50 megatons were set off. During this series Russia also tested the effect of these giant explosions on missiles in flight. The significance of this would not be known to the United States for several years.

Only after this major break-through did Russia agree to negotiate the Test Ban Treaty. The negotiations were conducted in virtual secrecy. But the Administration prepared the country for the Treaty with a full-scale publicity campaign based primarily on the dangers of radio-active fall-out. Newspapers, magazines, radio and TV carried warnings of latent dangers to children and the unborn. United Nations Secretary General U Thant said in a public speech that radiation poisons were "present in the bones of every atomic age child." Undoubtedly there was danger on this score, but it was not as great as the excited warnings implied. Secretary of State Rusk later told the Foreign Relations Committee that it was, in truth, "of secondary importance." The real reason for the treaty was "to prevent the spread of nuclear weapons."

On August 12, 1963, the United States Senate Committee on Foreign Relations began public hearings on the treaty, and a procession of military witnesses, hand-picked by the White House and Defense Secretary McNamara, paraded through the hearing room. Most witnesses favored ratification of the treaty.

But there were voices raised in vigorous protest, among them those of former Atomic Energy Commissioner Lewis Strauss and of the noted nuclear physicist, Dr. Edward Teller.

Dr. Teller was particularly vehement in his objections. He said, "This test ban has something to do with knowledge and. . . not so much with knowledge concerning aggressive potentials. It has something vitally important to do with knowledge concerning missile defense, concerning the vulnerability of our retaliatory forces. I believe the Russians have acquired this knowledge. I believe because they have acquired this knowledge, they don't need any more atmospheric tests, and I believe that is why Khrushchev is willing to sign the treaty at present . . . He has the knowledge, and he is willing to stop and prevent us from obtaining similar knowledge. If the Russians want to build a big missile force with which to attack us, they can do so legally under the present testing. What they need is knowledge, and that is what they have. What we need is knowledge, and that is what we don't have."

General Thomas Power, Commander of the Strategic Air Command, thereupon proceeded to startle and shock the Senate Committee by saying that "the only way you can prove a weapons system is to take it out of the stockpile in a random pattern and let the tactical unit take it out and detonate it." When asked if this had been done, he replied: "We have not tested any of the operational warheads in our inventory . . . We have never detonated a nuclear weapon warhead in an Atlas, Titan or Minuteman Missile."

He assured the Senate Committee that the treaty, if ratified, would preclude any such testing in the future. "It is the biggest danger in the treaty. It will leave us in a position where the Soviet Union has fully tested all of their missiles and nuclear warheads, but we have not."

The commander of SAC made it clear that the Air Force was opposed to ratification of the treaty and expressed the opinion that the American people should know why. He said that the Strategic Air Command took a position against the treaty because it held life and death implications for every American family. High yield nuclear explosions, such as the Russians had proved their ability to produce, might set off electromagnetic pulse phenomena which could cripple our missile electronic systems thousands of miles away. This might stop our missiles from even being fired from their silos. General Power's warning was as grave as Dr. Teller's.

A special Senate committee heard secret testimony from experts many of whom also warned against the treaty. In the final Senate vote every member of this committee voted against the Test Ban Treaty. The remainder of the Senate, those who had not heard this secret testimony, passed it. Many of them said they had done so because they felt a vote against the treaty would be viewed as a vote against peace; in fact, a Senator voting against the treaty would appear to be a "Public Enemy of Peace," in the apt words of one newswriter.

President Kennedy was delighted with his victory. He called the treaty "a clear and honorable national commitment to the cause of man's survival" and a "step to get the genie back in the bottle." As we learned later, he believed it was his greatest accomplishment while in the White House.

There are many who believe it may have been a great mistake. Barry Goldwater, one of the senators who heard the secret testimony, wrote later, "Cold facts continue to argue against the test ban treaty and suggest that the inability of this nation to test, particularly nuclear defenses in the atmosphere, is creating a growing survival gap between us and the Soviet Union."

Furthermore, one of the main reasons the President advanced for the treaty—the prevention of the proliferation of nuclear weapons to other nations—was proved wrong. After its signature, France exploded its own nuclear bomb, Red China built up its own nuclear missile arsenal, and other countries were free to do the same.

After the treaty was signed Kennedy apparently considered himself to be highly expert in the areas of nuclear missiles and nuclear strategy. He began a review of the relative strengths of the United States and the Soviet Union.

At that time America had a massive lead over Russia in nuclear weaponry. This superiority had been built up during the Eisenhower Administration and consisted of 200 Atlas, Titan and Minuteman missiles, over 100 Polaris missiles and about 1700 nuclear bombers. Russia at that time had about 50 ICBM's and 200 long-range bombers with no submarine-based missiles to match the Polaris. Our superiority in megatonnage that could be delivered to Russia was about 10 to 1.

In meetings with his Secretary of Defense, Robert MacNamarra, Kennedy discussed this superiority at great length. Together they made one of the most fateful decisions in U.S. history. They decided to "give away" our country's massive military superiority in missiles and permit the Soviets to draw equal to us on the theory that this would create a mutual balance of terror and work for world peace. It was Kennedy's idea that if each side had Mutual Assured Destruction capability, which came to be known as MAD, that the Soviets would then stop their military buildup.

How Kennedy could have made such a decision so soon after his meeting with Khrushchev in Vienna and his own vow to make U.S. power "credible," is today hard to conceive. Perhaps it was because of the huge amounts the U.S. would have to spend in the non-military nuclear powered moon effort and the inability of this country to spend the extra amount also necessary to maintain our lead in nuclear missiles.

At any rate, Russia was soon to take advantage of President Kennedy's youthful idealism and build up its nuclear capability. By 1967 the United States lead in military hardware was down to 4 to 1. But what really worried military experts in the United States was the rapidly declining superiority in total deliverable megatonnage from 10 to 1 to 2 to 1.

However, the MAD appeal was still strong. It was still believed by many that Kennedy's decision had been sound; that once Russia did, in fact, achieve true equality in missiles and megatonnage that Soviet leaders would be satisfied.

Others, more knowledgeable about Soviet leaders' true nature and intentions, were more fearful. In an interview in 1972, Dr. Edward Teller was asked what the results would be if the Soviet Union launched a surprise attack against the United States. He replied: "The question is when. Right now, they could do terrible damage. In a few years, if present trends continue, it is practically certain that it will be the end of the United States . . . I think that more than 50 percent of our people would be killed. I believe that the Soviets could so behave that there would be very few casualties in Russia because we would not have forces enough to retaliate. They have excellent defenses: air defenses, missile defenses, civil defenses. It is possible that, in a few years, we shall be at the mercy of the Soviet Union, unless present trends change."

Another similar warning was made in a study conducted for President Nixon in the early 1970's. A panel of outstanding experts studied every aspect of the emerging problem created by our country's decision to hold back on our nuclear forces and letting the Soviets catch up. It issued a statement that read in part: "Being second rate in the nuclear age . . . multiplies the chances—not of peace—but of nuclear war . . . the road to peace has never been through appeasement, unilateral disarmament or negotiation from weakness. The entire recorded history of mankind is precisely to the contrary. Among the great nations, only the strong survive."

The trends referred to by Dr. Teller have not changed. At the end of 1978 William Randolph Hearst, in an Editor's Report to his readers warned, "The Blunt Truth: The United States of America is now second best militarily, vulnerable to attack from a nation that declared its enmity toward us, and its goal of world domination, from the moment the communists seized control."

In 1979, an even more chilling warning came from a man even more fully informed and qualified to speak. Soviet leader Brezhnev gave a press briefing for United States Senators visiting Russia. Senator Paul Laxalt of Nevada summed it up: "When Mr. Brezhnev indicates to us, across a table, eyeball-to-eyeball, that he can do us in in 24 minutes, thats a pretty chilling message."

It is important to be remembered by the American people that the fateful decision that makes warnings like these possible today was made by a President of the United States. The decision was made with the noblest of purposes and, after Kennedy's death, the concept of MAD was sold to the American people as sound, at least in part, because of the legend that was built up around John F. Kennedy, the man who launched it. In view of the threat that faces our country today, it is clear that Kennedy's decision may have been one of the most disastrous in American history.